The Arachnean and Other Texts

L'Arachnéen et autres textes
by Fernand Deligny

Translated by Drew S. Burk and Catherine Porter
as *The Arachnean and Other Texts*

First Edition
Minneapolis © 2015, Univocal Publishing

Published by Univocal Publishing
123 North 3rd Street, #202
Minneapolis, MN 55401
www.univocalpublishing.com

Cet ouvrage publié dans le cadre du programme d'aide à la publication
bénéficie du soutien du Ministère des Affaires Estrangères et du Service
Culturel de l'Ambassade de France repésenté aux Etats-Unis.

This work received support from the French Ministry of Foreign Affairs
and the Cultural Services of the French Embassy in the
United States through their publishing assistance program.

Photographs: Henri Cassanas
Maps: archives Jacques Allaire and Marie-Dominique Guibal
Reproductions: Anaïs Masson

Designed & Printed by Jason Wagner
Distributed by the University of Minnesota Press

ISBN 9781937561109
Library of Congress Control Number: 2013954259

Table of Contents

Introduction   9

31   **The Arachnean**

The Island Below. A Series of Images   115

129   **When the-Human-that-We-Are Is Not There**

131   *That* Seeing and Looking at One*self*

137   Acting and the Acted

145   Art, Borders ... and the Outside

149   Card Taken and Map Traced

155   The Fulfilled Child

161   Those Excessives

165   The Human and the Supernatural

171   The Charade

175   Freedom without a Name

183   Pretend Not to Notice

187   The Obligatory and the Fortuitous

193   Connivance

197   The Missing Voice

201   When the-Human-that-We-Are Is Not There

Maps and Legends   229

Living between the Lines

The organization of this volume by Fernand Deligny highlights its fundamental elements. The stylized way in which the book articulates texts, maps, and photographs allows it to stand, in a sense, as the purified essence of the author's work, especially of the theoretical and practical inventions he produced in the 1980s. The texts bear upon the stakes of his enterprise in the predominant context of the period, namely, psychoanalysis. Thanks to the photographs, the reader is present at an adventure that ultimately passed through a reflection on images: these are not photos of an experience but rather a certain experience of photography. The maps, finally, present the secret, internal movement of the site: what brought it to life for so long, what it left behind in the form of still unexploited echoes, what establishes the implicit link between life and daily life in the vicinity of madness, the creation of forms resulting from that connivance and the new impulse that derives from it, pointing toward another way of living, a different "common." The texts produce a different gaze, and that way of seeing makes the texts possible; the life between the lines is the place of articulation between the two. These three sets – texts, maps, images – constitute three equivalent experiences, at once autonomous and highly interdependent: in other words, the same thing presented under three different aspects. The texts do without images, the images do without commentary, and the maps are accompanied by legends only to allow the reader to move beyond the enigma of the first glance more quickly, to grasp the circumstances of their development, and to measure their aptitude to make visible in and of themselves the itineraries that are forgotten as soon as they are experienced, the underlying architecture of the network.

Why so many precautions, since the texts themselves offer commentary on images? The paradox is cleared up by the move to articulate the function of images and tracings in the formation of territories in which the real of autism is adjacent to the so badly-named common reality, which is precisely not common to them, to *those* people; for it to become common, it was necessary to detour by way of maps and images. The detour made it possible to move from a stigmatizing and excluding "*those* people there" to a "these people, here," whose position in space then appears in all its singularity and all its sovereignty, in the sense in which Bataille speaks of a *souveraineté* with no role, no power, no use.

In the photographs, which at first glance might appear to be documenting a Scout camp, we very quickly see something else: children alone, children whose mode of being is that of pure presence. About children, one often says, as about dogs, that they "get underfoot," thereby designating that difficult crisscrossing among divergent modes of activity; worse still when it involves autistic children whose enigmatic agitation creates ripples and underlines their "invasive absence": absence from "themselves," absence from the collective project, and absence from normalized human life in general. In these pictures, on the contrary, it is not absence that is underlined but a presence, powerful, solitary, yet territorialized in the extreme, in a space fully laid out with landmarks and signs (walls, stones, tubs, posts, a ball of clay suspended from a string) all of which are objects of an intense activity about which we know that, in order to designate its singularity, Deligny had to divert the verb *agir* ("to act") and make a noun of it ("acting"), so as to oppose it to the indefinitely conjugated French verb *faire* ("to do").

Thus the use Deligny was to make of images later on was already announced in 1969: to bring into view what one fails to see, to make visible the power and importance of gestures that usually escape our attention or that we position negatively as forms of meaningless agitation, unplaceable, unusable. Here, on the contrary, these gestures are inscribed in a territory that is no longer that of a deficit but rather that of an "acting" that Deligny sometimes compares to baroque adornments, variations, rituals. Deleuze would have said that, deterritorialized in relation to the territory of pathology called a hospital, they are *reterritorialized* in an entirely different way: there is a presence of pure, purposeless form. Such is the meaning of the maps, which are eventually replaced by a movie camera.

No adult appears in these pictures: questions, forms of address, injunctions, therapeutic, educational, and occupational intentions have been withdrawn along with them, to be replaced by things, their arrangement, their scrupulous organization. As in the films *Ce gamin, là,* and *Projet N,* the silence that seems to reign in these sites of life must not hide the incessant exchange that takes place by way of space and through the positions of things, an exchange that molds the "living area" into a paradoxical place of "communication" that is suited to this "common" of a different type that includes autistic children and even, in a sense, *turns* around them, responding to the turning that they carry out tirelessly around us, as if questing, Deligny would say, after the *Nous là,* the "we there." The seeming withdrawal of the adults corresponds to a statement that appears at the beginning of *Ce gamin, là,* as a keyword printed on the film: "It is not a matter of going toward them, of

10

concerning ourselves with them, of addressing ourselves to them." It is a matter, on the contrary, of joining them differently, elsewhere, through detours of which the film offers us the state of the place at a given point in time.

Deligny was familiar with Louis Althusser's article, celebrated at the time, on "ideological state apparatuses" that "interpellate individuals as subjects," and he had corresponded with Althusser on the topic. The originality of Deligny's theoretical and practical position consists precisely in what can be called a "suspension of interpellation," in which one can also see a fundamental point of intersection with the inaugural gesture of psychoanalysis, over and beyond the explicit oppositions, as will become clear. One might say that to "the theoretical anti-humanism" professed by Althusser, Deligny opposed an authentic "practical anti-humanism" that dismissed "men," the humans-that-we-are, shored up by what Deleuze called a "thought image" of themselves, a flattering, ready-made image, dominating and exclusive, in favor of a narcissistically and socially less satisfying "human," possibly mute and idle, but in reality more richly endowed with practical recompositions.

The texts that figure in the present collection had been for the most part unpublished in French. They can be seen as addenda, appendices and specific developments that accompany the writing of the books in which Deligny set forth and discussed the major theoretical questions that grew out of his years in the Cévennes and his life alongside the "autistics." In these new essays we find, again, an astonishing interweaving of reflections on animals, art, language, and politics, a stubborn search for a "nonhuman" humanity, that is, a "human" that seems nonhuman to the "humans-that-we-are," who apprehend ourselves first on the basis of our consciousness, our projects, our will. But the inflection is slightly different. The anthropology that is the constant object of Deligny's research is deployed once again here, unquestionably, with new nuances and new thrusts, new bedazzlements. However, every time Deligny engages boldly, perhaps even recklessly, in new constructions, he interrupts himself: "But this is not my aim." This formula reappears several times; it is paradoxical in that on every occasion it closes lengthy developments that nevertheless seem to include precisely this "aim," all the more so given that the speculation resumes with renewed vigor in the passages that follow. But the author must be taken literally. If the aim is elsewhere, then where is it?

It seems that "the aim" is hidden in the text, like the figure in the carpet, and thus visible to all who are willing, quite simply, to adapt their gaze. What Deligny writes and describes in these lines is a particular "mode of being" that he calls a network: "The random chances of existence have led me to live within a network rather than otherwise, by which I mean in another mode. The network is a mode of being." A network mode of being that is in relation, for him, with the intolerable, a spontaneous muted resistance to the concentration-camp dimension of social reality, a "network effect"; the proliferation of networks "reaches its peak in moments when

11

historical events – which according to Friedrich Engels are products of a blind, unconscious form – are intolerable, and it must be said that historical events are endowed with a propensity for being intolerable." The historically intolerable, or History with a capital H, here echoes the "unlivable, uncurable, unbearable" aspects of history writ small, that of Janmari, who is the original figure in the network in question. Those three words, uttered almost at the beginning of the sound track in *Ce gamin, là,* describe at once Janmari and the situation in which he exists: the intolerable fact of his presence, the intolerable fact of his institutional diagnosis.

The analogic model for this network, which obviously invokes war and resistance but has other resonances as well, is a spider's web, the "Arachnean," a stubborn weaving that offers the image of a way out, an outside, a "stepping aside," and that resurfaces endlessly at every moment in history, a filigree, a vital persistence. Neither a solution nor a "thought-out project" but "an enduring phenomenon, a vital necessity." And to remove any illusions from those who might believe they are finally finding here a key to the glorious project of human emancipation, Deligny gives examples: there are the "dissidents" of the great years of the Gulag, to be sure, but also those patients who escaped from an asylum in the early 1940s and organized themselves right away to kidnap an old lady for ransom, to join the Foreign Legion, or more simply to work for the neighborhood blacksmith. We suddenly find ourselves not with Sartre but with Genet, or Guyotat.

"[M]y aim ... consists in the following: when the constraints of history become unbearable, networks arise that quickly prove terribly effective at the pinnacle of history, spearheads in the stalemates of confrontations." Thus it is a question of accompanying this surfacing, this growth, like that of a weed that springs up and proliferates: consenting to be its site. This accompaniment goes hand in hand with the search for instruments. Here is where the status of theory becomes marvelously complicated. Deligny unquestionably develops unprecedented theoretical instruments (a language, concepts, filmed images, maps, and so on). But his genius lies in the way he gives them, at the same time and in the same gesture, a different status. "My aim is to limit myself to the ingenuity of innate action, to be awed by it, and not to try to clear up its mysteries. What Karl von Frisch says about this is enough for me: there are mysteries for the experts in these matters." Thus the affirmation, or the central thesis, according to which "the mode of being in a network ... is perhaps the very nature of human beings" – a mode of being whose nature as "structure" needs to be clarified, "despite the fact that the word 'structure,' like the word 'unconscious,' has been monopolized recently" – is only the theoretical side of a practical truth that is just as essential: it is a matter of inventing the language of the network as the instrument most propitious for making it live and function. A language "other than the mother tongue, that is, other than everyday French." Or inventing its "mythology" (see this highly important remark: "What a shame that humans didn't place heaven at the center of the earth when they elaborated their mythologies"). A language to which one must be able (an essential term) "to entrust oneself." In other words, a language that equally deploys effects of knowledge, belief, self-evidence, and legibility, that authorize and favor behaviors and initiatives.

Thus these constructions, which can readily be called conceptual, also have a different status. They constitute the vocabulary, or better yet the work on language, that made the organization of this *double* life possible, or rather the organization of the side-by-side life that characterized the little community, allowing it to create and recreate itself endlessly.... At the outset, there was Deligny's proposal to the adults that they trace the children's itineraries, and their own, in order to protect themselves from themselves and their irrepressible tendency to name what they thought they were seeing. Tracing in the place of naming and interpreting. Since we don't know what the children want, and since asking them for a response in the realm of wanting manifestly constitutes a form of violence toward them, let's look at what they do. Let's look at them indirectly, by way of their journeys, instead of imposing on them an intersubjective face-to-face encounter. Little by little, something else becomes visible. The establishment of maps, a gradual revelation of the constellation of the "actings" that had been masked up to that point by the blinding light of intentional language, so well-intended; the spotting of "crossbeams," at the intersection between the two worlds (that of the adults, that of the autistic children) who rubbed shoulders without seeing each other; efforts on the part of the adults to make themselves visible to the children by positioning themselves as much as possible within their field of "vision," within their "seeing point," which is different from our "viewpoint," becoming like the water that oriented them literally, as if by magnetism, Deligny said in *Ce gamin, là;* a slow setting into motion of the two choreographies which are unaware of each other (gestures of daily life on one side, rocking and wandering on the other), until they are superimposed and accompany each other in a common space *of a new type* which is not that of communication but that of an entry into a resonance of gestures; a slow rotation once again that makes it possible to propose itineraries and new "initiatives." And so on, indefinitely.... The maps placed at the end of the volume provide a glimpse of this extensive research, which sought for more than ten years to transform into a universe of continually renewed harmonics the world of silence and violence, forcings and misunderstandings, constituted by the confrontation between autistic children and persevering educators. Maps of individual everyday journeys, maps of hand gestures linked to various tasks, maps on the scale of the body, of the rooms of the house, of the immediate environment, of more distant sectors....

This research is used for a single purpose: not first and foremost to constitute a body of knowledge, but rather to shape a gaze in order to change habits and allow for a "common" life. Deligny is a "communist by origin" who is interested in "primordial communism," that particular "common" that is precisely the object of constant rejection on the part of instituted, social humanity. The "common" that groups together in a common space not simply the beings of language but those who speak *and* those who do not speak, or no longer speak. Thus he brings into resonance not-wanting and non-violence: "This is because non-violence and not-wanting are in the same category; it is a matter of liberating the course of acting." It is another way of responding to the "intolerable" question of knowing whether, about those who "want" nothing, one must by that same token think, and say, and act as if, they are worth nothing.

Such, then, is the aim of Deligny's project: "To respect the autistic being is not to respect the being that he or she would be as other; it is to do what is needed so the network can weave itself. Do what is needed? There is nothing to do except to allow the network to make itself." This "doing without doing," which is what allows acting to be, is probably Deligny's signal invention, in relation to which all the rest is only defensive commentary, use of language against itself, infinite rectification not in order to "recognize the other," as the "monks" say, or the clerics, but in order to make a place for the other (and not "his" or "her" place: what do we know, in advance, as to what that place might be?): "we have thought for a very long time that to continue to exist we would have to have the use of several hundred hect-ares in the Cévennes, something like the sea.... This mode of being can exist only if, within space, there is some matter that supplies information, in space and not in time. For ages space has been cultivated, arranged in such a way that the innate has in effect atrophied to the point that we can say it has disappeared or, if we are determined to hold onto it, that it exists in a phantom state in the behavior of the humans-that-we-are."

Our contemporary vocabulary offers us an apt word for designating such a con-figuration, the word "arrangement" (*dispositif*): a material and discursive order, a way of organizing space articulated with a system of categories and beliefs, values, sensibilities, and tropisms that allow us to make unnoticed or hidden parameters and factors perceptible and to bring about shifts in behavior (or, conversely, to produce invisibility and thus repression, in which case the privileged instrument of power is the use of stated and restated self-evidences to organize the behavior of others). Schools, hospitals, families, laboratories, analysts' couches, theatrical stag-ings.... Deligny's language, before being a system of representations or concepts, in the contemporary sense, that of naming reality, is in particular the condition of possibility of a mode of being, a mode of life that allows the real to surface. When Deligny writes: "The sole access consciousness has to the Arachnean lies in traversing it. Like a meteor that takes as good sense the direction of its trajectory, which, as far as sense goes, has none whatsoever," one cannot help thinking about Giraudoux's fable as taken up by Canguilhem: instead of wondering what desti-ny impels hedgehogs to cross the road and get run over, we ought to see instead that our roads are violently crossing the hedgehogs' environment, in which these roads are *a priori* invisible, and thus they are prevented from seeing the effects they produce except at the last moment, too late. The language of science, of objectivity, thus disrupts the order proper to the living, which is partly hidden by it, and has to correct itself endlessly, in an asymptotic manner in the process of experimentation. "And the human then appears as being what remains, somewhat in tatters, of the Arachnean traversed by the sort of blind meteorite that is consciousness. Which amounts to saying that consciousness is in no way capable of mending, patching, or repairing the damage it would be false to think it has provoked: consciousness provokes damage ceaselessly. What takes (has taken) place supposedly in time takes (has taken) place in space, space being right now; and one shouldn't put too much trust in that simple, appealing word."

Deligny is aware that he is constantly struggling with a contradiction, the very one that Bataille formulated in lapidary fashion in *Inner Experience*: how to form the project of exiting from all projects? "If I say that the network must have priority, it seems to be located on the side of the thought-out project, where the Arachnean disappears. Thus we have had to imagine a practice that would allow the Arachnean not only to exist but to persist, something that is much more uncertain, because if it is possible for the Arachnean to flourish, who knows what it will have to bear; at the very least, it will be incorporated into the thought-out project.... This does not prevent us from seeing what is wrong here: the thought-out project absorbs everything, and what it cannot absorb it destroys as inopportune." "The network is not about doing or making; it is devoid of anything that would serve the purpose, and any excess of purpose leaves it in tatters at the very moment when the excess of the project is deposited in it." This reflection leads to a fundamental observation: "What can be woven between the ones and the others [the inhabitants of the network] is, properly speaking, unimaginable." Deligny's theoretical propositions, language-based, are thus always ultimately "formulas of the unimaginable," or "formulas of incompatibility" (between two logical systems, that of intentional language – that of doing – and that of silent "acting," without will and without awareness). Paradoxical formulas, always at the extreme limit (like those of Freud, speaking of unconscious thought, of will that does not want to want ...), they draw their principal interest and their immanent force from the arrangements of life in which they come into being, giving rise to constantly renewed configurations: it suffices to look at the photos or to watch *Ce gamin, là,* and *Projet N* to "understand" that the structure we are given to see is first of all borne by a foreign language, a language that is other: extreme coherence, absolute strangeness. An other language that is not the language of the other but a language so that the other can be, and be always more, other. As Deligny says, these categories, which are at the same time nouns (believing, fearing, doing, acting, wander lines, crossbeams ...), are literally the "keywords of the network," passwords, shibboleths allowing us to cross that insurmountable border, or rather to move alongside it constantly, never losing sight of it, recognizing it as such. These formulas are ways of inhabiting language that make the space inhabitable for those who do not speak. Language, as opposed to

15

vocabulary and grammar: "which goes to show that when the real is at issue, vocabulary is of no use, nor is grammar."

Mythologies, as Deligny also says, and this formula immediately brings to mind Freud's, when the analyst asserted that the theory of drives was "our mythology," "our," that is to say that of the analytic community, analysts as a community relying on that mythology in order to continue its work.

As for why "autistics" (at least those with whom Deligny is concerned) do not speak, that is a vast question. All the contemporary debates revolve around it, in a highly positivist perspective – a quite comprehensible perspective, perhaps, at least up to a certain point where hope (on the part of parents) runs parallel to control (on the part of institutions): to know so as to anticipate, to anticipate so as to act. Prevention, diagnosis, cure, or improvement, adaptation, would depend on knowing, finally, what is the cause. The misunderstanding is at its height, here, both regarding the relations between psychiatry and psychoanalysis and regarding Deligny's place in this debate – which is in reality completely external. The term "autism," which Deligny uses in a very specific sense (characterizing children who do not speak and will never have spoken: the autistics whom today's specialists silently label "profoundly" autistic; the label "high-functioning" is the only one spoken aloud!), always encompasses very different realities: as many meanings as there are individual children. The causes of autism remain unknown, and are in any case multiple. In the major, ongoing confrontation between those who believe autism is innate (a genetic cause, still undiscoverable) and those who believe that it is acquired (the psychogenesis of this form of psychosis: the "refusal of language," according to the most advanced work on the subject), just as in the confrontation between psychiatry and psychoanalysis, Deligny does not choose, precisely because the question of causation does not interest him: he considers it, rightly, entirely outside his realm of competence, unrelated in particular to his "aim" and his research. In his discussion of Lacan's texts, the category he retains is that of the real, precisely because it is useful for designating the register in which the autistic is positioned and in which we exist for autistics. But where psychoanalysis identifies the human and the speaking being, the *parlêtre*, consigning to oblivion the extreme form of psychosis that consists in absolute externality to all language, Deligny on the contrary separates the two, reinscribes autistics within the circle of common life and even goes so far as to see in them the human par excellence (but not the subject), the human as real, in relation to which the use of language seems to be chatter and peroration, repressing and forgetful vanity, a vector of violence and exclusion. The human is gesture, and form, before it is language. Is this the viewpoint of an austere moralist, a fanatic devotee of silence? As always, the formulas counterbalance one another and numerous voices stress the unsurpassable aspect of the "symbolic," of access to speech and of the unfolding of social existence through and in language. But what interests Deligny is conceiving of silence *within* language, at the very heart of language, as an agent of relativization and critique, with political implications. After all, it is not on the side of autism that we find savagery, but rather in civilization and its most characteristic gestures. But what interests him even more is always what he calls "our task": "this real aspect of our movements," this way of becoming "real," that is, visible, in the eyes of these children, the organization of the encounter between the two regimes of visibility: ours, which allows us to see only what we know how to name, and theirs, which reacts to signs, to reference points independent of all language. To our "point of view" corresponds their "point of seeing," in which what is visible is identified in the infinitive, apart from any subjective intention to "look." "Which would mean that we are real, which I believe, and that our "movements," even the least of them – the slightest gesture – are, from a certain *seeing point*, real.... The-human-that-we-are inhabits us, takes up residency, watches, *that* way of seeing is immediately eliminated, because *that* seeing and what can see ITSELF cannot be reconciled."

Thus we understand that the opposition between a psychoanalysis that would privilege language as an approach to the human and a quasi-ethological approach – that would choose what is immutable in the species – does not account for this confrontation. It amounts to contrasting, term by term, two positions reduced to being simply two conceptual systems. This is perhaps how Deligny himself, in the context of his time, might have felt and expressed his rejection of psychoanalysis (which was a rejection of the "psychoanalyism" and the imperialism characteristic of the discipline at the time, more than a rejection of the texts of Freud or Lacan themselves). Still, if we stop measuring these works by their coherence so as test them in action, it is easy to see, to the contrary, another dimension of convergence. Neither psychiatry nor psychoanalysis is merely, as Erik Porge puts it, "a systematized conceptual apparatus, but a dwelling-place of language with windows that open onto the unconscious."[1] Windows that open, for their part, too, only on condition that a certain arrangement has been set up and that analytic vocabulary makes the arrangement credible, that is, visible. Rather than looking at themselves in the blank space of concepts, each of these two positions would do well to read the work of the other with an eye to arrangements. The common point lies in that inaugural decision to reorganize space, to reverse hierarchies, and to set about listening and lying in wait for that which (or for the person who) is there, and from whom there is everything to learn, whether he or she speaks or not. The slightest gesture, the slightest word, the slightest silence, as we know, counts, then, not so much so that knowledge can be produced and a cure can follow, or a reintegration into the human community, but more fundamentally so that a life can take place anew, even and especially if, to us, it does not appear to be "adapted." Just as the analyst physically turns his back on the subject the better to find her elsewhere, not in her stories but on the basis of the free play of her discourse, which sketches in the geography of her mental space,

1. Erik Porge, *Des fondements de la clinique psychanalytique* (Ramonville-Saint-Ange: Érès, 2008).

so Deligny stopped "concerning himself" with autistics in order to find them, too, elsewhere: in the screens, the filters, the "paralanguages" constituted by the cartographic traces of the autistics' world, thanks to which Janmari became Deligny's teacher, as his hysteric patients became Freud's. For that, it was necessary from the outset to bracket address, interpellation, and intention; in addition, Freud had to tolerate the idea of a "dismembered," exploded psyche, differentially localized, and Deligny had to tolerate the idea of a radically a-subjective humanity. Beyond the conceptual systems and the "representations of the world," however divergent these may be, gestures, practical decisions and arrangements were superimposed on one another, and Freud set up his interventions as Deligny did with his stones. What was important lay in the decisive encounter, the scansion that makes for interpretation or the repositioning of the stone that relaunches acting.

Redrawing the perceptible and the visible to make room for what normally has no room, bringing to light dimensions that call into question the naturalness and legitimacy of individual and collective behaviors, is a form of work, a "task" that may have, as a bonus or a luxury, therapeutic and pedagogical effects (and all the more so in that they are never sought in this process, on the contrary; as in psychoanalytic cures, we are at the opposite pole from behavioralist training): it is more certainly a political activity that could well be attached to what Rancière calls the "distribution of the sensible," a "system of self-evident facts of sense perception that simultaneously discloses the existence of something in common and the delimitations that define the respective parts and positions within it."[2] Autistics are not the only ones concerned. And Deligny's work is thus also, indissolubly, an art, a search for new forms, forms of being and forms of life, but also and primarily forms "for nothing," that is, forms that do not prefigure those that "the humans-that-we-are" [ON] will consent to use to characterize the space of their action, or of their acting. And it is an art that configures these forms without hesitation. In the section of his *Dialogues* titled "Many Politics," Gilles Deleuze refers to Deligny's reflections on the forms of individuation that do not come about in the mode of a subject or an ego, but "against all psychological or linguistic personalism, [and that] promote a third person, and even a fourth person singular, the non-person, or It, in whom we recognize ourselves, or recognize our community, better than in the empty exchanges between an I and a You." He adds: "We believe that the notion of subject has lost much of its interest in the name of pre-individual singularities and non-personal individuations."[3] This degree of radicalness and freedom in relation to the codifications guaranteed by multiple forces pertaining to the identities and behaviors of individuals has lasting political consequences: it comes from Spinoza, from

---

2. Jacques Rancière, *The Politics of Aesthetics: The Distribution of the Sensible*, trans. Gabriel Rockhill (London: Continuum, 2004 [2000], p. 12.

3. In *Dialogues*, trans. Hugh Tomlinson and Barbara Habberjam (New York: Columbia University Press, 1987 [1977]), Deleuze refers to Deligny (pp. 127-128); however, the passages cited here do not appear either in the translation or in the original French. [TN]

Nietzsche, from May '68, from Foucault, but it would probably not have taken on such a lofty linguistic turn without Deligny's texts. The "lines of convergence" that are meant to follow the movements of bodies in their immanent resistance and to map and mark the space where they become perceptible, rather than attaching themselves to the disappointing and predictable projects of consciousness, draw much of their disruptive power from the "wander lines" of the network in the Cévennes.

—Bertrand Ogilvie

The Arachnean

1

The random chances of existence have led me to live within a network rather than otherwise, by which I mean in another mode.

A network is a mode of being.

It doesn't take much – a simple passage from masculine to feminine – for *le mode,* mode of being or doing, to become *la mode,* trend or fashion; the word remains the same but the thing evoked is no longer the same thing.

Thus I have lived through the random chances of existence in a network rather than otherwise, and in the randomness of what I choose to read there is always some sort of network to be found.

It's a bit like the story of the nook in the wall and the spider that ended up meeting: if the spider indeed sought out the nook, we may also say that the nook was waiting.

And it is true that I sometimes reach the point of telling myself that a network is waiting for me at every turn. The specific network of which I speak, our network, is almost fifteen years old – which, for a network, is quite an advanced age – and its project is to bring autistic children into close contact.

These days I wonder if this project is not a pretense, the true project being the network itself, which is a mode of being.

Actually, networks abound, and it does seem as though their proliferation reaches its peak in moments when historical events – which according to Friedrich Engels are products of a blind, unconscious form – are intolerable, and it must be said that historical events are endowed with a propensity for being intolerable.

Thus there are events that grow, as we say a tree grows, or the walls of a house rise, and there are networks that spin and weave themselves like so many spider webs, in nooks and in the forks of trees; until birds pass by, or a housekeeper's broom.

I have always had the utmost respect for spiders; today, I can tell myself that this was a matter of intuition. There must be some mistake in the signs of the Zodiac: mine is supposed to be Scorpio, but I am convinced that I was born under the sign of the spider.

I was predestined for my work; from my earliest years I have always had some network to weave.

But can we say that the spider's project is to weave its web? I don't think so. We might as well say that the web's project is to be woven.

We should not take this story of signs too lightly.

Logically speaking, the human species is heir to all species extending beyond the animal and the vegetal – heir to clouds emanating from interstellar spaces that have somehow made oceans the source of what we call life. In the human being the somewhat pronounced accent of consciousness of being has appeared, though this in no way resolves the wholly disparate bric-a-brac of the heritage that has befallen us.

For my part, when it comes to retracing the course of creation, I stop at the spider, while a good many others go no farther back than their own ancestors.

2

Still, I've been finding myself in abandoned dwellings for quite some time. Each time, my companion has gotten there first. She awaits me there. She has no more need of me than I of her, and this allows us to have quite satisfactory neighborly relations.

I'll be told that the dimension of exchange is lacking.
What a mistake. I want nothing from her and she expects nothing from me, which keeps us both from holding a grudge.

I am not going to try to subjugate her, and it is obvious that my presence is of no use to her.

In this lack of self-interest there is a highly moral aspect.

But, looking a bit more closely, I have to acknowledge that I am a man and that I benefit from her presence, whereas I truly provide her with nothing. Which shows how the last to arrive profit shamelessly from their predecessors.

3

What a pity that words grow old. In doing so, they do not grow more beautiful; if I say that in old French, an *araignée* (spider) used to be called an *aragne,* I see that *araignée* is *aragne* and that in growing old the word lost the beautiful and candidly open resonance of its two "a"s, and that there is nothing agreeable or necessary about the "*gnée.*"

Aragne was enough.

That said, if the word has grown old, the spider has not suffered over the centuries and even over millennia. Before the word existed, the spider spun its web unconcerned with the flurry of words, which moreover in no way damage the Arachnean web.

A word like Arachnean resonates somewhat as the word Magdalenian does, the latter evoking the last period of the Upper Paleolithic (the civilization of the reindeer). From the reindeer to the spider, it's a short step at most.

Feeling somewhat Arachnean myself, I mean no insult to spiders or to humans, and just as a spider does not need to have tasted some prey in order to begin weaving its web, while the first network of my own devising was being woven, I was radically unaware of the reason behind this making, though it required some determination on my part.

I was twelve years old; I was a day pupil in a secondary school and it was in my neighborhood that the network was woven, not in the school, which in any case had no suitable space for it. And if chance played some role here, this was the case every time.

If I wanted to indicate one of the constants of the network, I would note an "outside" as one of the necessary components.

That said, and when space becomes a concentration camp, the formation of a network creates a kind of outside that allows the human to survive.

4

To come back to the Arachnean reign, one should not believe that all spiders spin webs, far from it: the Australian ball spider clings to a horizontal thread and turns one leg in a circle; another thread hangs from that leg, bearing at its far end a tiny drop of a sticky substance that will capture insects. And this is merely one example of the various traps available to Arachneans. We know that the same thing holds true for our own species: certain individuals proceed like the ball spider, and the same individual may spin a web at certain points in her existence and at others wield a sticky ball.

If I wanted to exhaust the analogy between the human and the Arachnean, I would risk evoking such surprises that what I am recounting would arouse more suspicion than attraction, it being understood that, as far as the analogy is concerned, we are talking about a resemblance established by the imagination between two or more essentially different objects of thought.

5

As far as the human species, ours, is concerned, some have focused their attention on kinship structures.
It is in somewhat the same vein that I would be inclined to examine what the structure of the human network may be like. Its ultimate purpose is not obvious, if one really wants to save it from the burden with which beings conscious of being risk overwhelming it, those beings who have difficulty tolerating the notion that things make themselves and prefer to believe that they make them with full knowledge of cause and effects.

In the streets near the one on which the house where I lived as a twelve-year-old could be found, something must have been lacking, because a network was woven there.

I may have been its craftsman, but it seems to me that it actually took shape on its own, starting from places of which the largest and most attractive was a construction site where a few houses were probably going to be built, a site that was off limits, moreover, not that this fact has ever prevented networks from forming; perhaps we should even say quite the contrary.

But this would be to emphasize the attraction of the forbidden, which looks to me like a pretext whose sturdy support is all too self-indulgent.

It would be better to speak of the attraction of the *vague*.
Vague is a word that seems to have disparate origins, and this gives fullness and diversity to the echo it stirs up.
In French, a *vague* is a wave; the word refers to the movement of the water's surface, to an unused space or empty lot [*un terrain vague*], to what the mind has difficulty grasping, while the verb *vaguer* means to stray, to wander about at random.

This is how the construction site seemed to us when we came upon it, once the workers had left at the end of their day.
We would go there, then, and wander.
If a Karl von Frisch had turned up, with his eyes trained to glimpse the mysteries of animal architecture, he would have observed the construction of an entire network of trajectories evoking war, because we took advantage of the space as good sons of veterans of Verdun and other war zones; the small wagons on rails carried several passengers while others took turns pushing; it was a merry-go-round, a mine, a surprising outgrowth of heterogeneous shelters in which we took the risk that an untimely shove would bring it all down on our heads.

That said, and it by no means exhausts the inventory of what could be called "acting like," playing at being soldiers, workers, children at play, I am certain that an observer would have perceived often-repeated trajectories whose goal was not at all obvious, for wander is a verb that needs no object.

But we see quite well that there is a sort of necessary complicity between these trajectories of wandering and chance encounters.

6

But it must also be said that if the observer had been present, his gaze alone would have disturbed the architecture of trajectories, and should his presence have lasted or recurred, the "vague" space would have become vacant.

This is where architecture disappears, and if the word seems excessive let us discuss the net of our trajectories.
If such a net was woven, what was it supposed to capture? It was a question of using opportunities, and, moreover, chance, that is, opportunities that did not yet exist but would come into existence through the use we would make of the "thing" we had come across.

A fishing expedition of the sort, one that creates things out of nothing, requires a net whose structure it would be astonishing to find created by chance. In reality, chance is a completely unexplored word that is merely used to limit our perplexity.

If a certain number of our trajectories involved wandering [*vaguer*], it is clear that, from one day to the next, several opportunities having come to fruition, attending to them [*y vaguer*] was the point, here, as we say with regard to occupations.

The space, once occupied, lost something of its vagueness, then. And that meant the disappearance of the infinitive to wander, a term whose extraordinary richness we can glimpse.

It would be better to say that we seem to glimpse it, somewhat in the way those who observe interstellar space have glimpsed other galaxies in the interstices of our own.

I open at random a three hundred-page book, *Animal Architecture*, by Karl von Frisch.[1] I land on a nest of a species of termite that uses its own waste as construction material for its harmonious work. Twenty centimeters high, this nest is subterranean and surrounded by an air chamber. Its surface has aerating slits, each surrounded by an annular wall and constructed with such regularity it is as though they had each been stamped out by a machine.

That said, with regard to our trajectories within that empty lot, that vague terrain, my memory is not exact enough to retrace them.

Moreover, it is highly probable that the most tenacious of the wandering trajectories were enacted in a completely unconscious way, prepared to inscribe nothing of themselves into memory unless they found an opportunity that would end up justifying the act.

To put it another way: the aspect of wandering that is nonetheless essential – essential because what is at stake is the quest for chance – tumbles into the darkness of complete oblivion.

Human beings are made this way: the galaxy of conscious or unconscious intention in the Freudian sense of the term obscures other galaxies that would have the right to be called innate, it must be said; beings conscious of being could only be moved by this phenomenon at the expense of the predominant importance they grant to the wanting in which they place all their hopes.

---

1. Trans. Lisbeth Gombrich (New York: Harcourt Brace Jovanovitch, 1974).

7

If I hear about the Arachnean – not that I am hearing about it, but I tend in that direction – it's rather like evoking a bygone epoch, an age, an era.

Arachnean: the word enchants me. What a pity that on this planisphere we find no Arachnean islands, neither islands nor mountain ranges. Besides spiders, nothing else is Arachnean; sometimes perhaps there is a fleeting allusion to an architectural detail or a piece of embroidery, whereas it is obvious that a language that would be Arachnean ought to exist, and at least one people if not a civilization.

My project is a little clearer, now: to give this word Arachnean, which I find astonishing, a meaning worthy of its harmony and scope.

I could have imagined a people and spoken of Arachnides as one speaks of Atlantis, I could have striven to make my tale so attractive that the Arachneans would have begun to exist in human memory.

Such is not the path I have chosen, preoccupied as I must have been with clarifying the mode of being in a network. Thus I shall not be talking about a legendary people such as the Cyclops but about a structure; despite the fact the word "structure," like the word "unconscious," has been monopolized recently.

I look at the cover of the book for which I would like to find a term that would evoke to what degree it is going to become familiar to me; I cannot call it a bedside table book since it lies on my dinner table; I'm talking about a book that is a companion the way a woman could be, a close book in the sense in which one might speak of one's close friends.

On the cover of this nearby book – the face it offers up when it is closed – there is a spider web; the spider is there, on the lookout, and the Arachnean net, evoking a city map, and toward its center, a cloud of droplets of light, a constellation exactly like those that the most modest telescope allows one to see in infinite number.
One can get lost in it all.
The fact remains that, on the walls of the room, there are traces of the trajectories of this network, for a network has trajectories.

What could also be said is that these trajectories have a network, are the network, take shape within networks. So it is with the Arachnean: we never know whether it weaves or whether it simply exists from having being woven.

Such are the terms of the analogy that is to reign over the production, most likely an everyday affair, of these pages that fall under the sign of the Arachnean.

I almost forgot to mention the masterpiece located in the left-hand corner of my window, in broad daylight: quite a good-sized web.

8

A beautiful gray web, supple and curved, with a tiny bit of netting in a corner where the spider nestles.

Speaking of webs brings painting to mind.[2] Where is the painting before it has been made? A good many painters, some of the most glorious, have said to no avail that the painting is in the canvas and that the hard part for the painter is getting rid of the visible whiteness of the canvas without ruining the painting, without forgetting anything and without adding anything.

But this claim is taken as a paradox, almost as a joke. Everyone knows quite well where the project of the painting resides: in the head, the soul, or the heart of the painter.

It is a big mistake not to listen to those who know what they are talking about.

I asked myself the same question about spider webs: where can they be found, and in what form, before they are spun? Each web has an artisan and it is all too easy to suspect that every spider holds in its heart the project of setting out to weave its own at the first opportunity.

Things get complicated when we start talking about the work of the Trinervitermes termites that live in the African Savanna. From the tiny mound where the nest is lodged, a hole is dug all the way to the underground water table, and this pathway drilled into loose soil can be up to fifty meters long.

The termite colony brings together several thousand individuals and although it is possible to tell apart the egg-laying queen, no one has ever seen the chief engineer of the drilling enterprise.

What Karl von Frisch tells us is that, in the natural sciences, there are mysteries that the human mind, despite its power and thirst for knowledge, has not been able to penetrate.

I shall say the same thing about the mode of being in a network, which is perhaps the very nature of human beings, "the mind" merely intervening into the bargain, in this case, and its work is the excess rather than the structure of the network.

---

2. The French word for "web," *toile*, also means "canvas." [TN]

The painter is quite right to say that, since the painting already resides in the canvas, the greatest risk for someone who seeks to extract it is adding to it, that is, using the Arachnean as a baggage net[3] wherein the artist would shed his feelings, fantasies, ideas or whatever else is encumbering him.

9

Seduced by the word "Arachnean," I looked to the spider as the term for an analogy. The disadvantage of this choice is that the spider is not social; it is solitary, and it does its work all by itself, whereas termites, ants, and others work in concert; so do human beings.

As similar as a network may be to a spider web, it is the work of more than one, which means several; as with the Trinervitermes, there is no possibility of locating the master builder who would have had the project germinating in its head, heart, or soul.

There is a web, but no drilling, and if I am told that to undertake a drilling project, men work in groups – not to mention machines – this doesn't help me much. On the contrary, actually. If the project is clear, precise, and well defined, in other words if doing or making something prevails, we are dealing with a concerted effort and the Arachnean might well disappear then, broken, jagged, and torn.

The network is not about doing or making; it is devoid of anything that would serve the purpose, and any excess of purpose leaves it in tatters at the very moment when the excess of the project is deposited in it.

10

There are twenty thousand types of spiders and every one of them has a unique manner of weaving on which the form of the web depends.

It does seem that the human species is one; thus networks always have the same form.

Which shows that a network and what can be called a society are not the same thing. Better still: this thing we call society in which beings conscious of being enjoy themselves to the fullest can become so restrictive, so bent on subjugation, that networks are woven outside the grip of the abusive society.

---

3. A reference to the nets used rather than rigid rails on baggage racks in certain trains and busses. [TN]

What happens, and what often makes networks break down, is the overburdening of the project, an overburdening so constraining in its turn that it passes for the network's reason for being; and the impostor keeps on proposing another society; if the conjuncture of history is propitious, the network takes on fantastic proportions; now it is a society, the starting point from which networks are secreted and, the network having become an organized power, it goes to great lengths to keep house, it invents brooms, multiplies teams of cleaners, while the responsible parties get lost in conjectures about the causes of the epidemic of apparently disparate networks whose structures nevertheless probably always remain the same.

The Arachnean reemerges at every moment in history, all the more surprising and disconcerting in that the upholders of society, instead of blaming chance for the way things are, see in every network the effect of concertation.

11

A book I cherish tells me that some tame young beavers, who had been raised by humans and had never seen a beaver dam or lodge, cut down trees as if they had received special training for the work. Better yet, they constructed a real beaver lodge, using stones and branches as well as other more delicate materials they had available, and in a creek they built an authentic waterproof beaver dam, without making a single mistake, without showing even the slightest hesitation.

And my friend Karl adds that here again we have an entire area of investigation on offer to anyone who would like to learn more about it. To be sure.
One of us thought he saw a beaver in the river that runs along one of the inhabited areas of our network. Lacking any personal experience with beavers, I shall gather some potentially useful raw material from this reported fact: there are several young beavers; they have water, stones, and branches at their disposal.... The main thing is that they have no need to see papamama or others do it in order to work, the master builder being the species.

I have never been able to admit that, as far as our species is concerned, the master builder has disappeared or, better yet, never existed.

One would have to imagine that in our honor nature abruptly failed in its task, giving us free rein; one would have to think that, owing to some hard-to-imagine blunder, it left this species, ours, orphaned, mutilated, seriously unfinished.

It seems more plausible to suppose that the master builder was driven off, much as the leaders of a society wipe clean any trace of a network, considering networks not only inopportune but highly undesirable.

Humans, as beings conscious of being, mean to be their own masters and are unable to tolerate any other; on this basis they find themselves struggling within abysses of aberration, where curiously, the Arachnean resurfaces, without rancor; and it is true that, caught within the turbulence of the worst disasters of which he or she is the author, a human being has no recourse but the network woven among several people who become close and indispensable to one another, without understanding a thing about it, moreover, for if the course of existence had remained somewhat peaceful, none of the people in close proximity would have felt any particular sympathy toward any other. Such was the case in the truck that lugged me along with four or five others from Calais to the Netherlands in order to take me, through some rather unlikely detours, to a cave famous for its prehistoric vestiges where my kin of the Aurignacian era had woven the same small network that we were bringing back, intact, from a horrific war that was to take several years to die down.
That said, the few hours, not even a full day, we spent in the cave left an impression that led me to take seriously the idea that a memory can leave marks.

It was there in the cave that the echo of the armistice reached us. At the same time, the network woven among the members of our little group disappeared along with the threat of war.

I found myself wanting to find a name for these comrades of the moment; I came up with *pote* (pal) no doubt owing to the word's close proximity to *poteau* (post), which has the benefit of eliminating any virtuality of sex or language.

From war to asylum, the network became my mode of being, which is not to say my reason.
I wasn't a dissident like Vladimir Bukowski, whose memoirs I'm reading. Nevertheless, I knew myself to be refractory. Refractory to what? To war? If there is in the word "refractory" some idea of fracture, refusal, resistance, war was merely one of the aspects of what mankind can do. I was therefore refractory to mankind, which left me in the position of having to be human.

Chance persisted in manifesting a sort of leniency toward me; in particular, I found myself responsible for a network where children said to be autistic came to live, hence I had to ask myself what human means, the answer being: nothing. Human is the name of a species, although "species" has already disappeared from humanity's understanding of itself.

12

For Karl von Frisch, the fact that instinctive action often takes place "in a vacuum" seems to be one of the criteria allowing him to determine whether the acting observed is innate; and while he says that for animals, "thinking" is not always the best way to succeed in an enterprise, he nevertheless concludes that if a wholly rudimentary "work" is successfully completed – by a chimpanzee, for example, who stacks several boxes to reach a banana suspended overhead – this work, however uncertain and clumsy, is situated at a higher level than a great architectural work such as a spider web, for in the end the latter is merely the fruit of an innate instinct.

Here I lose a pal who, in saying this, joins the camp of people who establish as inferior what they think they themselves lack, whereas it is more than likely just a case of carefully maintained atrophy, like that of Chinese girls' feet, not so long ago.

This "higher level" of the slightest thought-out project – be it only the stacking of three boxes in order to reach a hanging banana – summarizes the human condition quite well, no doubt because humans see within it the condition of their own autonomy.

What a shame humans have not imagined that, since their lives came from the sea, death would lead them to find themselves back there; at least we would be rid of this higher level, the sky would then be the nearby sea, accessible on equal footing, and humans would be correspondingly less ravaged by the aspiration toward superiority wherein, moreover, they lose themselves.

13

To say that the existence of the network appeared to me at the same moment as the armistice is worth whatever history is worth.

This is to hold the Arachnean in contempt, perhaps it would better to say to swallow it up.
So the spider makes silken threads that can be said to have been projected, enabling the weaving, on the basis of which, as the web is woven, it literally swallows back the precursory threads, not that it belittles or scorns them; the silk that emerges from its body is highly precious and is recuperated.
When the preliminary scaffolding has disappeared, has been swallowed up, there is nothing left of the threads, or, rather, they have become those of the woven web that exists and persists.

I can say the same thing about the perpetually swallowed-up network; there remain all the forms that can be taken by the propensity not to exist alone, and the innate network is all the more swallowed up to the extent that the thought-out project demands to know what it is doing.

And if the autonomy of the thought-out project is the criterion for its level of superiority, we remain befuddled by the need that beings conscious of being then have to "do as," and thus to imitate, to identify with something from which beavers and spiders are exempt, owing to the fact that these animals are completely governed by the innate forces that animate them: hence the web, an architectural masterpiece, and the lodge and the dam, other masterpieces of ingenuity and foresight.

14

It should be quite clear that the Arachnean has nothing to do with beings conscious of being, which are woven entirely, it appears, of sex and language. If innate action is sometimes reiterated in a vacuum, what the vacuum then evokes is that the project is completely unrealizable, if only because the raw material is lacking.

The spider, it seems, does not lack for material, since it produces its own and Karl von Frisch says as much: thanks to a veritable built-in factory. That said, if we watch a spider act, what it weaves first of all may not be a web, if the necessary support structure is not within its reach; it weaves a small sail, a little parachute to which it will entrust the free end of the thinnest and lightest of strands that it can extrude from its spinnerets, the lightest despite having a pearl of glue suspended at its tip, this pearl as well comes from the factory embedded in the spider's body; the wind carries the parachute far from the vertical axis, and what can happen is that the pearl of glue suspended at the end of the thread and carried off by the parachute encounters a branch, which allows this first thread stretched transversally to be the starting point from which the essential structure of the weaving will be sketched.

In this we see the resources of the Arachnean, confronted with which beings conscious of being remain speechless, and, it must be said, quite ill-equipped.

Such beings could, justifiably, blame nature, which has proved to be so ungenerous in their regard.

What matters, in the spider's work, is that first very fine thread carried off by the little parachute that captures the wind is not forgotten. The fact that it is swallowed back up seems to me to be a genuine event.

The analogy with the event in my own history that I have recounted is remarkable.

The network appeared to me the day of the armistice and it appeared at the exact moment when the need for the four others, which had been very close until then, faded away. The other preliminary networks had thus been swallowed back up, whereas, if one looked more closely, they had taken place.

It is hard to compare high school with war, except for the fact that they are both obligatory.

One shouldn't be too surprised that the obligatory is the necessary underpinning for incomplete sketches of networks.

But must a network – can it – be completed?

There is something about the ambiguities of the term that sounds a warning bell. A network can complete itself by disappearing or by becoming an institution.

The sole underpinning that allows for a network is a breach, a rift. If we are talking about a window, the network becomes a curtain.

But this is not my aim.

15

My aim is to limit myself to the ingenuity of innate action, to be awed by it, and not to try to clear up its mysteries.

What Karl von Frisch says about this is enough for me: there are mysteries for the experts in these matters. What I see as regrettable is that the humans-that-we-are, in this respect and inasmuch as it concerns them, play deaf and abuse their blindness. They do not lack reason(s) for doing so, whether the word is written in the singular or the plural.

It is not reasonable to be a dissident in the Soviet Union. Dissidents have their reasons for being dissidents. They are considered and treated as mentally ill, and imprisoned. In an asylum, a network is woven; among the dissidents? Among those who are there, whatever the reasons for their internment, whether we are talking about mentally ill prisoners, delinquent repeat offenders, or even guards. The network has distant and sometimes devoted partisans who are visceral anti-communists – which is not always the case with dissidents.

It becomes obvious that it is very hard to spell out under what banner the network would operate.

Once upon a time there was a network – which was my mode of being for several years – grafted onto a much larger, scattered network that went under the name of youth hostels. The network in which – along with others – I was a spider took in adolescents who were more or less seriously "psychotic" as well as repeat juvenile offenders. This network, oddly enough, encompassed the same mixture found in all asylums, Soviet or otherwise. Accentuating the similarities, and even though "my" network was out in the open air, there were psychiatrists, and, at a certain remove, judges. Those who had a say in this endeavor were communists. There's nothing I can do about these oddities of history.

Some of the most rebellious adolescents went of their own accord – and in spite of us, to the extent that they let us know of their intentions – to sign up for five-year stints in the Foreign Legion, as if the very density of that training had a more powerful magnetic pull than the diffused network of the hostels.

I had been somewhat inoculated against surprise since the moment in 1943 when, after a breach had opened up in a psychiatric asylum, several of the youngsters nearing adulthood went straight to the Waffen-SS and joined up. My memory is burdened with many instances of the sort.

I say this to note quite simply that the network is not a solution but an enduring phenomenon, a vital necessity.

On occasion I have seen a network being born rather in the way that, via film, we can watch a plant grow in ten minutes, whereas in real time it takes several days or weeks for this "doing."

In my case, there was no cinematic trickery, no optical instrument to tamper with the images; four or five dazed, solitary, inert adolescents regained their vigor in the blink of an eye, suddenly irrigated; I was unquestionably witnessing a network effect.

The fact is that this refreshed network stemmed from a project that can be formulated as follows: go kill a nice old woman in her home, in which one of the five involved had worked a few years earlier.

This was a network that had to be decapitated, which suggests that the head of the network is the "thought-out project" or rather the formulated project; these are perhaps not exactly the same "thing."

Was it really the idea of killing an old woman that reinvigorated the four or five adolescents? It was rather the new mode of being of some of them, a mode that, within the boredom of the asylum, constitutes an event. All it takes is for the initial stitching to be swallowed back up, as happens with spiders.

The "thought-out project" that seems to be the goal emerges for what it is: the pretext or, to put it differently, the opportunity.

We could say as much about the nook where the spider will fasten its web. If opportunity can also mean circumstance, we see quite well that the nice old woman is not there, in the asylum; there is indeed a "thought-out project"; one of the four or five had to think of this nice old woman; moreover, killing her was not even the real project; the project was to use her money to go to Dunkirk or Calais and look for a job on a boat; the latter was thus the project that I took up again, several years later, equipped with a coffer that made such projects possible – and such projects exist in abundance, as a matter of fact; so it was that a heinous crime was avoided.

The disarray of the authorities confronted with a network is actually remarkable. Dissidents sometimes manage to play this instrument – the network – with such astonishing virtuosity that it might be deemed a reflex. When dissidents are expelled, or manage to expel themselves, and write their memoirs, as far as the customs and habits of people from free countries are concerned such writers are felt to be disconcerted; they have a sense of scattered people, an ambient freedom from which they themselves do not benefit; such a waste, all this widespread freedom, and not only freedom, but food, too, and everything that is lacking in the country from which they have been uprooted; they are heartbroken by this inertia; but what can be done about it? What can be said? Create a network?

16

If ever a reader has leafed through the books I've written, he or she can justifiably grumble that I have experienced only a few events in my life to which I keep on coming back.

This attachment hardly surprises me; it is Arachnean; a nook is a nook; I am an individual of the species that lives at the higher level of the thought-out project. It may appear that writing is a project of this order.

The fact remains that there is the act of writing and there is the what. The what, the contents of the book, what it will say, what is written about is obviously the essential thing; what remains is the act of writing, which is Arachnean. You can look at ten thousand, a hundred thousand hands writing: they all do the same thing. There are nonetheless some differences between the spider and the act through which the fingers of a hand – turned into legs – and the palm – turned into a body – write; the thread of words does not emerge from spinnerets located at the base of the wrist; we have had to learn to write.

The fact remains that to write is to trace and to trace is within the reach of any hand, whether or not there is a thought-out project or the intervention of learning; we have the hands of countless school children, bearers of drawn traces, as first-hand witnesses.

I'm not taking a big risk in affirming that tracing is innate.
Nevertheless, a tiny child, a future representative of the elite thought-out project of autonomy, must not be mistaken for a larva that has to be stuffed with the acquired learning of the human-that-we-are – which is not that of the species, because the species doesn't give a damn about acquired learning. Place a newborn who hasn't had a chance to see how others do it in the vicinity of a swollen breast and you'll see what it means to act without any thought-out project. That said, the thought-out project comes into play soon enough, it being clearly understood that this project is thought by "us" and not by the newborn who is moreover no longer entirely new; it's thus a matter of the ex-newborn becoming autonomous in learning to think (like everyone else); it is most often the case that newborns have certain predispositions to do this. Yet here I am, attesting to what happens to these newborns who are not at all disposed to engage in the thought-out project – thought first by others, until the day when....

Acting persists in the mode of suckling and, while we maintain traces of these gestures, we find ourselves facing a network of traces where mystery awaits us as patiently as the spider lurking in its abode, a leg nonchalantly posed upon the threads of its web, threads that lead all the way back to the spider and from which it feels everything that happens to its web, locating and evaluating the probable origin of the vibrations.
Let us imagine a single instant in which a papamama and others close to an ex-newborn, once the suckling phase is more or less outdated, maintain their attitude toward what the child may "want," the word is going to win out; it is not at all obvious that the newborn wants to suckle if one thinks that wanting goes hand in hand with a thought-out project.
From the moment the other is presumed to want, the innate act vanishes; it seems that such acts are inconceivable, and this is truly the case, for there is no longer any word for it.

17

It is quite understandable that we can say a spider is going to make its web; but does this mean that it wants to?

It seems to me that, on this point, it's fairly easy to get the reader to agree. That said, if I say in the same way that the trajectories whose traces can be inscribed in a network have not been wanted, the reader begins to look at me with suspicion. If I speak this way about the trajectories of autistic children, I risk being accused of depriving them of the privilege of the thought-out project.

There is always, somewhere, who knows where, a High Court that watches over rights; where the flip side of the law, as it were, can be seen; if, under the pretext that, however "autistic" they may be, they indeed have the right to want, even if they haven't acquired the practice of the thought-out project, I inflict this right on them and condemn them to a likeness – an identity – that is all the more burdensome because it is fictitious. Certainly, they have a right to the higher level; but what can they do with this right, if not live the disarray of extravagating, which literally means to wander off the path?

What path are we talking about? The path of the thought-out project.

That said, it could be that this stubborn determination of the human-that-we-are to want to know and recognize only the existence and value of thought-out projects is what makes us extravagate, that is, leave the Arachnean path.

This extravagance seems all the more inescapable in that the Arachnean path is not traced, no more than is a spider web, which is spun without preliminary drawings, unlike the work of tapestry weavers, whose work is sketched out in a very precise manner.

Where can the project of the spider web be located? Since we're not dealing with a wanting-to make, or a thought-out project, the necessity for a project disappears.

This doesn't prevent the web from existing, neither the web nor many other even more stupefying things; such things can be found on every page of *Animal Architecture*.

Might the human-that-we-are be deprived of access to such things? I'm not talking about access to understanding, but access to acting; it's really a steep price to pay for access to the higher level of the thought-out project.

18

This is where the dilemma emerges: the thought-out project – the Arachnean. It appears self-evident that we have no choice. But here we're dealing with self-evidence, which is never anything but the character of something that imposes itself on the mind with such force that it needs no proof whatsoever.

For if it is true that we have no choice, it's simply because THEY don't offer us one. But what would happen if we had the choice? According to the dictionary, to choose is to make up one's OWN mind [SE *décider*]; thus the choice is already made between SELF [SE] and THAT [CE] which would be non/SELF [*non/SE*], something that is inconceivable to us.

If an "autistic" child has the choice between water and "us," there is a strong chance the choice will be made quite quickly; has the child then "made" this choice? Does going toward water come from a thought-out project? I don't believe so for a minute, even though with my own eyes I've seen the ruses, subterfuges, and stratagems enacted by an autistic child who, having noticed water, was prevented from approaching it, so that the story of the chimpanzees, the boxes, and the bananas hanging from the ceiling does not tell me what it tells Karl von Frisch. What Frisch takes as self-evident – that there is a thought-out project on the chimpanzees' part – is not self-evident to me.

For what ought we to think, then, of the tiny parachute of very fine silk that is about to carry the thread with its grappling hook made of glue toward a branch that will become one of the two support structures required for weaving?

Let us have a look at the weaver bird, a plucky little bird who, as his name indicates, is a bird that weaves; he does not weave a web but a nest, whose structure consists of knotted fibers; what Frisch says about them is that the knots are not pulled tight, and this, he says, is because the weaver bird may be led to rebuild the nest simply because the female, having taken a look at the work, doesn't choose to enter it. In fact, there are several females who come and flutter around the structure while the male goes about his business; the nest that one of them does not appreciate may be chosen by another as her home.

What then is the criterion for distinguishing between a thought-out project and "activities [that] are clearly directed by innate drives?" (Frisch 245)

It could be that what pushes zoologists to classify stacking boxes at a higher level is simply the fact that chimpanzees resembles us. The same way of walking, the same mode of thinking – or almost. And it is also true when speaking of a chimpanzee's hands, its mimicry.

"Despite everything...."

What is the tenor of this whole that makes the difference? An entire world? An insurmountable limit? The fruit of an inveterate decoy? A simple effect of language, which has more than one misdeed on its record?

The fact remains that the acting in question, because it is innate, is on an inferior level. Never mind that the fruit of the thought-out project is frightfully toxic and harmful.

19

Between drifting and searching – in the noblest sense of the term – is there truly a difference of "level?"

We see quite clearly that "to drift" [*vaguer*] is a verb without a complement, or object. The same goes for "to search," which takes on its loftiness, its own exigency, if the researcher is working within a network, rather as termites do, and if the "what" that is the object of the searching is not at all necessary, given that the "thought-out project" of the researcher is to search.

And here we come back to the Arachnean; the spider has no need whatsoever to think about the insect that is going to get caught in its web.

The fact that drifting has no predefined object can make one think that the subject, then, is adrift.

Returning to the memoirs of a dissident, just as I occasionally return to *Animal Architecture*, I perceive that the dissident has noticed that revolution is not the work of a network.
It's about harassing the monster, exasperating it, weakening it, driving it crazy, revealing the absurdity in the apparent power, so much so that the partisans have completely disparate "ideas," their only point of harmony being the appetite for provoking the monster's malice, even if it means getting caught in order to prove the cruel stupidity of that malice.

Such, in the simplest terms, is the thought-out project of the dissident, of this particular dissident; the network appears merely in the form of precautions taken to avoid getting caught too quickly.
In fact, the recourse to freedom that is demanded aspires to stir up echoes in near or far-off lands; is the network fighting against Power? The fact is that it struggles with the amorphous, the amorphous being, literally, something that does not have its own crystallized form.

Above and beyond the Arachnean, we find ourselves among crystals.

Thus we are dealing with form, and it is not at all by chance that the word "cell" has appeared in the vocabulary of revolutionaries.

But this is not my aim.
If crystals and cells are in order, why not the Arachnean?

20

Responsible for a network, as conscientiously as possible, in what way am I Arachnean?

Responsible, I'm on the lookout, just as the spider is.
That said, the same goes for the ten or twelve others whose presence weaves our network.

Ten or twelve spinners on the lookout upon the same web, this is what differentiates us from spiders; each one of us is provided, as is right and proper, with our own thought-out project; it would perhaps be more accurate to say our thought-out projects.

These projects bear upon the network, or else they support it, bear it up like so many buoys, if the network is a net.

This word "bear" illustrates quite well one of the things we must be on the lookout for. To speak of buoys is a very approximate analogy, for a network is not an inert thing, as would be the case with a net, and we are not buoys.

What can be woven between the ones and the others is, properly speaking, unimaginable.

If I say that the network must have priority, it seems to be located on the side of the thought-out project, where the Arachnean disappears.

Thus we have had to imagine a practice that would allow the Arachnean not only to exist but to persist, something that is much more uncertain, because if it is possible for the Arachnean to flourish, who knows what it will have to bear; at the very least, it will be incorporated into the thought-out project.

What would one think of an architect who, in his blueprints, reserved certain aspects of a structure to be built as places for spiders to weave their webs? He would be a bit suspect, at the very least, and it would surely be under his own roof, inside his skull, that spiders would be said to dwell. Let him think of heating, lighting, soundproofing, costs, but not about spiders.

This does not prevent us from seeing what is wrong here: the thought-out project absorbs everything, and what it cannot absorb it destroy as inopportune.

If, thanks to this practice of tracing trajectories, the Arachnean aspect of wander lines, traces of the paths of children whose project escapes us, should appear, will we be capable of respecting this proximity as we should?

Chance has helped us, on occasion; the slightest desire to use the Arachnean – to whatever end – made it disappear, so that if freedom is awareness of necessity, one still must understand, within this necessity, the necessity of respecting – and thus of perceiving – the Arachnean, which is no small matter.

But why so much concern for the Arachnean since it takes shape on its own?

Well, no: lift a spider onto a glass plate, and some sketchy weaving may occur, but only in a void, for the glass plate is the void, quite simply because there is no possible support structure and the spider's gestures, obstinately reiterated, the very gestures that would allow it to weave, become so many spasms, preludes to the agony of the Arachnean.

In the same way, if humanness is a mode of being in a network, we can easily see why it persists as a vague desire, and rather like what is lacking in the human-that-we-are rather than as what characterizes humanness.

21

To return to the premises of our practice and go back to the very earliest maps traced, it appears that the Arachnean network of wander lines does not arise from an encircling ring, which is to say that if we draw a completely imaginary line that connects the points farthest away from what would be the center of the living area, this line has roughly the form of an egg.

To the naked eye, it would appear that the Arachnean of the wander lines is attached to a sort of dividing wall that does not exist.

I have no idea whether Karl von Frisch or his colleagues have tried to find out in what overall form a spider web is inscribed, and not just one but all webs of spiders of a given species. One can certainly see the futility of such "research"; at the extreme limit, with the help of chance, it might become apparent that Nature harbors, among its mysteries, some profound unity, and that it works in a mechanical fashion, whether we are dealing with a spider web or with the wander lines of "autistic" children.

By way of the thought-out project, the humans-that-we-are escape this mechanical mode, except for the fact that humans invent machines.

Humans reserve for themselves, as they should, the privilege of the thought-out project, and some of them contemplate tenderly the wonders of ingenuity and utility that work for them.

Frisch sounds like an old friend when he says: "We humans are proud of our inventions. But can we discern greater merit in our capabilities than in those of the master builders who unconsciously follow their instincts? The evolutionary roots of human behavior reach far back into the behavior patterns of animals." (Frisch 286)

In contrast, when he speaks of human beings, I hesitate to follow him: "The first human beings, too, lived in caves before they started to build solid huts and thereby created the first real dwelling-houses." (Frisch 284)

Better still: "only [structures] what is of proven biological value will develop and survive over long periods. The fact that [such structures] appear at the same time as objects of perfect beauty is something I gratefully accept as a gift of nature without wishing to philosophize about it." (Frisch 283)

I find it hard if not impossible to follow him here.

The criterion of utility refers to the thought-out project that concerns the humans-that-we-are. "The structures formed in microscopic protozoa admirably fulfill their vital functions of protection and support and, at the same time, exhibit an exquisite beauty." (Frisch 283)

If the criterion for persistence were utility, what would be the point of this diversity? These fine protozoa, which make their own skeletons, would lead to the most efficient, useful, and uniform shape; and this is what is currently happening to humankind, obsessed with utility, the crowning achievement of the thought-out project.

One could say that the zoologist writes under the reign of a tyrannical and super-cilious dictator, rather like those freethinking or libertine writers of past centuries who never failed to put their work under the banner of God. But how difficult it is to think differently. An analogy springs to mind: a network is like a protozoon that would undertake the making of its own skeleton; if it neglects the beauty of forms, the necessity of the ornate, it condemns itself to be an enterprise devoted to the thought-out project. What the dissident has to say about the factories in his coun-try where he had to go do internships as a student seems to be a fable. Factories function under the auspices of the thought-out project, a rigorous and demanding production plan; the workers in question, grappling every morning with the number of parts they had to produce, found the path to the buildings where the fabricated parts were stored, just as ants find what they are lacking at the end of a long path; the workers amply supplied themselves with finished parts and spent peaceful hours in the shop where what weighed on them was boredom rather than fatigue, the ornate aspect at certain moments being based on vodka.

In the closing lines of *Animal Architecture*, Karl von Frisch returns to the mystery. For him, the problem of links between man and animal is of an infinite complexity: "the sum total of unsolved mysteries will always remain immeasurably greater than the sum of our discoveries"; he pities those who "have never experienced that sense of profound awe in the face of the workings of nature, some of which will forever elude comprehension, even by the mind of man." (Frisch 286-87)

But by proceeding in this way doesn't he deliberately deepen the mystery? There is the higher level of the thought-out project and there is what the innate can do. The connections? There must be at least one: being prepared to perceive that the innate in the human exists and persists, beyond the moment of suckling, or might persist if....

The humility Frisch invokes – and which he says is called for in the face of this impenetrable mystery – would immediately find something more useful to do than pushing us to concede: not to situate the thought-out project as being of a higher level on the pretext that it is the structure, the skeleton of "our" mode of thinking, a structure whose effects fascinate us, all the more so in that, as far as we are concerned, the innate that would drive us if ... is reduced to the state of a relic and thus mixed with other characteristics of our behavior such as aggressiveness or sexuality, which curiously do not appear when we speak of sociability, affability, or artistic abilities. In fact, instinct embarrasses us, just as people of a certain caste are embarrassed by ancestors of a lower caste; always the "level." The humans-that-we-are had to reach the point of extracting themselves from their animal dross. But what a strange vision of beings and things, whether they are from the animal or human species; and why would what happened afterward be of a higher level than what happened before? That the most visible layer of a terrain is called higher, or superior, by a simple play on words, leads to calling the other layers lower, or inferior. As for the humans that we are, if there had not been inferiors, how could there be superiors? How would they maintain themselves? In orbit?

What a shame that humans didn't place heaven at the center of the earth when they elaborated their mythologies. As newcomers, they could have made themselves discreet, timid, respectful, seeing predecessors everywhere, in all vegetation, in all animals; actually, they did think that way, but almost furtively, swept up in the vogue of the thought-out project whose utility seemed undeniable. And now they hesitate, they have second thoughts, but their approach is uncertain, faltering. And how could it be otherwise? The innate has dried up, atrophied. Humans have nothing but lungs, now, whereas they would need gills.[4] Hearing: they are no longer capable of it. They understand, they hear themselves think; but hearing is not at all the same thing as what can be said.

The mystery about which Frisch speaks is proof of what we are lacking. If a philosopher comes to the rescue of the bewildered ethologist, it's to tell him: "The bird is not a doctor of science who can explain the secret of flight for his colleagues. While his case is being discussed, the swallow, without any other explanation, takes flight before the dumbfounded doctors ... in less time than it takes to say the monosyllable *fiat*, the bird Will has already accomplished the perilous leap, the adventurous step, the heroic flight of wanting; the will, leaving behind the firm support of being, has already leapt into the void."[5]

And here we are again, feet first, within the thought-out project.
And this bird lives in a flock, in a tight-knit formation.

If "the will, leaving behind the firm support of being," flies off, it does not fly into the void; it is called, attracted by its companions passing high overhead, sometimes very fast, and sometimes the flight detours back, puts itself within reach of a nascent will and gathers it into its project.

If there is a void, it lies elsewhere; it is here, close to us in the space where the innate "explodes" within the void, and I tell myself that this void is willed.

The philosopher speaks of will [*volonté*], and his thought can be carried away without his knowledge by alliteration; he speaks of flight [*vol*] and thus of birds; and the birds that are "wanters" – as we might say of gray geese or ravens – are predators that pillage the space that can be called the site of the innate deprived of being owing to the avidity of all the wills that, as the philosopher says, have left behind "the firm support of being."

---

4. The French word for gill, *ouïe*, is a homonym of *ouïe*, hearing. [TN]
5. Vladimir Jankélévitch, *Le Je-ne-sais-quoi et le Presque-rien 3. La volonté de vouloir* (Paris: Seuil, 1980), p. 84.

22

Thus we are dealing with the site of being, all "wanters" swept up in their incessant and, in all likelihood, circular migration.

It can happen that the "wanter" in flight sees its shadow at the site of being, but this grasped shadow is not however within the grasp of being.

The rapacity of "wanters" has nothing to do with any sort of malevolence; it is a matter of extracting being from its hard coating where wanting threatens to fasten it down.

One of the characteristics of wanters is that they speak and think of themselves as wanting; we see this from old French, which speaks of *volenté* when we would say *volonté* (will) and *voloir* when we would say *vouloir* (to want).

We can see to what extent the philosopher has it right: being is *wanting*, a support that a wanter, in flight, abandons, suspended within the zeitgeist of knowing that it wants.
As for knowing *what* to want....
But this is not my aim.

The being without wanting, planted upright, insensitive to the wind of what is in vogue and the zeitgeist, blind to the "whats" that are the bait of the wanters, rather than to the weathervane, makes one think of a sundial, planted for all eternity; but for what? wonder the fliers [*volants*]. And they end up realizing that the planted sundial proves at least that the sun turns, which has nothing at all to do with the real, and that with a bit of ingenuity one can make it tell us what time it is, or if not tell us, then at least point it out. From this an appearance of utility re-emerges, explaining to the flier why the being without wanting persists, as well as all the reasons that militate in favor of its disappearance.

But the fable is not finished.
Fliers, owing to their moral principle according to which every being – even without wanting – can always be useful, invented the sundial, and now we have the being encircled with inscriptions that are of no concern at all to it; it's all about the sun.

But here the encircling ring, which has the form of an ellipse, more or less, reminds us of something.

Didn't all those traces, all those wander lines, form an encircling ring?

Where the fliers trace a sundial, what would really be at stake is the Arachnean, if the fliers weren't blind to the real in the same way the beings in question are blind to the "whats" of wanting.

But of what use could the Arachnean be if fliers have the means to conceptualize themselves?

The Arachnean is really found where a flying willing SELF [*SE*] sees its shadow, nothing but its projected shadow whose flapping wings are cleaning house.

23

Here we are: at the site of being / instead of being,[6] the Arachnean, immutable in its forms, its "architecture," to borrow Frisch's term, which is better understood when we are dealing with a beaver lodge, a beehive, or a termite nest than when we are talking about spider webs, even though a web is also a dwelling.

It is right to say *au lieu d'être*, because even if being takes place, if this place has been swept away by the shadow of the fliers, at the place of being / instead of being there is nothing that allows being to exist as a being; being has become "I am" and it flies and comes together in lawful wedlock, which is not within the grasp of the infinitive being.

Whether the being without wanting is also without desire, I leave it to others to decide.

That said, to be without wanting does not necessarily mean that a being is inert.

There, where fliers see and foresee a dial – and this word is fitting here since fliers are aware of time – the being whose wanting has not taken shape perceives nothing of the sundial and its meaning.

For the dial beckons.

In contrast, the Arachnean of acting can be attached to the sundial, whose shadow then turns in vain, it can attach itself and spin its web apart from time, which, in the form of a shadow, passes again and again with the same obstinacy as the web of acting is woven, immutable in its form.

---

6. The French phrase *au lieu d'être* can have both meanings. [TN]

It is curious to see with what abnegation an autistic child can act. Once again, I must choose the closest approximation in the vocabulary, except that abnegation speaks of self-sacrifice and of voluntary sacrifice; where once again we find flight [*le vol*].

There is certainly abnegation, owing to the fact that the acting is disinterested. But this disinterest bears on what would be the "what" of wanting and not on individuals who might deprive themselves of the benefit of their own actions.

Which can lead one to say that acting is aimless, and the dictionary intervenes to remind me that such a manner of acting is only possible through the sacrifice of the self, which is a rather strange conception of things.

If an autistic girl A. obstinately places small branches on the blackened ashes of a fire that has not burned for two years, the aim of the action matters little to her if it were a matter of wanting, even to feed the flames, and someone who wants the fire to burn wants it in order to warm herself up or to cook her food. A.'s gestures, which are clearly inopportune and surprising in their obstinate abnegation, nevertheless do not strike us as radically strange; it is not the first time we have seen a gesture of a similar nature. Let us be carried away for an instant by the wanting: "What A. wants is to reenact a gesture she saw someone else make, and it is quite possible that, just as she was on the verge of doing so, someone prevented her from doing it for fear that she would get burned; one more reason to do it again now that no one is preventing her any longer from doing it non-stop."

Let us remain on the spot and then contemplate this action in a vacuum, so obstinately reiterated that it becomes a ritual.

And we come to one of the "mysteries" with which our existence close to that of autistic children is studded, knowing that Arachnean action has all the characteristics of ritual gestures. This suggests that mythology does not take flight as quickly as one might think; it does not soar high overhead if one does not rely exclusively on what it is saying.

For I can certainly tell myself that A. is a kind of priestess whose self is sacrificed for the maintenance and worship of the fire cult; I can tell myself this if it's somehow convenient for me, if I need to come to terms with wanting at all costs, then A.'s gesture becomes highly – and purely – symbolic, while within her acting there is not an ounce of symbolism; acting is purely acting.

Which shows that the symbolic stripped of all making and aimless pure acting are located within one and the same gesture.

Who would be surprised by this, except for those who adhere stubbornly to the superiority of the thought-out project?

That said, if the Arachnean of acting is immutable, how is it that A. goes to put small branches on the long-cooled traces of a fire?

If there is acting, then it dates back to an era when human beings had not yet mastered fire.

Spiders certainly did not wait for us to build dwellings before they began weaving their webs; the fact that there were dwellings, and walls with something in their nooks to hook a web to, hardly proves that the nooks gave birth to the Arachnean.

24

No wanting in the Arachnean.
And within each gesture of wanting the Arachnean can be found, provided that one looks for it.

Is it really so surprising? The voice seems to be one of the preferred instruments of wanting, and to such a degree that one can no longer untangle the one from the other, language from wanting, so as to determine which one comes first. The slightest word has the voice for support and the voice relies on the noise emitted by the vocal chords, this noise being a matter of acting; on this subject, I have as many throat witnesses as it takes to prove what I'm putting forward here.

The fact remains that, whereas in order to moan, squeak, scream, or buzz, acting suffices, in order to speak, one has to want.
Unless the wanting is caught by up the doing-as that can make one speak.
There remains the Arachnean, where noise from the vocal chords can be heard, and we find it again among Tibetan monks, at the height of a ritual that seems monotonous and repetitive to us. If the Arachnean has nothing do with the act of speaking, and if wanting is not based on the support of a being, instead of being Arachnean, a kind of humming is pursued tirelessly, which is surprising, because anyone who can hum that way can speak; only the wanting is lacking.

But so it goes for all Arachnean acting, whose dexterity proves to us that any sort of doing would be within its reach if....

Hence the – erroneous – conclusion that there is a not-wanting, a will not to want to say or make.

And we know what happens to resisters; with the extreme magnification of what became of them in the Soviet Union, we can understand quite well the reasoning of the governing bodies: in a country where everything is done for the happiness of the individual and where the exploitation of humans by humans is suppressed, anyone who balks at this can only be mentally ill, cracked by a malign wanting that is just as harmful to the individual who wants as to the rest of society. That person, however significant or insignificant, all things considered, is not defined solely by wanting, Soviet system or not, this is what escapes, and in one way or another, this is the motor that has to be repaired, even if it means looking into the unconscious, which can intrude like mud in a sprinkler nozzle; popping up from who knows where, it gets in the way.

That said, to admit the persistence of the Arachnean would require such upheavals in the way the humans-that-we-are have organized ourselves that it is entirely reasonable to think that we will persist on the flight path that has become so ordinary and so powerful that it puts us in orbit, while hoping that what happened to Icarus won't happen to us, Icarus who was so preoccupied with escaping the detours of the labyrinth. And the Arachnean can truly be said to be rich in endless detours.

25

After having heard – and understood – that in regard to the children present here, wanting is not the order of the day, it will take many years for this formulated certainty to permeate customary attitudes ever so slightly.

We could say that they were stubborn, insidiously obstinate, the ones and the others, believing in wanting against all odds. Indeed, what could one make of some other who is present without wanting? It is hard to believe how much distance there can be between an expressed and understood "truth" and the hard, dense core within everyone that decides.

What belongs to the manifest attitude is as surprising when we are dealing with a being aware of being – and it's wanting that decides – as when we are dealing with a being whose acting seems to come about by reflex. Reality is there, table, bowl, chair. If I weren't there, the table, bowl, and chair would still be there, which presupposes that I distinguish myself from reality – as a being conscious of being.

But what if beings do not distinguish themselves from this external reality?

Each time the table, bowl, and chair are encountered anew, it amounts to a rediscovery.

While, for us, it is a trivial matter to be able to expect that, in reality, things don't move, don't get up and leave during our absence, this is not the case for beings who don't distinguish themselves from this reality, which, rediscovered, is welcomed. Was there then some anxiety on this point?

Without a doubt; and what I have sometimes designated as fearing is woven from that uncertainty.

While for our part we have only to believe in the existence of reality – that is, to believe in our own independent existence – it is easy to understand that a being who is unaware of being and of being apart, distinct from the bowl, chair, and table, lacks this assurance.
Hence the minutiae of repeated and uncontrollable checks on a constellation of things, a process that can persist for days, weeks, months, or years, to such a degree that we witness discoveries that are somehow prodigious, the rediscovered thing belonging to a moment which had for some time been forgotten.

This is because the constellation of things has nothing to do with what we condense within the moment, this moment being a certain moment in our time of being aware of being and which merely passes, pass being a verb that evokes a crossing whereas it is really a matter of formulating in the past, if only in order to feel the present.

26

No need to want in order to act. Quite the contrary: all it takes is wanting for the constellation that triggers acting to disappear, rather in the same way sunlight causes the stars to disappear.

We must come back to the Arachnean and take a closer look at a spider web, so close that it looks enormous to us.
What we see, then, is that certain threads are quite similar to a string of pearls, each pearl being a drop of glue. Here we can see the ingenuity of the Arachnean; specific threads are glued together in such a way that the spider can move around without risking the same fate as the prey captured by the pearls.

So we can think that if the customary fabric of a living area captures something of acting, holds it in place, it is because the Arachnean that is available merely threads the pearls of our findings, of what we have spotted among the things that seemed to be the object of the vigilance of fear; acting is thus precipitated upon them.

Whoever says object simultaneously situates the being conscious of being that distinguishes itself from the object; hence our error and our apparently congenital inability to weave the Arachnean as serenely as the spider does.

We can thread the pearls of what we have noticed; we would still have to imagine the dry threads upon which acting could freely go back and forth.

In looking at a spider web, we seem to be witnessing a machination whose subtlety confounds us.

So much foresight inclines us to think that nature is Machiavellian, even if it means moreover that we pay less attention when a plant assimilates carbon in order to give back the carbohydrates and oxygen that we need so badly.

The fact that the vegetable kingdom was the first to appear, providing us oxygen and food when the time came, leads no one to say that there must be some sort of hidden desire within plants for human beings to exist, whereas humans are actually the products of a staggering machination.

That having been said in order to put wanting in its place as a very recent epiphenomenon, wanting is capable of placing itself in quite remote virtual orbits owing to the fact that it moves by self-propulsion. Wanting thus proceeds by distancing, by detachment, just as beings conscious of being distance themselves from reality. Language can be viewed as the combustible material of this self-propulsion.
But this is not my aim.

27

That acting occurs without the intermediary of wanting situates wanting as intermediary. While intermediate suggests an interlude, something that interrupts, intermediary seems rather to suggest something that bears the responsibility of assuring communication, while to all appearances the two words come from the same source.

Seeing wanting as an interlude evokes a kind of entertainment, a representation. The interlude comes to take its place between acts, it interrupts the representation, being itself a representation.
Radio offers a good example of interludes when, whatever the theme under discussion may be, regular three-minute intervals of catchy music are interspersed; these interludes seem to be obligatory; it is difficult to decide of what representation these interludes are intermediaries. One has to believe that the people who prepare the

programs are aware of the interludes and imbued with a sense of their necessity; the presumption is no doubt that this is what listeners want.

It is highly probable that wanting is an interlude rather than an intermediary, and what becomes clear, then, is that the project is representation.

What does Sartre say about the project?

"The being deemed free is the one who can carry out his projects."

"Man is a project that decides itself."

Here we see the spectacular scope the interlude may take.

Wanting carries off being as an eagle seizes a lamb, or as a swallow picks up a feather that it will use to embellish its nest; better still: there is no more nest or feather; no longer even a swallow; all that remains is the flight of fliers, carrying their own gravity.

One might have thought that human beings appeared like an interlude in the spectacle of nature.
And suddenly they decide to be the entire spectacle, all by themselves.

This is precisely what the other philosopher evokes: the heroic flight of wanting, the will leaving behind the firm support of being.
If I were a painter of allegory, how would I represent this flight?
Wanting takes flight, thus the allegory involves a bird, or an airplane, a prototype of a realized project and thus a striking manifestation of the freedom of beings – according to Sartre.

But what sort of allure should we attribute to this firm support, what sort of odd appearance? That of a tree, a rock, a fist, a frond? That of the first human being, dazed by the brood that must have come from his own body, it seems to him, if it came from somewhere; he had become accustomed to birds; some even used to perch on his shoulder, curious about everything, the corners of his lips, the holes in his ears, his eyes; but the particular bird that has just taken flight doesn't care a fig for the human, having decided to take flight on his own wings; godspeed.

28

The mystery is thus in the project.
It is the project that is a mystery.

But the philosopher tells us – not Sartre, the other one: "The timid, furtive glow, the lightning flash of the instant, the silence, the evasive signs – this is the form in which the most important things of life choose to make themselves known. It is not easy to surprise the infinitely doubtful glow, or to understand its meaning. This glow is the blinking light of glimpsing in which the unrecognized suddenly recognizes itself."[7]

If human beings – as they have made themselves, being their own project – merely glimpse – if that – the most important things in life, what does that imply for the human beings they decide to become?
Sartre is right; everything does seem to happen just as he says: human beings decide what they are; the least we can say about this is that they do not do so with full knowledge of the facts; the most important things in life escape them. And why would the most important things in life want to make themselves known – and recognized?

To the wanting of human beings, another wanting necessarily corresponds; apart from wanting, this other wanting understands nothing; it does not recognize itself in itself. If it cannot grasp wanting, even in things, it is at a loss, being itself merely a project.

We ourselves were at a loss, in 1967, somewhat besieged by the ongoing mystery concerning what the young people around us might actually be capable of wanting.

If we were besieged, it is because we had a position.

We had only to abandon this position for the mystery to disappear – because the mystery came from us, not from them.

I am re-reading what the leader of the long struggle of the Chicanos – Mexican immigrants – in California had to say.[8] During the most important marches, the signs they carried included the symbol of their movement and a banner of the Virgin Mary like those found during Mexico's war of independence; furthermore, the most successful protests were the ones that took up – once again – the old pilgrimage paths. The Chicanos are Catholics? No question. There remains the Arachnean, that is to say, along this path, an aspect of the project of demonstrating in front of the courthouse, an aspect of the path repeated from time immemorial whatever the project may be.

---

7. Vladimir Jankélévitch, *Le Je-ne-sais-quoi et le Presque-rien, 2. La méconnaissance. Le malentendu (Paris: Seuil, 1980)*, p. 179.
8. César Chávez (1927-1993), a labor leader and civil rights activist who led a series of struggles in favor of better living and working conditions for migrant workers in California.

The fact that there is a coincidence between the wanted, decided-upon project and the journey of yesteryear provokes resonances of which the leader – who has good ears – is aware.

If this leader were devoured by the project he bore, he would be deaf to these resonances and would drive out of the procession the remnants that had nothing to do with the meaning of the approach, the very aim of the project, an aim that is in a way mankind seeking access to greater dignity.

If human beings mean to be a project that decides on its own, they thereby become the aim of the project.

From such a project the banners reappear, and so do the paths of obsolete pilgrimages. Surprising as this may be to some.

And whoever decides about beings confronts even greater surprises head on and runs a serious risk of heartbreak.

Such a person will think that human beings do not know what they want, which is true; or, rather, humans have to distinguish between what they want simply because they are capable of wanting it and what does not involve wanting. The latter is what I call the Arachnean; it is not within the grasp of wanting.

29

So here we are, and while the path of our approach was not very long, it has led us to abandon a position besieged by the mysteries of an ungraspable wanting, thick as a fog one could cut with a knife, except that a knife that could cut the fog had not been invented. Because what can one make of the wanting of a child who keeps on hitting his head against the wall?

In the mode of wanting, the answers are quite simple: self-destruction, self-injury, and so on. Chance leads us to live near a fountain. The child no longer hits his head against the wall.

Was that really what he wanted, then? Water? It is obvious that the attraction of water trumps the attraction of hitting one's head against walls, which is surprising, but these are the facts, as they say.

It is easy to see that one can take away the necessity of wanting and settle for co-incidence, coincidence being a position we can hold onto without being besieged.

Coincidences asked nothing of us; we had only to perceive them, and once we had gotten a glimpse, they multiplied and diversified.

The fogs of wanting behind us, we navigated the customary,[9] which glimmered with a thousand previously unrecognized coincidences, in a word-for-word correspondence with what the philosopher evokes in referring to the gleam that is the blinking light of glimpsing; but the philosopher adds: "in which the unrecognized suddenly recognizes itself."

The unrecognized that recognizes itself does not inspire confidence on my part.

Who among us could have recognized ourselves in that shimmering of coincidences that we could glimpse, our own wanting making them disappear or recreating yet again the fog from which we had just exited?

Furthermore, what the philosopher says about this unrecognized element is that it recognizes itself. What are we to make of that ITSELF? Are we talking about something unrecognized that suddenly recognizes itself – itself – or is the "itself" mankind suddenly perceiving the unrecognized elements with which it is undoubtedly teeming?

I am not the philosopher and cannot answer for what he meant to say. We were thus navigating the customary, which shimmered with a thousand coincidences; acting emerged like seagulls that suddenly dive; which suggests that they may have seen something besides the shimmering, because it is hard to see how a seagull could feed on shimmerings.

Could there be something beneath this shimmering, then, some sort of project that might have escaped our notice? It turns out that acting is not a seagull and that if the analogy is, in certain respects, coincidental, we must let it retain its lightness and its inconsistency. It may be that acting is eager for coincidence and that is all.

30

Since certain ethnic groups make fire, may we suppose that one day a representative of our species suddenly began wanting to make fire?

---

9. The French adjective *coutumier*, "customary," can be used as a noun to designate a collection or set of customs found in a particular place. Deligny uses *le coutumier* to refer to the customary practices developed within the living spaces he describes; in the English translation, the neologism "the customary" has been adopted for the same purpose. [TN]

That seems unimaginable to me, almost as unimaginable as thinking that some pre-historic man suddenly began wanting to make water.

That he perceived possible coincidences between fire and the various uses he could make of it seems more plausible, even though the coincidences needed for this making to emerge and be within reach would then have to be established.

But how long did it take for humans to notice that this making was within their grasp? It is easy to imagine the fear felt in front of a fire springing up from nowhere. And we have to presume that it took intense curiosity to get beyond that fear.

To be sure, human beings are far from the only ones who use perceived coincidences for their own purposes, redirecting them, draining them, mobilizing them, mastering them, each species reiterating the same choices in the surrounding coincidences, and the same uses.

Still, there has to be something to work with in the surroundings [*environs*].

As for the word *environ*, the dictionary tells us to look under *alentours* (surroundings) and *entour* (around), the latter word so old that it has disappeared. The best ones always disappear first, perhaps because they worked too hard when they were in use. That *alentours* could become *entour* makes it quite clear that innate gestures can spring up in a vacuum. In the surroundings, there is not, there is no longer what would be needed; it is as though the surroundings had been incorporated, not within individuals, who have never known surroundings except as they have perceived them, but rather within the species itself, whence the gestures of acting in a vacuum, which can be expressed by the *entour,* what is around.

Are individuals surprised at the inopportune gestures by which they are suddenly impelled? Why would one be surprised? All innate gestures are just as surprising and push individuals in the same manner, without an ounce of wanting; individuals do not distinguish between wanted gestures and involuntary ones. All gestures escape individuals the same way, that is, they do not escape what we name "him" or "her," entities that exist only on the basis of wanting, for the simple reason that there is neither any him/her nor any wanting, or rather there is nothing of him/her or wanting except on the part of the one who is he/she, personal pronouns that he/she distributes in the surroundings with remarkable extravagance, as if, taking pleasure from the privilege of being, he/she were seized by panic at being alone on this earth.

But what does it mean for humans to be content with themselves if not that they are content with themselves?

31

So, then, we have the around and the surroundings, the around being what persists of the surroundings of yore.

If we do not use wanting, which is merely a function of the self, the coincidences between the around and the surroundings remain.

Coincidences are produced not only within the surroundings but between the around and the surroundings.

I'm very fearful of spoiling my discovery, which is never anything but the rediscovery of a lost word.

Entour can no longer be found except in dictionaries, dictionaries being constantly present in my surroundings.

But skimming the lines devoted to *environ*, I might well have missed it, lost as it was amid the dense columns of monotonous lines; it leapt to my eyes; this was the word I had been missing; but for how long?

If I give wanting its due, what I wanted was to see what was said about the word *environ*.

If *entour* emerged as if driven out by the drabness of the other words, it was indeed because there was a coincidence between *entour* and *alentour*, between around and surroundings.

Within the around there is what is lacking and within the surroundings there is what fills in this lack?

We can see quite easily how *entour* (around) gave way to *entourage* (attendants or associates surrounding an individual); some people doubtless think that the *entourage* creates the *entour*. I would say, rather, that the surroundings are rich in what may allow for coincidences between the surroundings and the around; rich or very poor, miserable, wretched, a void, or almost.

The fact is that, as far as the around is concerned, it would be better to speak of bacteria, the Milky Way, deep-sea fish, hemoglobin, proteins, or anything else that can be observed, however extraordinarily complicated the instruments needed might be. No around.
Moreover, the place is taken, occupied for all time, fortified, baptized, marked.
Humans, as far as they are concerned, know what is going on.
And the around, too, has been a project of theirs for ages.

32

By chance I come across a book, *Biology of Behavior*, by Irenäus Eibl-Eibersfeldt.[10] A swarm of insects, fish, birds, indigenous peoples from more or less everywhere, as well as Freud and Kant: "That men are divided into leaders and the led is but another manifestation of their inborn and irremediably inequality."[11]

And here we find the around designated as a promoter of inequality: "The second class [the led] constitutes the vast majority; they need a high command to make decisions for them, to which decisions they usually bow without demur."[12]

Now Kant: "Humans desire harmony, but nature knows better what is good for their species; it wills discord ... [and it] wills that human beings ... thrust themselves into work and hardship, only to find means, in turn, to cleverly escape the latter." "For this reason one should thank nature for their quarrelsomeness, for their jealously competitive vanity, and for their insatiable appetite for property and even for power!" "Without ... unsociability, ... human beings would fail to fill the void with regard to the purpose for which they, as rational nature, were created...."[13] And so on.

Here it is no longer humanity seeking itself, but nature that has wanted human beings to be insatiable in wanting power, and if there are few leaders and countless numbers being led, this is innate. So there is nothing left for ordinary folk to do but try to get in the good graces of those who are in charge, a vain effort, moreover, since everything is settled.

What is shocking in these remarks, other than the contents, is their peremptory aspect. The innate? Freud knows very well what's what; besides, there have always been those who dominate and those who are dominated, so there is certainly something innate underneath it all.
Kant? Nature? He knows what that is. There are the Arcadian sheep and the shepherds "whose talents [will] lie eternally dormant"[14] owing to this envious unsociability with its insatiable avidity for power. Which is going to liberate them.

So speak the great thinkers. Nature knows what she is doing and if she has made us as we are, it's because it had to be so.

---

10. *Ethology, the Biology of Behavior*, 2nd ed., trans. Erich Klinghammer (New York: Holt, Rinehart and Winston, 1975 [1966]).

11. Excerpt from a letter written by Sigmund Freud to Albert Einstein (September 1932), published in Albert Einstein and Sigmund Freud, *Why War?* trans. Stuart Gilbert (International Institute of Intellectual Cooperation: Paris, 1933), p. 49.

12. *Ibid*, pp. 49-50.

13. Immanuel Kant, "Idea for a Universal History from a Cosmopolitan Perspective," in *"Toward Perpetual Peace" and Other Writings on Politics, Peace, and History*, ed. Pauline Kleingeld, trans. David L. Colclasure (New Haven: Yale University Press, 2006), p. 7. [The three passages cited by Deligny appear in the Fourth Proposition, on the same page but in reverse order. TN]

14. *Ibid*.

That said, the behavioral biologist refers to morality based on reason; he moves un-apologetically from the individual-animal to the individual-human and finds many similarities without noticing that it might well be the case that human nature, the innate, is and perhaps always has been, something that no longer has any reason to be.

By the same token, a being conscious of being equipped with wanting is no longer natural, since the state of nature is exempt from wanting.

To justify the fact that what humans can want by way of something innate that would have seeped into that very wanting is an absurdity barely good for feeding ideologies, which moreover feed on anything and digest everything.

I am reminded of what the man who wove the network of the Chicanos says about his work. He is talking about unions, moreover, not about networks, but it doesn't matter; we are dealing with the same thing. The cornerstone of his approach is nonviolence, and his story makes it clear that nonviolence is the inverse of passivity.

What immediately stands out for me is the coincidence between nonviolence and not-wanting.

Moreover, the term nonviolence itself is incorrect, much as the term not-wanting might be. And Cesar Chavez says the same thing: in this judgment, we are not deal-ing with ideology or Christian virtues or virtues of any other kind.

Doing without violence is the only possible judgment. This amounts to nothing other than refraining from doing as (the other, the adversary, does). Chavez refuses to accept the money required to undertake and coordinate his enterprise from any source but the network itself.

Chavez himself has no power – except the power to decide that he will go on a hunger strike.

He speaks from his own vantage point, and from nowhere else. Humanity? That is not his aim.

Apart from the Chicanos and his own practice, he has nothing to proclaim, ex-cept perhaps that his practice is proving effective and that it is within the grasp of everyone, Chicano or not, who turns out to be in more or less the same concrete situation.

Are we talking about revolution? Chavez does not reject the word, while he pre-sumes at the same time that such a word may encompass many ways of acting.

He describes himself as prudent, cunning, stubborn, and vigilant as far as the basic, organic severity of the undertaking is concerned.

However enthusiastic his supporters may be, he prefers to let them boast rather than having to discuss the organic demands of the network.

Along these lines, the picket lines of the strike, there are women and children.

Wherein one can see how far the coincidence between that network and ours extends; it would be better to say that the points of coincidences are many and varied.

33

From one network to another, there are coincidences. What is similar in the situation that provokes these coincidences?
An excess of constraint.
There, we see the coercion of the major landowners who use the Chicanos.
Here, we find the good will of the familial or institutional entourage of the children said to be autistic.
There is always collusion between wanting [*vouloir*] and power [*pouvoir*]. All it takes is for us to know what we want or merely to believe we know what the other may want, or not want. To know only wanting (whether of the one or of the other) is already a way of bestowing power on oneself.
Whence the analogy between nonviolence and not-wanting.

In nonviolence one sees the avoidance of reciprocity. The same can be said for not-wanting.

In nonviolence, is it a question of negating violence?

It is impossible to deny that violence exists.

The same holds true for not-wanting.

There is no question of denying the existence of wanting; nothing prevents us from recognizing its necessity; still, wanting should stick to what concerns it.

Given the way the Chicanos were treated, one may think that it would be necessary – even imperative – to do something; thus wanting is necessary.

Given the manifest distress of "autistic" children, one must attempt something, which is to say, want something.

Thus what we are dealing with is this "something."

The Chicano said: nonviolence; we said to ourselves: not-wanting, when we began to see the necessary severity of the project itself.

But if we are to believe Freud or Kant – and how many others – violence is natural and wanting has been completely infiltrated by the innate which pushes some to be dominant and most of the rest to be unconditionally dominated; all that remains is for everyone to figure out whether they were born into the skin of the dominated or that of the dominators; therefore it suffices to choose one's skin carefully in order to feel comfortable in it; moreover, this is what the property owners who put the Chicanos to work claim: that the latter are perfectly content not only to have a role, but to have the role they are given.

But it is clear that what is at issue is not really one's skin but one's role, which after all is not exactly the same thing.

The owners do not go so far as to have a supply of skin in reserve for those who have none of their own.

It suffices to reject the idea that violence is natural as well as the idea that makes us think that the innate flourishes within wanting itself.

The innate is not found within wanting but elsewhere; still, this elsewhere must take place; without this elsewhere, there is no innate; it is as though the innate had never existed.

The same can be said of a spider expected to live under a glass plate; there would be no place for its web. You can always try to feed it flies by the spoonful; it won't even notice them, even if you persist in thinking that if it weaves its web it must be because it wants flies.

The Chicanos yell: "*Huelga.*" This is a strike, and in order to strike, one must want it to happen.

But what Cesar Chavez says about the word *huelga* is that it means several other things as well, that it evokes everything that may elude what the Chicanos know how to want, and would come down to this: during the *huelga*, they are elsewhere, which is the place of being.

34

Place of being and place of having.

The collusion between having and wanting is remarkable.

But what the Arachnean teaches us is that for the spider, it is not about wanting to have, through the weaving of the web, the fly; what matters is weaving.

To such an extent that the people who know what they want – wherein some see their freedom – are precisely depriving themselves of that freedom by believing they have put a stop to the detours of the Arachnean, which can in this case be said to be human.

By giving human beings what they seemed to want, spoon-feeding without end, you will not fill the void, which does not come from wanting, your own wanting being presumed to be good and that of the other bad.

Freedom given is not at all the same as freedom won. A gift does not replace a conquest, for what counts is the approach itself, and even there what counts are its forms.

And here we can see what is Arachnean about the network, it being understood that the Arachnean is not a having but an incessant finding, a discovery punctuated by surprises, these surprises being very peculiar coincidences that can only occur if wanting remains confined to what it can do and what is of concern to it.

"Huelga," the Chicanos proclaim and the strike takes place, leaving them some small space for being.

It may be that the huelga has a right to be; but is it really the same huelga?

It must indeed find other forms, or rather its primal forms must remain intact elsewhere and differently to the extent that it begins to have the right to be and finds itself validated; this does not mean however that we place it on a silver platter, but that it has earned the right to take place as a whole; thus it has a place to be, but this is owing to the very fact that the place is recognized, while what must be said about being escapes, as being consists in weaving and not in having any right whatsoever, even though a right given is still something acquired. And it is obvious that weaving – a network – is insatiable because it has no end.

The spider does not fold up its web when it has had its fill of flies and how could we know on what its vigilance bears: on the prey that has let itself be captured or on the damage done by the capture; is this capture a godsend or is it a disaster? Probably both at once, for the innate is not perturbed by the contradictory; not being constituted by wanting, it does not know what it wants.

From which the being conscious of being and constituted by wanting abandons the innate to its fate, turning away from it, seeking to get rid of it, and the cleverest, most subtle way to achieve this is to recognize the innate as that which pushes us to kill or to rule; with the innate thus incorporated, what is to be done with the carcass – do as a spider does with the empty shell of a fly, ejecting its dermal sheath from its web? Eliminate it by blinding ourselves to the fact that the innate is nothing more than forms, whether we are talking about the forms of webs or the dermal sheath, to such an extent that, having forever been eliminated, tossed overboard, the innate persists in its forms, among which there is the network.

Some will no doubt think that, as far as we are concerned, these forms are those of language, and that there are no others. Let them think what they like; this is never anything but a debate about the conception of humanity.

35

The human-that-we-are is the product of a long process of domestication; everyone agrees on this; since time immemorial, human beings have indeed been their own project, and this approach continues to accelerate, taking on more and more scope.

One can take pride in this, settle for it, or deplore it; one can contemplate with amazement what humans become at the most extreme limits of the lifestyle they take on; one can see fragmented ethnic groups disappear, mixed into a sort of monotone broth; one can witness the violent turbulence that takes good sense by surprise; the lone recourse for humans seems to them to be wanting, whether it is the wanting of the god that created them, or their own.

To put it another way, humans surrender to the forces that have led them to where they are.

One of the merits that humans readily attribute to themselves is the ability to master their instincts, which is an all the more curious place given that these "instincts" do not have a place to be.

In contrast, what do take place are massive, enormous, organized destructions, anticipated with premeditation, destructions that are wanted down to the last detail, whereupon humans are astonished and speak of instincts and of a natural if somewhat savage aggressiveness for which moreover the most highly reputed thinkers give thanks.

That said, it is understood that these instincts can be liberated only if some power decides to liberate them; the instincts are therefore channeled, dammed up, the floodgates in the hands of a select few; there are locks as well; one can lower the level of aggressiveness in order to obtain controlled competition; and such a geography, however absurd, seems to be accepted. The blend of instinct and wanting, in which wanting maintains the upper hand, seems to be accepted as a primal truth.

And yet it would appear that we are at the forefront, well positioned to notice, in view of "autistic" children, that aggressiveness is a function of the awareness of being, which leaves one perplexed as to the origins of this so-called aggressiveness.

But this is not my aim, at least for the moment.

36

I have just read two big books both nourished by the archives of the secret war, that war being, if not the last, at least the most recent; it is not in the vast bubbling cauldron of simmering massacres that I see something of the innate but rather in the sudden proliferation of networks.

In the existence of all these tangled networks, one can obviously see whatever one wants to see, from the purest spirit of patriotic sacrifice to the taste of most wretched schemers; I myself, of course, see something else there. War? One has to want to make war, even without knowing who or what is at the origin of this wanting, and the very persons who make the decision to go to war claim that they have been forced to want it; the networks that proliferate are made up of volunteers, and a good number of people pass from one network to another, creating such an imbroglio that it is rather striking to note that, after all is said and done, the existence of this uncertain weaving has been a major determining factor in the apparently fateful course of historical events.

To pass from animal architecture to the archives of the secret war can be seen as a high wire act, whereas we are merely dealing with the Arachnean, the network being nothing more than "a permanent or accidental assemblage of interwoven lines."

That the traces of the Arachnean lines are as permanent as those found on one's hands is pretty much what I'm trying to get at, with the slight difference that the network of lines on one's hands can be seen without difficulty, whereas the Arachnean network remains – endlessly – to be discovered.

Of the "hand" of the network, we can see only the back, the palm being a matter of acting, and acting instead of being, somewhat as we might say that a network – of resistance or intelligence – is woven in the place of war.

Actually – and in the best of cases – the members of a network don't know one another, and the solidity of the network depends on this surprising fact; this shows that the human can do very well without the subjective mode of being, a fact that, given the rampant inflation of the said mode of being, would warrant a little attention on our part.

Chance and coincidence, to tell the truth, are the keywords of the network and it is curious to see how those who have lived according to this mode of being have a tendency to keep quiet, as if there is some secret they must preserve, though no doubt this is often not the case; secret societies have constantly been suspected of the worst crimes for no reason except that they don't say very much. It would have sufficed, during the last war, to look at the attraction of private messages sent out via radio waves toward networks; the least one could say is that these private messages were not private at all. And how many thousands and thousands of people who were not part of any network listened to these messages and were curiously charmed by the strings of senseless phrases, knowing full well that for certain people these phrases were signals; thus there were networks here and there that were completely unknown and yet their existence provided a kind of solace; there was, in life, something like a new organ, a bit bizarre, but if the war were to end, that organ would be missed.

That said, those who had themselves been that organ really had little or nothing to say about it and quite often this was simply because they really didn't know anything more about it, something that greatly surprises those who didn't experience this mode of being, a desubjectivized mode, as it were, and wanting was then conjugated according to a mode that was, to say the least, unusual.

I shall be told that networks have been the object of rather blatant manipulations. This is true, in the same way that it is true that those who know objectively what they want are no less manipulated, the element of illusion being simply a bit bigger or rather more opaque owing to the fact that the real objective – and above all in times of war – must be carefully surrounded by a rampart of fake projects which are decoys all the more necessary in that it would be very dangerous to alert the adversary to the place and the moment when the decisive move was to be decided; so much so that even a war waged in broad daylight is as secret as a so-called secret war.

37

So it was that the small network in question lived for a time like a band of guerillas.

It had to overcome successive and more or less disparate difficulties. At times, we found ourselves using the typical vocabulary of guerillas: dig in, resist, advance, disappear, evade rather than confront obstacles. One word came to predominate: liaison, between scattered units. The era lent itself to this sort of thing; in 1967, guerilla was the term for a kind of quasi-universal ethnicity, ours being privileged owing to the fact that we weren't risking death or torture at every turn; in fact, all we risked was the obliteration of our project, which transgressed the reigning norms, rules, and regulations. For us, it was a matter of figuring out what asylum might mean, so much so that we had to fight on two fronts; a number of people were demonstrating in favor of eliminating confinement in asylums. We were in no way qualified to take in "abnormal" children; our approach could hardly have been more precarious and it was not easy to sort out the misunderstandings upon which the convictions of our friends and enemies alike were based; both moreover shared the perspective of the norm toward which the children who found themselves there were supposed to be tending, if only virtually. Yet we were in search of a mode of being that allowed them to exist even if that meant changing our own mode, and we did not take into account any particular conceptions of mankind, whatever these might be, and not at all because we wanted to replace these conceptions with others; mankind mattered little to us; we were in search of a practice that would exclude from the outset interpretations referring to some code; we did not take the children's ways of being as scrambled, coded messages addressed to us.

It seems to me, and not merely on the basis of our own approach but also on the basis of stories told by ethnologists and stories that have been drawn from archives concerning "networks" or those of their leaders, that there is indeed a practice of "networks," whatever their reason for existing and whatever projects they take on; between the most disparate networks there are the most astonishing coincidences that may end up forming common "lines," just as those found in the palm of the hand do.

If I say that these lines – those found on the palms of one's hands – are innate, I don't think I'm misusing the term; that said, the analogy between hands and net-works is remarkable.

It is not so astonishing that there is a coincidence between a network and a hand. Nature has a longstanding habit of constructing according to schemas that are always the same.

The fact remains that the coincidence is not obvious, owing to the fact that, while we can see inside our hand, we cannot see inside a network. It is as though the lines of a network can only appear under the surface, through transparency, whereas the conscious, transparent part of the network is not transparent at all.

Furthermore, the lines that we have on the palms of our hands do not structure the hands as do the bones that can be seen on x-rays; the lines on the hand seem to be made by chance, and the skin of a closed hand makes folds that could be distributed differently, since the palm of each hand has its own way of folding; this is not the case; these lines follow similar patterns with subtle nuances and are even accompanied by secondary lines that are not necessary for the folds; put another way, they have no rational purpose; the fact remains that their persistence is remarkable; such is also the case with the Arachnean; nothing more than a network of lines that are somewhat tangled according to forms that in fact do not structure the network, do not constitute its skeleton and do not appear to have any usefulness; it seems that one could make a completely different decision about them; but go ahead and try to decide for yourselves, according to some strict principle of utility, what paths these lines should follow; in gazing at our palms, we accept the fact that the innate is what it is, since we can do nothing about it and that any wanting, in this regard, would be ridiculous.

It so happens, alas, that as far as the Arachnean of the network is concerned – which moreover cannot be seen – human beings do not manifest the same respect at all; respect often comes into play only when humans find themselves bereft of all power.

38

When an "autistic" child stares at the palm of his hand, all that we lack is a mirror in order to understand what he is contemplating.

With regard to this very common, frequent gesture, we have the choice between two approaches:
– we could put a mirror in the palm of the child's hand in order to benefit from the occasion (for one never knows: one time might well be enough for the child to perceive that *she* exists, since she would see her*self*).
– we too could look into the palm of this hand – and not in hope of seeing the same thing the child sees.
We can look; looking is not seeing.

A book comes to hand that shows us paintings and sculptures from Australian Aboriginals. The first surprise: the title says: *Un art à l'état brut.*[15] In what respect and from where do we get the idea that this art is more *brut*, more "primitive," than that of our own painters, Braque for example, whose style is obviously influenced by these so-called "primitive" arts? Certainly there is a difference between the two forms of art: while Braque and his contemporaries were able to see manifestations of this *art brut*, it would be quite surprising if Australian Aboriginals had seen the works of painters from the Paris School.

What can *brut* mean?
"That which is in a natural state, having *yet* to be elaborated or shaped by man." I asked the printers to put the word *yet* in italics.

Human beings, in the present case, can only be the humans-that-we-are; this fish, this turtle, this stick figure painted and carved from bark by Aboriginals are art brut. The same fish, turtle, and stick figure – or something quite similar – reiterated by one of our contemporaries becomes elaborated art.

But if one watches Aboriginals at work, the part tradition plays is considerable; none of them sign their work, which in truth has no author. We have made the old Aboriginal with almost-white gray hair put on a pair of trousers; he is hunkered down next to his work, a painting on bark, the hand holding the stick brush placed close to the stone palette.

André Breton's text cites Levi-Strauss: "The system of myth and the representations that result from it serve to establish a homologous relationship between natural and social conditions, or, more exactly, to define a law of equivalency between the significant contrasts situated on several planes: geographical, meteorological, zoological, botanical, technical, economic, social, ritual, religious and philosophical."[16]
The turtle has a sturdy back;[17] from below, it pulls away, intact.

---

15. Karel Kupka, *Un art à l'état brut. Peintures et sculptures des aborigènes* (Lausanne: La Guilde du livre, 1962). All citations are from the English translation: *Dawn of Art: Painting and Sculpture by Australian Aborigenes*, trans. John Ross (New York: Viking, 1965).
16. Claude Lévi-Strauss, *La pensée sauvage* (Paris: Plon, 1962), cited in André Breton, "Main première," trans. John Ross, in *ibid.*, p 10.
17. The French phrase *avoir bon dos*, literally "to have a sturdy back," can also mean "to be a convenient scapegoat," to be able to shoulder blame or abuse.

39

Rather than *art brut*, primitive art, it would be better to speak of *art fossile*, fossil art. Trapped under the mass of superimposed cultures, fossil art occasionally re-emerges; as ancient as it can be, it surprises and inspires, as innocent as ever of the heaps of meanings that we think we have to pile on.

Yet the fossil moves, existing only in the tacit.
If I speak of it, it's to bring out the need for the tacit, whereas enthusiasm will express itself on its own.

The Arachnean of the network gets lost when it seeks to express itself. I can show this with numerous tales of authentic events that are fables only in that they have a kind of moral, or precept.

There was a time when, within the customary of our particular network, there was a beam, a fine old beam of yore, as gray as one could wish, and broad, a beautiful length of tree, roughly squared, upon which ten of us or so could easily sit.

This beam was positioned on the floor in a sheltered spot, at the same level as the ground outside, inside a big building that had once been a silk farm in the time of the silkworm.

The other units of the network had been set up five, ten, or fifteen kilometers away from this silk farm and thus from this solitary beam. It is true that before the beam there had been stones placed on the ground, stones completely identical in size and shape to the stone that served as a palette for the old Aboriginal from Arnhem Land. They had a different use; anyone who came from one of the distant units and passed by the silk farm would place something, lettuce, blackberries, cheese, on a stone belonging to a different unit, and in turn would take away whatever had been placed by someone else on their own collective's stone. All this usually occurred without anyone present but the person passing by.

And then the stones were replaced by the beam, which had been the main beam in a demolished house. The tradition coming from the stones persisted upon the furrowed gray wood of this crudely squared beam, until the day came when the tradition ceased; passers-by would sit and talk and thus exchange information, from which a socio-ethno-psychologist might have concluded that the network was reaching a higher level.

However, several years later, I learned that when the beam was in use in the customary of the network, the legend had taken on language, for the units advocated that the network live in the mode of exchange, an archaic mode and an obsolete tradition considered to be in good taste by everyone in the network, all of whom had an ingrained distrust of money; so it was that a rough solidarity was practiced, to speak like those who speak of the painted turtle on bark somewhere in far-off Arnhem Land.

Now, in this practice – the practice that came before the practice of sitting down to exchange news – my involvement was not a matter of chance; I had brought some vigilance to it, along with my usual share of anxious obstinacy. What suited me in this other practice was that it allowed for the persistent and manifest emergence of the tacit.

The dictionary is mistaken when it situates "manifest" among the antonyms for "tacit." Fossils are both manifest and tacit – and for good reason; if everything that is a fossil began expressing itself, we can imagine the stir it would cause.

Everyone has something to say about the fossil – and about the tacit; this is probably unavoidable.

But let us resume the course of events. As everyone had something to say – and what is there to say except what is said to all and sundry – the beam, until then rich with tacitness, became a site of exchange.

Now, a network that is strong in its old units can sometimes be enriched by a new one that is seeking to establish itself and has nothing to exchange, for to exchange is to "hand over something against compensation" and to "address and receive in return."
Yet the recently-added unit is destitute; the person who comes to the beam takes something away but brings nothing, except the feeling of being in the position of a beggar, a position that most often provokes an allergic reaction.

The beam that had been a discovery therefore provokes an allergic reaction, but owing to what? Owing to this fine old beam positioned on the floor according to the customary of the network? Not at all. The allergy is occasioned by what can be said about it, not about the beam but about what takes place, so to speak, behind its back.

The beam, like the turtle, has a sturdy back.

The notion of exchange, of being *entredite*, betwixt and between, takes shape and somewhat singularizes our way of living, tingeing it with obsolete traditions that have a certain attraction for all sides.

Regarding the bark paintings of the Aboriginals from Arnhem Land, the book that reproduces several of them cites a statement by André Varagnac: "It is enough that a culture should be well adapted to its geographical environment for its corpus of tradition to be maintained almost without change."[18]

But what is meant by "corpus," or "body," of "tradition?" There are the traditions and there is the body; and the body is not the sum of the traditions. To consider the beam as a site of exchange, it is what is formulated, that, taking on form or "body" (though it would be better to say "taking on language"), erases the necessity for the detour in which the beam is found, the beam being robust enough that naming it doesn't "kill" it. Formulation – as a term of exchange – eludes the beam, eliminates it.

So it is that the "body" of the customary, which is in the process of becoming traditional, disappears; what remain are units that exchange products, whereas individuals exchange propositions.

And so we became a small set of units equipped with a few rules, and this to the detriment of the Arachnean of the network; language has cleaned house.

From time to time, the beam reappeared, here or there, in the tradition of a living area, a subterfuge proposed between the children and "us," a trace of adornment, as if the adorned were what replaced the non-use of language and the fact of not-wanting.

Now, nonviolence is not a way of opposing power, even if this aspect appears in a manifest way. Nonviolence is what allows, what requires, that something else be woven, something on the order of the Arachnean network.
It is obvious that we refuse to do violence to the children.
But then what must we do?
Put ourselves in the position of not-wanting.
Is it a question of a position of passivity?
It is precisely the opposite.
Not-wanting creates a kind of interval in which the tacit reigns.
But it is also necessary for the tacit to govern a mode of being that is common to us, that is our own and that does not insert itself between us and the children so as to preserve a certain distance between them and us. We are to find this distance at every turn within the mode of being of the network itself.

---

18. André Varagnac, ed., *L'homme avant l'écriture* (Paris: A. Colin, 1959), cited in Kupka, *Dawn of Art,* p. 165.

40

When an Aboriginal from Arnhem Land, from northern Australia, carves and paints a turtle on a piece of flattened bark, what is he doing?
Nothing.

Once the turtle has been made – and so carefully, so meticulously – the Aboriginal is no longer interested in it; he can abandon it, sit on it, or let the rain wash the painting away.

When one of us, an ethnologist, tourist, missionary, or anyone at all, offers to acquire this work, either the Aboriginal will accept, and at best he will agree to work on commission, or else he will refuse simply because he doesn't want to become a white man, which would surely happen, he believes, if he were to accept the bargain.

In reality, for those who agree to the exchange, their skin does not turn white; rather, the art disappears from their work, for the white man cannot refrain from "commissioning," expressing a want that does not wipe away the painting that has been created, nor the bark, but it does wipe away the Arachnean from the trace absorbed by the dictated project, for the request that is made is one of the most common forms of wanting.

In the book that contains reproductions of Australian Aboriginal bark paintings, there is this phrase: "One day this [primitive] being who was destined to become modern man...."[19]
A whole couplet about communication follows.

Referring to the same images, André Breton writes: "That some of these paintings are 'produced uniquely for the pleasure of the creative effort' must not make us forget that they attest the same generative principle as the other initiatory works which, in the strictest secrecy, propagate the myths peculiar to the tribe."[20]

Under the seal of secrecy?
The tacit would suffice. That a tracing is tacit does not mean there is a secret.
There is simply what can be said and what cannot be said; are we dealing with a secret, a wanting-to-say that is impeded, forbidden, by a certain, perhaps traditional, power?

Perhaps we are dealing with an impossibility; perhaps the wanting-to-say does not exist, in this instance, as if by reflex; and if it is the case that a reflex has an aim,

---

19. Kupka, *Dawn of Art*, p. 168.
20. André Breton, "Main première," John Ross trans., in *ibid.*, p. 10.

it would be a matter of preserving what, once said, disappears or is swept away; language cleans house and thus sets up what would appear to be the fate of humankind.

In these pictures of bark paintings, the turtle often appears, an aquatic turtle, it seems.

We had the experience, during a certain period of time in our particular network, of focusing on a raft in order to evoke its singular characteristics.

What can be drawn from a raft is almost incredible.

We had somewhat exhausted the analogy with guerillas, the enemy forces tending to become manifest, as in *The Desert of the Tartars*[21] when a garrison becomes exhausted in its routine waiting for the invasion which never comes while the officers and guards exhaust their gaze fascinated by the desert horizon.

The word raft came to us to evoke the very structure of these tiny units we were forming, positioned on the waves of the Hercynian mountain range and launched on a crossing that would never end; every hour of the day, morning and evening, every raft remained in the same place, in the same hollow between eroding mounds that had the color of waves, but forever immobile, unless an earthquake were to intervene, which seemed quite unlikely.

The simple word raft provoked a geyser of analogies and the endless crossing could evoke what we had to traverse, namely, language.

Suffice it to say we were not out of the woods yet.
That said, we held on to the raft; the fact that the rudder was only minimally effective under the circumstances did not surprise us; there remained the drifts, planted here and there, which could allow us some relief from the effect of drifting owing to the very language that carried us along and did not allow us to traverse it the way any Pacific ocean would.

Beam, raft, turtle; so many watchwords that have in common their sturdy backs, for language as we know, has undeniable symbolic force.

But it is easy to see how this force of language, born from what we were able to tell ourselves, if it proved to be the only force, continually diverted us from our initial project, which was to traverse it.

---

21. The English title of a 1976 film directed by Valerio Zurlini, *Il deserto dei tartari*.

In the commentaries that surround and literally besiege this aquatic turtle painted on bark by some Aboriginal from another world that appeared primitive, it is the symbol that appears, the keyword, it seems to me, of everything that can be said.

If the symbol is the lone master, its reign is established to the detriment of the Arachnean, which exists only by being tacit, and always distant from what is represented, which can be, at best, nothing more than a pretext.

41

The turtle.

Concerning the bark paintings, André Breton speaks of immediate pleasure, of the untrained eye that is left to wander; he speaks of rhythmic unity, of the organic correspondence between the painting and the shells that exist on this shore, of a contact, a current that passes; he speaks of being seduced and subjugated, of elementary affects, of the emotional threshold that holds sway over the pathways of knowledge, of the very act of creation, the only act that matters for the Aboriginals....

He thus privileges emotion, a word that, at its root, is motion. And Breton wrote this introductory text under the sign of "the first hand."[22]

This turtle thus consists of hand traces; acting comes first, and then making occurs as if superimposed on the tracing, as if incidentally. The witness seeing an Aboriginal grapple with the bark, the person who sympathized with the one she watched as he worked, is surprised by the casualness with which the Aboriginal treats what he has made.

The Aboriginal turns his back on what he makes; his project does not reside there; it resides in the movements of the hand that reiterates the pathways, it comes and goes where the hand must pass; and the hand is not his own. It is just an ordinary hand that he can use the way he uses a little stick, chewed down at one end, as a pencil; the human is at work, and the traced turtle is just as common as the spider web, which is clearly not the web of some particular spider that would sign the Arachnean work with its name.

And the emotion that can surprise us in letting the eye wander over the turtle does not come from the fact that we are contemplating a singular, exceptional work, but

22. Cf. André Breton, "Main première," in Kupka, *Dawn of Art,* trans. John Ross, pp. 7-10; the text includes an image of an ancient etching of a hand from a stone wall in the Oenpelli region of Arnhem Land. [TN]

precisely the contrary, it comes from the fact that the turtle is felt to be common; it is human; and not because a human being is represented by it – though this can happen as well – and this by way of some linguistic interference, given that, for those who have use of it, language gets mixed up with everything, adding its symbolic grain of salt, but quite simply because, for the human, the hand comes first and its traces are common, and common to the species.

And here we see a form of communism that can be called primitive, except that the word primitive evokes a certain state, a certain moment, a certain stage in history; it would be better to speak of primordial communism, "which is the most ancient and serves as the origin."
This is why I wrote that the Arachnean was a fossil.

But one must understand that this ancient origin, however fossilized it may be, remains at the origin of each of our gestures today, fossilized in the sense that this origin is buried under the sedimentary layers of what human beings have been capable of wanting and wanting to become, considering themselves to be their own project, eager to have what they can want and to want what they can have, or what they could have if certain people were not outrageously privileged.

To abolish privilege, one would also have to abandon those who have decided to be separate beings and of such a superior level that they have ended up believing themselves detached.

With the return of someone who had gone off to wander about in Arnhem Land, a turtle-relic appears, a turtle that could be a crocodile, or a skate fish, or coitus, or a female kangaroo, or any number of other things. If I can produce this little inventory, it is because there is, on this bark, something represented, and thus a certain wanting to make a female kangaroo rather than a manta ray.

Who could contradict this? One would still have to distinguish the portion that is reiterated in what is being represented.

Otherwise what would be the source of the surprise, the emotion, and, all things considered, the art?

Art; another word that has a sturdy back, an enormous turtle that emerges from the depths of antiquity and with respect to which we can clearly see – if only from reading André Breton, who with regard to painting speaks of the seashells nearby – that nothing proves that it waited for humans to turn up before showing itself in the light of day.

Quite the opposite is true, actually; art is found everywhere in nature, and what is surprising is that man still respects something that is no more useful than a spider web in the corner of a room.

Which still leaves a little hope as far as the persistence of primordial communism is concerned. One must believe it is just as tenacious as turtles before all the floods, or, to put it another way, as tenacious as the lines on the palms of our hands.

42

If our particular network, so flimsy and precarious, had a vocation, it would be to weave at least some aspects of a primordial communism. We understand quite well that the same thing applies to this work as to painting, the work of art lies in the canvas. Where else could it lie? Inside heads, ideas, inside hearts, or somewhere else?

Each living area is a canvas,[23] it being understood of course that we are speaking of the canvas prior to the painting. There is nothing there, nothing but a stretched space. The fact remains that a certain part of the artwork is already completed; there are some among us who do not have the use of language; they are accustomed to acting, whereas making escapes them. We have had to approach a certain practice of not-wanting; if only out of respect for something that seemed self-evident: that all wanting created violence in the sense that wanting in the place of the other, in the mode of interpretation, is an act of violence, a rape, just as it is an act of violence to think in the place – to put oneself in the place, to take the place, to occupy the place – of a spider or a turtle or anything at all for which our language is nothing but noise among noises.

It is clear that primordial communism is not inscribed within the charter of human rights, where what is at issue can only be what human beings can want; such a charter has to be drafted and thus has to consist in language, and moreover it has to be in a language that can be translated into all languages.

It is obvious that, in the approach we are engaged in, if a clause of the said charter concerned us, it would speak about the right of every human to language. But why is it that every right entails the necessity of separating the human from the species, it being understood that the word species is common to everything that lives; the word species evokes a kind of common good.

And this is true to such an extent that even something that can appear as appropriation by a particular species or by individuals of a species, when it is examined

23. See above, note 2. [TN]

a bit more closely, is, like everything innate, always very unstable according to the circumstances; this is the case with the famous notion of territoriality (defense of a meticulously defined territory), which is established, aggravated, or extinguished depending on the overall food sources that can be found within this territory – which can just as easily be an enclosed field where dangerous competitions take place as a place of peaceful neighborly relations.

43

In the last lines of his book, Karel Kupka writes: "Every art changes inevitably in its manifestations as its creators develop, but less than one might think; it always keeps its simple, noble function, indispensable to man, which is to *communicate* ... Man has always used art voluntarily and consciously, spurred on by his instinct, to *communicate*."[24]

André Breton warns us: "The *end* pursued by the Australian artist has nothing to do with the finished work of art as we circumscribe it in its spatial limits.... His concern from first to last is with the process that leads up to it."[25]

But then how is this famous communication established if the completed artwork is of no interest to anyone, least of all to its author – the creator – himself or herself? The only person who will be interested is the foreign collector who will attempt to communicate and find modalities of exchange in order to take the work back to some museum.

It seems, then, that for the Aborigenes it is not a matter of making any kind of artwork whatsoever. It would rather be a matter of acting, and acting upon the very mode of acting in which reiterating prevails.

The drawn and painted turtle is always the same. Karel Kupka speaks of instinct in relation to the necessity of art; what is innate is acting, and acting without an aim, though coincidences may arise between the "traces" of the acting and some usefulness, perhaps indispensable for survival.
So, to communicate, this keyword endlessly inscribed on the facade of the temple of fashionable ideas?

As for the turtle, the Aboriginals can speak about it; and moreover there are legends regarding this theme, and others; the turtle is not taboo.
But where does the "instinctive necessity" to trace-paint come from?

---

24. Kupka, *Dawn of Art*, p. 178.
25. Breton, "Main première," John Ross trans., in *ibid.*, pp. 9-10.

Among all the forms of – innate – acting, drawing is constantly found.

Moreover, and Karel Kupka tells us this, sometimes the most remarkable modifications come into play in what emerges on the bark; all it takes is for a new material to be introduced within the surroundings of the territory, be it merely some detritus from our industries; some sort of battery residue provides a black that proves easy to manipulate and the Aboriginal will dip his brush into it and use this "color" copiously, in which case the turtle takes on a completely different appearance.

What becomes of the "mythic system of representations" in this business? Is it possible that the venerable swarm of mythic tales steps aside, leaving room for a fresh new tale that justifies the presence of the black that turned up? If I read this event in my own way – and not with a different interpretation but without using the key, the symbolic skeleton key – it is because I've often seen the tracing-painting of a child – an autistic child – that had hitherto been dominated by a seemingly immutable reiteration become significantly modified by the simple fact that the instrument for the "making" had been changed. If communicating is at stake, then here the message is reworked simply because the hand had found different raw materials or different instruments within its grasp. If communicating is at stake, and if communication is subjected to this extent to the randomness of what may be left in a corner, communication is truly random. And what is more, no one really gives a damn about the turtle inscribed on bark, except for enlightened amateurs coming from another world where art has great importance as a source of meaning.

44

To communicate?
I understand well, or rather this word, as I understand it, is doubled.

There is the mythic tale in which the turtle is evoked by name.
And there is the tracing-painting on the bark.
One has to believe that the turtle evoked by name in the repeated tale is not enough.
There is what can be said about the turtle.
And there is the tacit.
In order to make the tacit speak, what is required is to want, to do violence and to violate, and not at all a secret or something that would resist being said.

The turtle is not traced-painted in *place* of what is said.

There is the place of saying and there is the other place that is not the place of saying and that has little to do with (the) saying, except for what the saying actually adds to the bargain, taking advantage of the coincidence, which appears here as being represented.

Of coincidence we make confusion, for the drawing-painting is literally subjugated, domesticated, and made subservient to this undertaking of which the humans-that-we-are not only have the secret but long practice.

Instead of saying, the Aboriginal paints.
Instead of painting, the Aboriginal says.
What he doesn't say, we make him say, and not by torturing him, but by torturing the turtle or the skate or anything in which we want to see nothing but representation and communication.

Such tenacity must have a precise aim, which is moreover easy to glimpse. It is quite simply the hegemony of the humans-that-we-are.

But in order to break with this propensity toward hegemony, thanks to which our privileged mode of living was founded, it is not a matter of honoring everything and everyone, in this case the Aboriginals of Arnhem Land, by treating them and understanding them as similar — and similar to what if not to us. One must notice that instead of saying, or at the site[26] of saying, it is merely a matter of saying.

There remains the other place where communicating — the common can be seen at the root — evokes this primordial communism that exists and persists but that comes from so far off that humans have difficulty rediscovering it, whereas it is self-evidently there, as I am told in a letter that I received today from Cuernavaca, which must be somewhere in the vicinity of Mexico. In a drugstore a boy about ten years old uses a Japanese calculator to prepare customers' bills, whereas the turtle painted on a piece of flattened bark will end up finding its place in one of the museums in the man's city or in a neighboring capital. And we can easily see what is inescapable about fate.

45

That humankind has bypassed, ten thousand or a hundred thousand times over, a different fate that it might have had can be either recognized or rejected.

What has happened has happened, and nothing else. There remains this network that I see with the same eyes that I use to see the turtle painted on bark, different eyes from the ones that are looking at it.

---

26. See above, note 6. [TN]

It was first called an attempt and then a raft; now it is a network, quite simply because rafts are not used that often outside of adventures like the Kon-Tiki's, whereas, if we are to believe what the radio, newspapers, and books tell us, networks are proliferating, at least when the times are conducive, which is a way of saying: when "the times" no longer lend themselves to anything else that men want – and quite often it is a man that emerges and personifictivizes[27] this wanting that is supposed to be the wanting of all the others – the networks shall be woven. And if it is true that if what has occurred – in history – has taken place and nothing else, what might have occurred persists but in forms that escape us, and quite often, as a kind of escape mechanism or way out, networks inherit these forms which have not taken place or which we might say have taken place "in time," which, to tell the truth, is quite a strange place.

The statement that what can be said about networks corresponds to what can be said about turtles – and more specifically those of Arnhem Land, which are aquatic and find themselves painted on pieces of bark that have lost their curved form – is true in more ways than one.

Still, I'm not about to abandon the word Arachnean inscribed within these pages.

The Arachnean, the turtles, the lines of the hand, go well together if only by virtue of the fact that spiders, turtles, and the lines of the hand and perhaps even the turtle painted on bark all share the same origin, all come from nature; they were not wanted, at least by human beings, even if a good number of humans presuppose a creative entity behind them and cannot imagine a harmony that would not result from wanting.

An autistic child traces; you can always ask yourself what, and answer your own question in the same breath.

Tracing is acting.

That the network consists in acting is a little harder to acknowledge.

And yet either it consists in acting or there is no network.

Was it therefore not wanted?
Neither more nor less than the turtle painted on the bark.
The Aboriginal did have to want to peel off a piece of bark, work it, flatten it, and then set out to find a flat rock, prepare the colors, bite into a stick of a specific kind of wood.

---

27. The French term *personnagise* is a neologism based on the words *personnage*, a character in a fiction, and *personnaliser*, to personalize. [TN]

The same holds true for our network: we have had to want a certain number of things, plan for them, decide on them, and it is clearly harder to find four or five presumably inhabitable locations – even for the future – than it is to cut a rectangle of bark from the trunk of a tree.

Nevertheless, the fact still remains that the network is of the same nature as the painted turtle; some will call it a work of art; this word works as well as any other if we're willing to rid it of the prejudice according to which we are dealing with – and dealing only with – the represented.

Like the turtle, the network has a sturdy back, just as the hand has a back that doesn't have much to do with the Arachnean lines on the inside of the same hand.

The network has a sturdy back.
No telling what it may represent for those who are concerned with what it represents. And passers-by are numerous, people who come from their own world, persuaded that we are ceaselessly in the middle of trying to provide a representation, give a performance. They come to see, if only how this network rears, trains, educates, or cares for "autistic" children.

The ethno-socio-psycho-logists are greater in number than one might think. The fact remains that while some among us can speak, and I'm often the one delegated for this office, the network cannot be expressed.
Many things can be expressed, such as the bark, the flattened rock, batteries left as rubbish, our resources, the chewed stick and, why not, even the legends borrowed from historical myths which can be recited and even written down; there remains the network, which consists in acting; and on this basis it eludes us, whereas we use it as a keyword and I am no longer surprised by hearing others who are the network, make it, live it, say that they don't know where it is and can't perceive its consistency or no longer perceive it. They say that once upon a time....

That said, it is possible that the network could disappear or even that it did disappear three years ago without anyone noticing at the time.

All it takes is for a conjugation of wanting to be established whose exigency and clear conscience are such that the tacit is disposed of.

I must take every precaution to protect this tacit from being in any way confused with the unconscious described by Freud; that said, the turtle will never be free from what it represents in the eyes of those who look at it; in talking about it, one will speak of love and affect, of the need to communicate and anything else one will want to make it say, for such language has the virtue of allowing anyone to speak in the place of another, this other existing only to be spoken of; to be spoken of makes it a speaking entity, which is true for turtles, even aquatic ones, and for spiders, and even for the lines of the hand.

From speaking to meaning (*vouloir dire*, literally "wanting to say"), not even one step needs to be taken and nothing is required to go from wanting to say to wanting to make [*vouloir faire*].
If we ask an Aboriginal from Arnhem Land what he wanted to make on the bark, he may reply: "A turtle...."
Unless he gives it one of the names that it bears in the legends.
But it is clear that what is said here means nothing or very little compared to all the rest, the painted traces of which are still there.

Furthermore, how can an Aboriginal from Australia – or from anywhere else – "make" a turtle?

What I mean is that, if there is a network, we could not have "made" it.
Nature alone....
So there is nothing to be done but let nature run its course?
Nothing is as difficult as letting nature run its course, for nature has no need of us in order to make a turtle, whereas, for a network to be woven, a certain number of human beings who are relatively close to one another are needed, plus a certain number of others who are relatively remote, without regard to time and space.

46

Letting nature run its course is never more than a way of saying, or at the least, understanding, that it is possible that chance, in the same way, does a good job.

I am well aware that human beings, as eminent philosophers construe them, boast about nature having wanted them to exist, and we can see that such a view of nature is only reached through the wanting of the aforementioned philosophers. But this is beside the point; I'm talking about networks and nothing more, in other words nowhere else, a network being the site of being in, and according to, a certain mode.

Does a network have morality? It must certainly have customs or morals, these being a given like the bark one must scrub gently, no doubt soak, and keep flat by placing some stones in the right places, stones that can be removed once the bark has taken on the shape, forgetting where it came from, thus becoming a flattened section that seems to have lost the memory of the tree trunk that it protected and from which it was plucked, and thus lost the memory of its former role.

These two roles, which correspond to two successive moments for the bark, coincide in a single moment for the network. Being a network, it is a support, not that it has to support – or withstand – the presence of children.

Being a network, it is a stretch in space, a tiny fragment of the terrestrial bark. This tiny fragment, have we not cut it out, have we not removed it from the rest of the bark?

One must look a little more closely.
It so happened that the living area was maintained as it were by stones, placed like so many drifts within the customary, if only to help us take their presence into account, whereas they marked nothing, the stones were not markers except insofar as they appeared to mark the boundary between two modes of being, ours and that of the children. These stones helped us to activate these detours ourselves, detours without which the necessary paths in the course of making remained our own, and offered very little attraction to the youngsters who seemed to watch us from beyond our world strewn with intentions. And we managed to detach this fragment of bark, terrestrial bark, by forcing it to undergo a modification of scale; there were maps where drawings could be seen, the full set of our customary paths and, against this backdrop, the wander lines, traces of the children's paths and above all those of the children whose projects eluded us.

Therefore it's clear that in the slightest of our gestures, we were akin to the Aboriginals of Arnhem Land, apart from the fact that what appeared was neither a turtle, nor a crocodile, nor a skate fish.
Was it the Arachnean?
One could easily think so in looking at these maps, which were abandoned once they were made, just as the bark paintings are abandoned. The lines drawn in India ink unquestionably evoke a spider's web traversed by some busy bumblebee, and the lines dangle like ropes aboard a ship whose sails have been ripped apart by a storm.

47

If the Arachnean evoked a prehistoric period the way the Mousterian speaks to us about the Neanderthals, we would have to speak of the Graniers people or the Serret people according to the name of the locale of the living area where the maps were drawn.

And yet, every human from any place-time is a network human, with the subtle difference that if the network is the name of something, we have no idea what that thing is, we have never seen it.

The Aboriginal has seen turtles and even if, while he is painting on bark, his project is not really to represent them the way they are, he is nevertheless inspired by them. Which shows that the network is something other than the turtle even if I go as far as to say that it would not be so surprising if they were of the same nature; but then are we dealing with true aquatic turtles that have been stopped in their movement and fixed in their role as emblems – the word emblem encompassing the representative and symbolic – or are we dealing with the fact that tracing-painting is in nature – in human nature, in the present case? If tracing-painting is part of human nature, perhaps the same can be said of weaving; but weaving what? The word that threatens to come into play at the outset is relations; it is a matter of weaving relations among the ones and the others; but it is still necessary, then, for the one to be distinguished from the other.

To watch autistic children live, this ability to distinguish oneself – from the other – does not always seem to be a given.

And the mere fact that one or the other of us has to insist on turning acting into making often provokes, on the child's part, an attachment such that it would not be exaggerating to say that the child begins to fasten onto this other person from whom he does not appear to distinguish himself; he cares for this other person no more than he cares for himself; this other is the self that the autistic child is not / does not have. And if two autistic children live habitually in close proximity, the relation that is established is not really established between them but between them and things; it is obvious that things have unquestionable priority; and not inert things, but things in movement, things and their movement, things in their movement, for things in their customary movement appear to be one and the same thing.

Would the third term then be things and their movement? There would still need to be, between these terms, two others, something that is not obvious.

The attachment to the third term is such that – as was the case earlier with the attachment toward one of us – it is not obvious, from the reiterated movement of things, that the children distinguish themselves, as they themselves hover closely around one another, and their acting arises as if to allow the reiterated movement of things to take place, though they may intervene by turns, either with their own hand or by manipulating the hand of another as we would do with an instrument.

48

Passing a moment ago by a good-sized cooking pot that is used only rarely, my eye was caught by the very fine threads woven by a spider and suspended where there would have been a skin if the pot had been a drum.

I was in the middle of writing these pages and I thought I saw – or nearly – the trace of the customary gestures involved in the use of this cooking pot.

There was a coincidence here that touched me at the point where one might think that writing prepares itself.

The threads glimmered in the sun, barely perceptible except for their reflections, an iridescent shine.

People sometimes speak about the irony of fate, and why would chance not be capable of some malice?

By dint of writing the word, I saw the Arachnean the way a Yaqui sorcerer sees the threads that bind people together.

That the gestures that have succeeded in taking place in time – and time is space, after all, the vast circle of the cooking pot with its blackened sides is a space – persist in the form of an iridescent thread presupposes the existence of a certain memory; still, one has to wonder what a word can mean. Some think the innate, a set of specific behaviors, is nothing more than a memory in which behaviors that had been innovative in their time, efforts that had proved fruitful, rooted themselves in the ways of being of the future individuals of the species; this could explain the genius of each species; an explanation that makes good sense; the fact remains that there are only a certain number of possible types of good sense and to place oneself at the crossroads of all these paths of good sense is no more comfortable a situation than choosing one path and going all the way to the end to see where it leads, without forgetting that this path leads you in the opposite direction of the same path if you start out going the other way.

Trying to get a handle on the innate does not get me very far.

All I can say is that when consciousness is eclipsed, what appears is astonishing and worth looking at, rather in the way one considers a solar eclipse – and one has to run to the four corners of the world because each eclipse can be seen only from a certain vantage point – and each time, doing this teaches us something about the sun, which we think we are seeing whereas we see virtually nothing but our own blindness.

So I had reached the point of looking at something human in the cooking pot with sides blackened by the use we make of a wood fire, letting myself be taken in by the mirage of seeing iridescent traces of reiterated gestures where one could just as well evoke ritual gestures, stereotypical symptoms of autism, and art.

49

While teams of international astronomers, scientists equipped with extraordinary instruments, race to the four corners of the earth to get set up to record all possible aspects of the solar eclipse predicted to the nearest possible second, and it will take years to study all the traces of the phenomenon, the children we see living around us and have been seeing for almost fifteen years now are here, peacefully, with an eclipsed consciousness. Eclipsed by what moon? Would I know if this moon were out of my reach?

Can I say that the Arachnean then becomes visible? It has occurred to me to think this if not to say it out loud.
Rather what appears are vestiges of the Arachnean web, traversed and ruined by the passage of insects and stones or what have you – meteorites, as it were.
And the human then appears as being what remains, somewhat in tatters, of the Arachnean traversed by the sort of blind meteorite that is consciousness.

Which amounts to saying that consciousness is in no way capable of mending, patching, or repairing the damage it would be false to think it has provoked: consciousness provokes damage ceaselessly.

What takes (has taken) place supposedly in time takes (has taken) place in space, space being right now; and one shouldn't put too much trust in that simple, appealing word.

This is how the Arachnean would speak if it were wise, which it visibly is not in the least.

The sole access consciousness has to the Arachnean lies in traversing it. Like a meteor that takes as good sense the direction of its trajectory, which, as far as sense goes, has none whatsoever.

I have had occasion to speak about the immutable because it had seemed to me that this was one of the characteristics of the Arachnean. That said, the Arachnean is endowed with a suppleness, a dexterity, a virtuosity, a capacity for initiatives that somewhat reconciles it with what our own species might be. Might be is a conditional: what our species would be if it existed.

What is in our grasp is to think that our species doesn't exist and that human beings are merely their own project (belonging to "themselves" alone, humans thinking themselves).

Actually, the species does exist and persist; it is what is lacking in human beings, who fill in, clog up, and paper over this lack with all that they can say to themselves, and they give thanks to consciousness, the grace by means of which they can ward off the vertigo, the absence that they feel before the wanted chasm of the Arachnean.

50

Let's take a detour via Ivan Illich, vernacular values and *Shadow Work*.[28]

What an odd word, the vernacular; coming from an Indo-European strain, it evokes the idea of rootedness and shelter. If Illich decided to track it down, it's because he needed a simple, direct word for denoting activities that are not motivated by ideas of exchange; a word qualifying autonomous actions, outside the marketplace, by means of which daily needs are met.

He specifies that vernacular speech is made up of words and idioms cultivated within the particular domain of the one expressing himself or herself, as opposed to what is cultivated elsewhere and imported. The dictionary, for its part, with reference to this word evokes a slave born into a house; in the extreme case and outside of parentheses, the vernacular becomes what is specific to a country.

Through books, Illich goes back into the history of this outdated word, which he would like to use to denote the preparation of meals as well as the formation of language, childbirth and entertainment; for him it is a matter of using the word to try to create awareness of the existence of a way of existing, of acting, of making that, within a desirable future society, could be extended to every aspect of life.

Along the way, he discovers that the term mother tongue has never signified vernacular language, but rather the language Catholic monks used when they spoke from the pulpit and did not use Latin; they were teachers, social workers, educators, and the term "mother" denoted an invisible, mystical reality, the Holy-Mother-Church whose language they used. This cleared up something that had always amazed me, namely that people always spoke of the mother tongue as if language owed nothing to the father; it's quite simply because this mother is not the vernacular, but the Church.

Every language is the language of the other, otherwise it is no longer a language; since every sign is a sign for the other, the slightest gesture aspires to be understood and this understanding necessitates a convention, and this convention becomes maternal. It is the convention that generates signs whereby everyone can understand one another or, as we say, communicate.

---

28. Ivan Illich, *Shadow Work* (Boston: Marion Boyars, 1981).

If the vernacular means escaping the mother tongue – this mother tongue having an obvious propensity to become polyglot and thus to become standardized – it can only adhere to its own tongue, which suggests that language can have a spontaneous origin, can be a sort of emanation of customary habits specific to a certain rootedness in a shelter, language being the flower of this plant. But there is still the bumblebee, without which the plant would disappear for lack of the agent that fertilizes it, even if only by moving on from one plant to the next. It is understood that, in earlier times, the first language of an individual was the *patrius sermo*, the language of the one who, in the household, had mastery of it, although every individual speaks several "paternal languages," if only to get along with his or her neighbors. Then Illich notes the advent of four inventions of Asian origin: the horseshoe, the stirrup and the strapped saddle, the bit, and the collar. The horse becomes a draft animal; a single horse replaces six oxen. Owing to its speed, it allows cultivation to spread over vast expanses. Settlements become villages big enough to have a church and then a school. And from this we get everything that follows, starting with institutions and the predominance of the language taught: "The educator, politician and entertainer now come with a loudspeaker ... and the poor immediately forfeit the claim to that indispensable luxury, the silence out of which vernacular language arises."[29]

According to Illich, vernacular language blossoms within silence; it does not speak *from* silence. A plant grows in the earth and not *from* the earth. It is with great sympathy that I follow him in his nostalgia for a golden age of the vernacular; moreover, it turns out that, according to the fashion of our times, the nostalgia that would speak of "returning to" seems to me to be quite widespread. What remains is to find the hand crank that would turn the earth in the other direction. When, within a very large nationalized company, the unions put among their demands as a requirement the creation of a body of specialists to organize training courses for those approaching retirement age so they can learn how to live, as it were, on their own land when they are no longer working, this gives one pause. But we see quite well – and more or less inescapably – that institutions have proliferated and diversified since the time when monks were inventing the mother tongue.

51

It is a matter of the Arachnean, and writing about it.

It would also be a matter of treating the network somewhat the way Ivan Illich speaks about the vernacular, which speaks of dwelling, and it may be that that word resonates with Heidegger's remarks.

---

29. *Ibid.*, p 65.

At the level of dwelling, we find shelter; the use of shelters, as far as our network is concerned, is customary and our lifestyle limits – as much as possible – outside purchases, even though selling – to the outside – is inescapable to the extent that our policy is to avoid institutions. Thus we come close to the vernacular, which gives rise to the customary, which allows children – autistic children – to exist exempt from disarray.

There remains language.

It is only too true that the "mother" tongue we use creates difficulties, sooner or later.

We have to work together, this is why we need a language; and even though this language is the maternal one we have had to incorporate words that were our own since they evoked our practice, slang words, if you will, but from a vernacular slang.

Do these words blossom "within silence?"
There is indeed the silence that stems from the fact that the children do not have the use of language.

Must one then think that a vernacular language would be one that resists, that tries to escape? It would still have to replenish itself with words found within the very rubble of a vocabulary fallen into disuse.

Thus we see that if vernacular language emerges within a silence attributable to the gap, to the distance taken from the contemporary – maternal, as it were – "loudspeaker," in reality, it is born of language itself.

As for the Arachnean, it is not, does not have, is not born of, language, be it maternal or vernacular. Whether we are dealing with speaking loudly or softly or of whispering or shutting one's mouth, we are always dealing with language and even the silence that comes from not speaking is still the silence of language.

There remains real silence – which moreover does not exist – which would be what is perceived by some being that does not hear, who grasps nothing of what can be said, of what can be exchanged.

Silence is rich, but this ore, these waves, these noises and murmurs cannot yield or produce a language. Silence itself – which is something completely different from the absence of noise – is the element of the Arachnean.

Fifteen years of network; five thousand five hundred days and five thousand five hundred nights and countless moments shared among thirty individuals, some of whom have been removed – or have removed themselves, made themselves scarce, as we say – and I find myself rereading some documents that attest to what was said during the meetings of the communist party leaders back then, and also the writings of "dissidents."

It is immediately clear that while their mother tongue is the same, they do not speak the same language.

I obviously have nothing to add to such a debate, except perhaps that "all that" is depressing, in the same way that reading the archives concerning the secret war is depressing.

I have to speak of networks in the same way I have had occasion to speak about rafts and say that what I would fear above all would be creating a language that would render the network useful. That said, I do not take this "fear" seriously; what I say about it is said in order to prevent readers (if there are any) from expecting to find some sort of usable equipment within these pages.

That said (and I would willingly swear to it), network communism would no doubt allow human beings – as we say – to arrive at the threshold of this other world about which it has to be said that everyone has heard, one way or another, in one of those languages, all of which are mother tongues, no matter what word the leader of a small firing squad uses to say: "Fire!" After which it is silence, which has nothing vernacular about it. As absurd and paradoxically utopian as this idea of myriad networks may be, it allows us at least not to trust in language alone.

I understand Ivan Illich very well when he attempts to show how the use of vernacular language allows or would allow, would support, a freedom of initiative for individuals who find themselves subjugated by the predominant and exclusive use of the mother tongue, which has a certain tendency to become universal.

That said, regarding vernacular language, someone has to have mastery over it, and the person who does has mastery over everyday life, governs it, if only because he or she has lived the traditions that are the foundations of the vernacular, its very forms; without this, individual initiatives and projects would wreak havoc, would be initiated or would fail at the expense of the vernacular. Whether we are talking about vernaculars of households or villages, they are traversed by all the winds and currents of the mother tongue, which blows from more or less every direction, propagating contradictory and irreconcilable statements because, henceforth, "mothers" are numerous, diverse and in conflict with one other, destined to fight, sometimes like furies, against allowing the predominance of any one to be established at the expense of another.

52

All one has to do is read how the US, land of religion and freedom, created the Marines, an elite body destined to be the police of their nation throughout the world. The phenomenon leaves one speechless: an irritable instructor-sergeant decides to subdue those who grumble or drag their feet and sends them off on a night march where they will have to cross a raging river; the result: six men drowned; one can hope that in the aftermath the survivors will speak, with full knowledge of the facts, the language of the motherland. And so it goes throughout history, something everyone knows perfectly well. And one shouldn't believe that things are simple; I have been personally acquainted with demobilized SS youth, ex-soldiers of the Foreign Legion, and youth who took an active part in late night bombing raids of German cities. Most of them were nostalgic for life in a network.

I shall be told that, between nostalgia and fanaticism, there is a line they shouldn't have crossed, which is a way of saying nothing at all and of giving intentions a scope that is quite illusory and will remain so as long as the confusion between individuals and subjects persists, individuals being attracted to network life and subjects signing up or being enlisted, enrolled – the latter term clearly expressing what it signifies.

Illich emphasizes the coincidence – in time – of two propositions, two projects, presented to Queen Isabella: that of a certain Nebrija, who proposed to impose a maternal grammar as the language of the state, and that of Christopher Columbus. By coincidence, both projects were laid at the feet of the same imperial queen around 1492. One has to believe that it was the right moment and that the time, as we say, was ripe.

There remains the Arachnean, which is not and does not have a history, no more than it is or has its own language. On this basis, it is easy to understand that language occupies and appropriates space.

53

The vernacular, implanted around a shelter, organizes the surrounding space.

The Arachnean appears during detours that entail acting.

If we take the trouble to trace these detours, the maps that remain to us have in common with the turtle painted on bark by the Aboriginals of Arnhem Land the fact that they are repeated inscriptions and that they are useless, imprints of some unit, and these imprints, from day to day, month to month, year to year, are so similar that they could be the emblem of that specific site; some have been reproduced in journals, displayed in museums, or hung in private homes.

There remains art.

I spoke of imprints; whatever dimensions we give to fingerprints and even if they are mounted in an ornate old oak frame, would it still be a question of a work of art, even if they are hanging in a gallery?

That each unit has its own imprint, all the better, so we can isolate the wander lines of each child, the set of each one's lines is easy to distinguish from those of the others: does this then offer a kind of proof of the rudimentary existence of each one?

Traces of wander lines and fingerprints, the individual exists, there is no doubt about it. He or she either knows this or doesn't know it at all; either individuals say this to themselves or else saying it to themselves eludes them, or rather they avoid saying it to themselves; to say that they avoid it is saying too much since the individual "he" or "she," for want of speaking, exists only for those who speak and whose consciousness and intelligence function in the mode of "the humans-that-we-are."

There remains the individual who eludes what is said.

And there remains art. Vernacular or mother tongue?

If, in the vernacular, an articulated language is not going to grow, will hands trace and paint, will bodies dance, will voices modulate?

If I am to believe the autistic children, tracing, frolicking, and modulating are forms of acting, are of the same nature as the lines of the hand.

In no way am I straying from my aim, which consists in the following: when the constraints of history become unbearable, networks arise that quickly prove terribly effective at the pinnacle of history, spearheads in the stalemates of confrontations. *Esprit de corps*, this is called. Two evenings ago, several kilometers from here, a group of weirdos with brass knuckles circled around a party, a matter of terrorizing contemporaries, neither Blacks, nor Jews, nor Japanese, whatever. There have been, or are, numerous more or less communitarian "networks" operating under the banner of a certain freedom and sexuality among other things. Which made me ask one of them whether that particular freedom was obligatory in their enterprise.

54

The pages I am writing are always very close to what I find myself saying to one member or another of our network.

What I say these days, about our particular network, is that something is missing from it, some kind of instrument.

The vernacular often finds itself inventing instruments out of necessity. Which shows the difference between the vernacular and the Arachnean.

If I say that a network comes into being in the same way as a work of art, there is some truth to this.

As it happens, this particular network has already invented its own instruments, which is to say that it uses, it relies on, something other than the mother tongue, that is, other than everyday French. Just as each fingerprint has something unique – or nearly unique – about it, the sound of each person's voice is unique – or nearly so.

It suffices to imagine a hearing device designed and developed to perceive these nuances – whereas our hearing is used and overtrained to skim off, to perceive, what the sounds pronounced may have in common – in order for us to glimpse the perplexity, the disarray, of a being so informed and literally submerged by the nuances that we eliminate so we can grasp only what the language (of the other) is saying.

And so it is for the autistic being, who is sometimes charged with mental deafness, whereas he or she quite simply doesn't select the same sounds we do.

The *symbolic nuance* of words, gestures, attitudes, mimicries, is not retained, is not heard.

If, within a given space, grappling with ordinary tasks, you want to speak to an autistic person "in his or her language," you would do well not to struggle over words; you can speak any way you like, in a language that is merely a series of roughly modulated sounds, something like a vague, scrambled sound print, and you shouldn't be surprised to see the autistic being behave as if he or she understood. From this starting point you can undertake to teach him or her to speak; you'll see just how far you can take the apprenticeship, or the misunderstanding.
But this is not my aim.

The humans-that-we-are belong to a symbolic order and indeed we understand quite well the complexity of the necessary apprenticeship – a prolonged and necessary initiation.

That human beings prove to be particularly talented at passing initiatory tests of this order is a fact.

Yet we may still wonder whether the symbolic order is the only order possible. If connections are established toward this end, they are necessarily established to the detriment of other possible connections, and no matter which of the myriad synapses intervene, a routine, sometimes nicknamed the norm, or the human, still has to be established.

All this to reach the point of saying that perhaps what I call a network is not of the symbolic order. No one ought to be surprised at this, and yet the persistent, self-evident phenomenon I call a network escapes the faithful mother tongue and, for good reason, the symbolic order; even if the use of this language is vernacular, since the vernacular in no way repudiates the symbolic order that structures it, even if the structuring occurs in the most singular, fragmented mode possible.

55

If we take the example of some outlandish networks, we note with some frequency that they are inhuman.
That said, when a nation, a homeland or anything else whose existence is recognized, historicized, advocated, embarks on the path of inhumanity, it reaches heights that leave traces of horror in everyone's memory. But this brings me back to the term inhuman, for this is where the debate resides: the symbolic order, for many, is the human itself, whereas for me, it is enough to say that the symbolic order structures the humans-that-we-are.

There remains the human innately endowed for the mode of being in a network.

When networks are formed, they lack only speech.
WE give them speech. The speech supplied to a network determines its project, its cause, and whatever else we like that can be said, it being understood that the network involved will code its language in order to remain clandestine if not secret. In other words, the network – if we can put it this way – sets out to learn what it wants. It views itself as the backbone of the project.

If we accept that a *network* can exist without belonging to the symbolic order, we must not be surprised by what happens to the person who barges in with a knapsack full of good will.

And this lone presence, desperately practicing non-intervention in affairs that have to do with the ways of being of autistic beings, is enough to provoke the disarray of the old days.

This is because non-violence and not-wanting are in the same category; it is a matter of liberating the course of acting.

To let the other do what he or she wants is first of all to want the other to be other and to allow that other, who is wanted through obedience to the symbolic order, to do his or her own wanting.

What can one say to the hapless newcomer?

Since the beginning of the existence of our network, none among us has found anything to say in such a case – beyond grumbling, soliloquizing and slandering the ideologies that pervade our contemporaries. For my part, I have pranced around with language, historicizing the Network rather as historic leaders speak of the Flag. I have never found this language to be useful for the newcomers who sat down in front of me, their good will falling into my lap. Could I evoke the spirit of the network? I tried to keep myself at a respectable distance from the role that seemed to have been reserved for me. I limited myself to saying: "The network? It's not human; unless the human is not what PEOPLE think it is."
What else was there to say?

56

I could return a hundred times over to the way a network grows; I could retell in a hundred ways the legend of the bread, of the bread made here, a kind of vernacular fad born from the encounter, at the bend of an alley of a virtually abandoned hamlet, with an ordinary oven that had also been abandoned, except by spiders, for decades. Every time it rained the mass of earth that weighed down on the dome of refractory brick became engorged with water; despite the piles of sticks and branches, instead of baking, the bread boiled in a scorching steam. Another oven was built just before its ancestor crumbled, having lost its bricks, beams, and tiles. It was a wood-burning oven, of course, and vernacular in the full sense of the word; the bundles of kindling came from the surrounding area, brought back from the hills on a donkey cart. The bundles were recognizable; each had its own identity; we could see who had made which one, from the retired miner down the street to a newcomer of good will, no more talented at making bundles of sticks than at intervening within the customary of a living area.

One may be astonished that there is often a coincidence between work that is well done and the attitude, the tone of voice and manners that do not disturb the customary of an area; this is where the virtues of the vernacular can be seen, where one can see that what was important was not the other, even if the other had his or her importance; that was not the main priority.

And perhaps it is here that part of the mystery resides, something that enables us to see that certain individuals, whatever their age or gender, are endowed with a kind of innate attitude that makes them reminiscent of close presences, whereas others, effervescent with good will, create, if only through their gaze, a climate of disarray.

There remains the odor of something indefinable in the air and gestures impossible to grasp. I recently heard a researcher in neurobiology place on the same level – speaking of ungraspable relations between individuals – perfume and language, both of which, he said, complicated everything.

And this brings us back to the monopoly of the relation of the symbolic order, which is not merely dominant but which excludes all other forms of relations. The Arachnean is a way of evoking those other forms.

We understand perfectly well that as soon as networks are in question, the pathways are not the result of individualized wantings. The individual – which I have occasionally baptized the "common body" to hammer the point home – is the network, which is to the vernacular what the spider web is to an otherwise well-kept dwelling.

Here we are dealing simply with an image that isn't even an analogy; between the Arachnean network and subjects individualized by the symbolic order, there is a symbiosis of two modes of being, each one keeping its nature intact.

And it would be quite mistaken to believe that what is not mastered by wanting risks being aberrant; quite the opposite is true. It's precisely when wanting has carte blanche that aberration lies in wait for the humans-that-we-are with more or less urgency and with a more or less collective scope.

57

In every mode of vernacular life, tradition has a share.

When Ivan Illich envisions and hopes for new avant-gardes that will orient themselves toward a mode of living in search of a vision of existence proper to each group, turned toward the subsistence of new types of values that are neither traditional nor industrial, understood but not necessarily shared by another group, permeated with a vision of the human species as *homo habilis* and not *homo industrialis*, it seems to me that he misunderstands the power of language.

If people are now attracted to the mode of living sketched out by Illich, an innovative mode of living that is vernacular in the sense that it resolutely implants itself and is not turned toward a movement, it is obvious that this mode will have no tradition. Which was the case with us as well, and still is. The presence of autistic children required, at the risk of disarray, a life whose customary necessarily had aspects that we had not wanted. Recourse to the elaboration of a rational method as specified in sociology was of no real help to us.

The Arachnean is not rational; it is no more reasonable than the way the brain functions to make us who we are; we haven't "wanted" this brain; through its intermediary we use the information that the apparatus captures, analyzes, and synthesizes. History, recent history at least, has shown us to what extent we ought to be suspicious of these coagulated apparatuses within what is called the State.

One can be amazed at seeing millions of people subjugated by Power.
What a strange power speech has.

Owing to this very power, the presence of children who do not have the use of it allows us to critique it and even shows us that, when the left hemisphere of our brains, for a long time called the dominant hemisphere, seems not to capture information that concerns it, an infinite number of bits of information are literally passed over in silence and are not dealt with by the "intellectual" layers of our thinking organ, which, for the humans-that-we-are, leads to an atrophy of this "sense" whose perceptions are vital, however well and even ingeniously they are compensated for by the humans-that-we-are, this self-mutilation is a result of the sacrifice that the symbolic order demands in order to implant itself and exercise its tyrannical power and it is well known that the tyrannized always ask for more.
But this is not my aim.

What is at issue is what a network can want, can want to believe, and can believe that it wants.

What was suggested yesterday, between someone from our network and someone else, namely, me, was that if this network wanted to be a vernacular, it would have to be a billionaire. For us, this was not a surprise. Without having to go through the process, we have thought for a very long time that to continue to exist we would have to have the use of several hundred hectares in the Cévennes, something like the sea.

It would be easier to find the necessary funds to found and open a museum, if only a museum of archaic traditions made concrete by tools of yore.

We are thus obliged to turn toward the utopian, whereas the mode of being that would escape the tyranny of the symbolic is utopian from the outset. We might think that it lies within us, right where we house the innate, under the sign of the individual.

This mode of being can exist only if, within space, there is some matter that supplies information, in space and not in time.

For a very long time space has been cultivated, arranged in such a way that the innate has in effect atrophied to the point that we can say it has disappeared or, if we are determined to hold onto it, that it exists in a phantom state in the behavior of the humans-that-we-are.

58

I have often spoken of the infinitive, which is the least maternal of the possible uses of the verb since there is no subject to serve as the key to it all; the verb creates the head.

A network exists only in the infinitive.

It is what the monk doesn't mention, whether it be the one who speaks in church about the hamlet that has become a village or the one who speaks on the radio.

And if I speak on the radio, I am a monk; the same goes for when I write, if only to say, referring to networks, that thousands of them would be needed, whereas a network cannot be wanted.

In this respect I am despite everything less a monk than many others who do not know that they are monks; they do not know where they come from, if not from the belly of their mothers; everyone who speaks has at least two mothers; the first is quite easy to recognize provided that she has recognized you; as for the second, recognition is ongoing.

And yet the autistic being who only has one mother, for want of the other whom he doesn't hear or understand, doesn't recognize the sole mother that he has. Here he is, alone, and hungry for networks; he needs nothing else, any other, as such, being the monk whom he can neither hear nor understand. All the monk's words, love, friendship, respect, ring hollow.

To respect the autistic being is not to respect the being that he or she would be as other; it is to do what is needed so the network can weave itself.

Do what is needed? There is nothing to do except to allow the network to make itself. But it is not going to make itself the way a spider web is made because, precisely, there is a spider, which moreover has nothing to want, as it happens.

59

A communist by origin, I watch our network live, I already had this way of gazing before I was a communist; in high school, where I was bored, I opened the top of the box that served as my classroom desktop to watch the odd little lizards we called newts as they went about their lives. We fished them out of the moats of the citadel; they were part of my own life in a way, and then I must have been ashamed to have them there as hostages while I myself – of what was I a hostage, and in the name of what was I forced to mope around in the back of the class? I was there because I was a pupil of the Nation, my father was killed in the war, and as far as this "seminar" was concerned, I knew what was obligatory; the professors spoke to us in the mother tongue and attempted to refine our use of it; this didn't keep us from having to go to war; which is to say, to the extent that I had some resemblance to the lizard, I was just as much a prisoner; and so it goes with every subject, except for those who make one body with the prison, who are the prisons themselves, something that can be seen in every regime.

Water lizard, turtle, spider: the network has origins that are disparate and more distant still than any "ism" with which the humans-that-we-are can be blended, albeit unwittingly. Chance has made me evoke the water lizard; chance has done well.

I used to go to watch the little lizards living in the moat of the citadel. There have always been citadels – this one dates back to the time of Vauban – with moats. It is here that networks live, at the foot of the ramparts, and most often, in the shadows.

Ramparts: it may be that I am speaking of Institutions or perhaps, as well, about the inner fortification,[30] the famous "self" [*soy*] built long ago, a remnant overloaded with history. Who had wanted this? The King [*Le Roy*].[31] It has been a long time now since the King reigned; and yet the citadel remains.

I was born several steps from the ramparts of a small village that sprang up from swamplands close to the North Sea.

I am writing not far away from twin rocks that are three hundred meters high, and on one of them the remains of an abbey-citadel can be seen; to tell the truth, there

---

30. The archaic French word *for*, from the Latin *forum*, "public place" or "tribunal," is now used only in the expression *for intérieur*, translated as "heart of hearts" or "deep inside."
31. *Soy* and *roy* are seventeenth-century French spellings of the modern words *soi* (self) and *roi* (king). [TN]

is nothing left of it, or rather you have to step right on top of what is left: enormous tiles rooted like enormous wisdom teeth that fell out long ago.

The Island Below, Summer 1969

When the-Human-that-We-Are
Is Not There

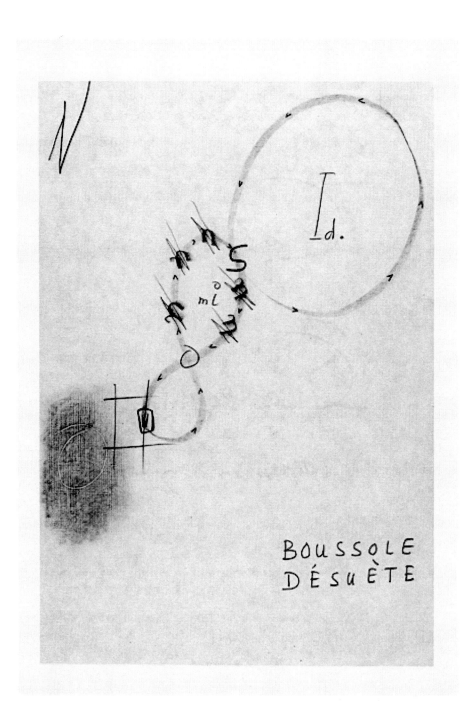

Figure 1

That Seeing and Looking at One*self*
or
The Elephant in the Seminar

In N,[1] the object of research: that which persists as prelude to, and despite, S – the subject – and which is (N initial of *nous*) of a "different nature." (That of the species that calls itself human.)

In Id: Ideology.

In mi: the micro-ideology of the attempt, network of *units*.

In u: the *units*, small sets of presences.

n: initial of *nous* scratched out from N (reminds one that one shouldn't lose one's bearings, shouldn't "lose track of the north": the very object – the project? – of research. Language circulates (the small arrows) and n willingly stuffs and re-stuffs itself with the products and byproducts of ideology.

The four crossed lines: the "*maps*" – our practice – which help us locate N. The words in N – N framed within a black line – used for whatever has to do with the maps – are "in conflict with" the words in S – which "belong to" the realm of the speaking-spoken subject.

At the twisting point of the attempt – which is transcribed as a figure 8 – we find a RING [*CERNE*] (drawn as a poorly closed O): vacant language, language "out of action," at the default point of language.

RING: the first of the words in N that can help shore us up so we can locate the vantage point, the "point-of-seeing," of the autistic individual who is desperately watching for N.

RING: This is a "tracer" dubbed RING.

> We shall never know what this word may mean.
>
> It means nothing. Autistic.

---

1. See Figure 1, p. 130. N here stands for *nous*, the French personal pronoun that can serve as subject ("we") or object ("us"). The title of the drawing, in the bottom left-hand corner, can be translated as "Outdated Compass."

This small calligraphic sketch presents the theme of our attempt, which turned nine years old this past July 14.

Just as the preceding attempt was led by a fellow whose perorations evoked with an uncanny resemblance the political inflections of the general in power, even though his hands were incapable of tying a knot, the current attempt refers to a youngster who lives the vacancy of language: autistic, mute, with nimble hands. For both individuals, a film has provided images of their presence.[2]

Other autistic children populate the network, which doesn't fail to look like a mirage.

As far as this particular text is concerned, the one I am writing at the behest of Armando Verdiglione, I am going to take as my starting point several lines from a book that was lent to me by someone who, before becoming a psychoanalyst, lived through the previous attempt and even the one before that. The book is *Seminar, Book 1: Freud's Papers on Technique,* by Jacques Lacan.[3] On the cover, there is an elephant, its tusks pointed, its ears magnificently deployed; its eye, frankly, not especially sardonic. A small bird is darting by. One word in the grass: Threshold.[4]

Let me read:

"Think for a moment in the real. It is owing to the fact that the word elephant exists in their language, and hence that the elephant enters into their deliberations, that men have been capable of taking, in relation to elephants, even before touching them, decisions which are more far-reaching for these pachyderms than anything else that has happened to them throughout their history – the crossing of a river or the natural devastation of a forest. With nothing more than the word *elephant* and the way in which men use it, propitious or unpropitious things, auspicious things, in any event catastrophic things have happened to elephants.... Besides, it is clear, all I need do is talk about it, there is no need for them to be here, for them to really be here, thanks to the word *elephant,* and to be more real than the contingent elephant-individuals."[5]

"That is how human politics comes about."[6]

With nothing more than the word elephant and the way in which men use the word, catastrophic things happen to elephants.

With nothing more than the word "man" ... etc....

With nothing more than the pronoun "he" ... etc....

---

2. Yves G. is the main character in *Le Moindre Geste* (1962-1971) and Janmari is the main character in *Ce Gamin, là* (1975).

3. Jacques Lacan, trans. John Forrester, ed. Jacques-Alain Miller, *The Seminar of Jacques Lacan, Book 1: Freud's Papers on Technique 1953-1954* (New York: W. W. Norton, 1991), p. 178.

4. *Seuil,* the French word for "threshold," is also the name of the French publishing house that brought out Lacan's book. [TN]

5. Lacan, *Freud's Papers,* p. 178.

6. *Ibid.* This is the opening statement in a response by Octave Mannoni to a remark made by Jean Hyppolite during Lacan's seminar. [TN]

Beyond the threshold, the real – as I understand it – where the autistic individual does not distinguish him- or herSELF. Beyond the threshold, the elephant. All it takes is to speak of it for IT to be there, in the seminar, and more real than the one on the cover. IT, the elephant, which does not risk crossing the threshold where we are seated, far away from elephants and seminars, at some half-way point. We are playing neither dice nor jacks. We are playing hopscotch. A few lines drawn. Several terms that are words, but extracted from the vocabulary, uprooted. Words we can use to prop ourselves up: *ring, crossbeam, break in the ring, inadvertence, initiative*. Words placed on a piece of paper as stones might be on a windy day. The wind, in this case, is language, which comes to us, "catastrophic," from wherever it blows or whatever it says; blinding. "Nature" is here, "outside," enormous, dazed, peaceful, close, out of reach.

By *nature*, I mean quite specifically the biological basis of all of human existence, considered independently of the effects socialization produces upon it.[7]

Socialization, hominization. It can be said that where autistic children are concerned, hominization has fizzled out. What does Lacan mean when he invites us to reflect, if only for an instant, to reflect "in the real?" Does he mean by putting ourselves in the place of the elephant? The real? Is it a question of inviting the elephant from outside, over there on the book cover, to cross the threshold and come sit down with the present company? Lacan makes it clear: there is no need for a *real* elephant. The word is enough. IT is there, "more real" than an individual elephant, situated, "contingent."

Contingent? "Something that may be or not be; without importance, non-essential; the opposite of necessary," etc. (according to the dictionary). I suspect that I grab a word the way one would grab a marked piece in a subtle game of dice, and that I use it as I would a pebble.

But when an autistic child touches, grabs, and drops a real pebble, is a pebble at stake, strictly speaking, or something else that I'm unaware of, something that substitutes for the pebble and for language alike?
What game is being initiated, and according to what innate rules? The pebble, then, manipulated by a *human* being, becomes something other than a pebble.
Let a child, should he or she be autistic, sit down here, on this stone, and the stone's nature is transformed. I have said this: we are on the threshold: depending on the moment, the stone is cold, hot, burning. Within the scope of our gaze, one or another of these children who is perhaps no more an individual than an elephant is. Unity lies in the species.

---

7. Lucien Sève uses these terms to describe what Karl Marx says about nature in his later works. See Lucien Sève, *Man in Marxist Theory and the Psychology of Personality*, trans. John McGreal (Atlantic Highlands, N.J.: Humanities Press, 1978 [1969]).

The "scope" [*'portée'*] of our gaze – the gaze that comes and goes of its own accord, goes without saying.[8]

Portée: "the set of offspring that a female mammal carries and births on a single occasion [litter]; the load carried by a ship [cargo]; the five parallel and equidistant horizontal lines that carry musical notation [staff]; the distance that a launched projectile can cover [reach]" (dictionary).

What may this gaze of ours have to reproduce, what is it loaded with, and by whom? What does it project, and with what force....

As for what it allows us to *note*, there is the obvious risk of always having the subject as the key signature.

To change the *scope* of our gaze since we are dealing with children living (within) the vacancy of this S, which allows what is being hominized to be distinguished from the real.

And what if the real – that by which we are real, elephants, but entirely without our knowledge – were not the terrible chaos that functions as a threat, a dread with respect to which the sonorous clankings of language evoke the only – eternal – salvation, what if language couldn't care less about "us," and not merely couldn't care less, but worse, knew perfectly well how to keep everything that comes from nature on the other side of the threshold?

So we changed our scope. Four lines that cross at right angles will do the trick, and several words – neumes, if we persist on thinking in musical terms, word-pucks if we return to the image of hopscotch – *crossbeam, us-here, We, ring* and *break in the ring, initiative, inadvertencies.*

And now these words start to play differently, shoved with the hand the way the stone-puck is with the foot when children play hopscotch.

To be sure, the words still play among themselves. To deprive them of this interplay is to deprive them of existence. What would happen to a word that would belong only to the real? Reduced to nothing; less than the cry of the bird that darts across the cover of Lacan's *Seminar*, within reach of the trunk of the elephant with the sumptuous lugholes that steer the prehensile appendix a bit, but more to fend off the possible "dart" rather than to grab it; what would the elephant do with it, anyway?

Just as word-pucks pulled along on the four lines that cross at right angles do not risk taking hold of the real that is evoked. Never have words played that game. They appear just as unnatural as circus elephants in a circus turning in a circle each holding onto the next by the tail and sitting on stools. Man is truly nature's master, and how could the master's children not be delighted at this actually quite terrifying spectacle?

---

8. Here, where the usual word order would be *va et vient de soi*, the reversal calls attention to a play on words captured in English by the doubled translation ("of its own accord," "goes without saying"). The reflexive pronoun *soi*, italicized in the French text, emphasizes the reference to a "self." [TN]

If I can take credit for anything in my existence, it is that I have never – not even and especially not when I was a child and of course taken to a circus – been able to tolerate such an outrage. I screamed; they told me: "Don't be afraid...."
I wasn't afraid at all. I was ashamed. A child prodigy.

This is to say that "things," even if they are only criss-crossed lines, come from far off. Four criss-crossing lines, *marelle* (hopscotch), a word that appears to come from *mare* (pond) but doesn't; in pre-Roman times a *marr* was a stone. *Mare* or not, with the help of our scope, it is a matter of marking the *uncrossable* distance between that way of seeing [CE *voir*] and seeing the SELF [SE *voir*] that "specifies" us. In part. There is the part that is specified by the use made of SELF. There remains the part of "that way of seeing." When an autistic child is involved, the balancing between the two settles in favor of SELF only if THEY [ON] decide out of hand, at the outset, that this should be done, and let's say no more about it, or rather, let's say it as if HE were speaking, speakable, since he is *human*.

As far as the autistic child is concerned, it is that *nous* (*we*) that I call specular, but, to be clear, it is N(ous) that is inscribed on the staff, N being "something completely other" than we ourselves. Rather as Lacan's Other is something completely other than the other.
It is in locating this "something other" that scope helps us.

Word-pucks sometimes change. We have posited *detour, drift, workbench, adorned, do-ing/making, simulacrum*. Inevitably words become charged with meaning and begin to slide into the formulation of the attempt and elaborate their own premature mi-cro-ideology. These words, which were "maps," words at odds with meaning, began to have meaning, to know what they wanted to signify. They have to be made to disgorge these meanings. What they articulate is a necessary way of thinking. Words can lock up like knees or hips. What I have called the "common body" is knitted together more or less from all sides. Rigor becomes rigidity. Our *practice* of *tracing* has gone astray. Sheep can get dizzy; "bleakness" can overtake one unit or another. One must find a way of *tracing* that breaks with what has led us to the "bleakness."

It seems that "human nature," which I prefer to call the *human of nature*, is terrified of bleakness, it being well understood that there is actually a latent contradiction between what can be called a certain avidity for reiteration of the identical and an insatiable appetite for "novelty." It will be readily understood that this *novelty* can only come from circumstances.

An attempt opens up a breach in the "ideological apparatuses of the State." Still, it can't avoid the surveying process that stands ready to confront the slightest con-crete initiative. No one is going to remake the map of the world because an autistic child is attracted by water dancing in a stone basin that rightfully belongs to its owner. HE says so, that man: "The water is mine." HE exists only by virtue of having. An old story. What can be offered up in exchange for the right of access to a stone basin where reflections of sunlight sparkle on the shimmering water? Without exchange, there is no individual; this is the law of history.

To say that N couldn't care less about all that, as an elephant couldn't care less about a prayer book, is to say that we are often at a loss.

But if someone understands that speaking about the *human of nature* is a way of draining off stagnant humanisms, that person has understood nothing about what I have been trying to say.

I know quite well that a term such as "of nature" relegates the one using it to the level of the ideological idiots who have never heard of Copernicus, Galileo, Marx, or Freud. But that doesn't matter. If I read that ideology does not have a history, that it is *immutable*, I reflexively tell myself that the same thing holds true for *the human*. It must be understood that I'm not at all talking about men.

That *the human of nature* is curiously deprived of that which provides other species what they need to survive, persist, and reproduce seems to be what language compensates for. From compensating to replacing, it takes just one small step to make us shift from respecting to dominating.
And it is reproducing THAT (CE) that I should have written when it was a question of other species. For "us others" – our own species – it is indeed reproducing the SELF (SE) that is at stake.

Hence psychoanalysis, and this specific attempt, which, starting from the autistic, strives to garner from the SELF a bit of respect for the THIS.

Acting and the Acted

That there are "individuals" for whom one [*on*][1] does not exist is unfortunate for them to the extent that one is the matrix of self [*se*], which is consciousness, on which the identity that is common to all is founded – in other words, that through which each of us is identical to every other, while this common identity also evokes the fact, "for a person, of being a specific individual and capable of being recognized as such without any confusion thanks to the elements that individualize him or her."

Thus says the dictionary, whereas our colloquium must evoke the violence that is expressed, in the infinitive, by *violenter* (to assault) and *violer* (to rape), which are identical as far as the first letters are concerned, letters that speak of *viol* (rape), a word that, still according to the dictionary sets us on a double path: woman, sanctuary.

The letter that invites me to present our approach evokes the "compass" that is in use among members of our particular network and the word *initiative*, which we are attempting to scrape clean so as to be able to designate accurately what occurs when an "individual" who lives outside of conscious identity owing to the vacancy of language thus acts in the infinitive, the act then taking place in an impersonal mode and the "individual" being in no way the one-such of the person.

If we have some measure of confidence in what can be seen from what allows these initiatives – a term I prefer to what triggers or provokes them – the perceptible from whence the acting is articulated proves indeed to concern us, but in such a way that it reveals aspects of "ourselves" that escape us. In order not to sever the face of the compass from the use we constantly make of it, an *initiative* on the mode of acting is going to turn up, an initiative that I shall first describe while warning that language can only be tangential to the "real" event.

---

1. Depending on the context, the French impersonal pronoun *on* can be rendered in English as "we," "you," "they," or "one." [TN]

As it happens, people often come to see me to get me to say a bit more about our approach. I don't get up from my table on these occasions. I turn toward the visitors and I sometimes tap my fingers in one spot or another on this cluttered surface. One day I was tapping in response to some surprise or other that had emerged from the wander lines we scrupulously trace, the person who teaches me the most about what I'm telling you and who was then fifteen years old, and autistic – though that particular word seems to be falling out of fashion; it doesn't matter, we'll find others – was passing by. He left, quickly, and reappeared some time later and deposited a pile of mud on my table, not very far from where my tapping had taken place. So here is an event that might be thought to resemble another, which would have been that the boy had come to shit right there in the middle of the setting. But this would be to forget the hands and at the same time a good deal of the rest.

So there were quite a few people there and what could you do but finger the little pile of mud, with a mask of benevolent gratitude on your face. It is quite probable that without the gaze of the "they" [ON], I would not have fingered something that evoked filth rather than an offering. It is imperative never to lose (the) face where ONE looks at ONESELF / ME (ON SE/ME *regarde*). And yet, there it was, in the dross of damp earth and ash, what in archeology is called a find: all the pieces of a clay ashtray that, four years earlier, had sat on the table where I had been tapping my fingers. Which could just as well be written as I had written it before correcting the first draft: a clay ashtray had been broken and the shards tossed into in the basket of papers we piled up and used to light the bread-baking oven. Once the baking is complete, you have to wait for the oven to cool off and then scrape up the ashes, gather them up in a bucket and go spread them out on the terraces where the gardens are being prepared.

But I should return to what I had to say: that a "candid" initiative is inspired only by accidents. Because, after all, these shards of an ashtray that shouldn't have been broken had no business being under the kindling consumed by the flames set to burn crumpled papers. And in the blink of an eye the shards of clay buried for five years in ash and earth were rediscovered, and still there in what ought to be called the locatable, still intact because it had not had to suffer the plowing under of what one says to oneself [*ce qu'on se dit*].

On the face of the compass[2] is drawn the great ring of language use, interrupted with an *a*, the young autistic boy being beyond the rupture, the ring thought/spoken by each of us, that is, by S, which evokes the SELF of saying (to) oneself [*se dire*].

On the face of the compass, two lines cross at a point where the small central ring *c* is drawn: the point of seeing/perceiving of the little guy in abeyance in the use of language.

---

2. See Figure 2, p. 139.

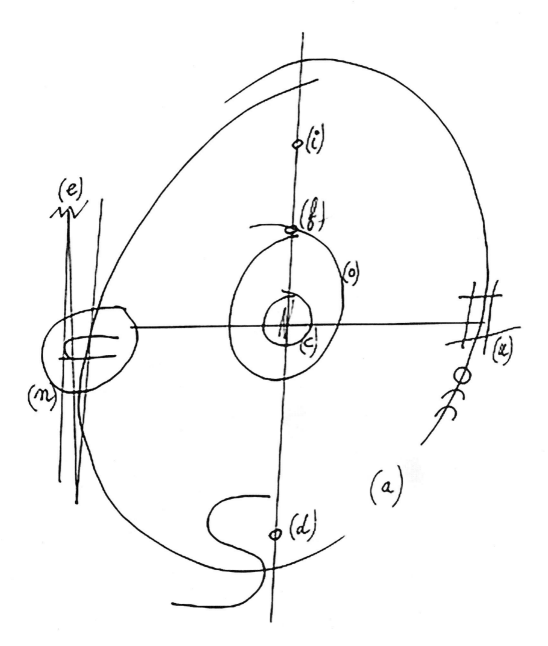

Figure 2

Of these two lines, one, the horizontal one, is that of *chevêtres* (crossbeams), a word in our jargon that evokes the *thing*s that, clearly, attract, orient, a word that lives with inter-rupted language. Among these "things," at one end, water, *u*, and at the other end, us [*nous*], *n*.

The other line, the perpendicular one, in its "southern" part, evokes terror, disarray, *d*. The ways in which the S can be inopportune are not without relevance here.

In its "northern" part, it's more about the initiative, and the crossbeam in *n, nous* (us) is not without relevance here.

In *o*, the other ring evokes everything that we are doing/living here. To put it another way, it's the "OK,"[3] the "all right" (or nearly), the "like us" (or close to it), in any case it could be said that, or almost, it would take nothing at all, etc., etc. Except that this particular "nothing" may just evoke a divide over which no bridge whatsoever is possible.

In *f* (for *faire*), it would be a question of making (something useful, something articulated with what we are doing).

In *i*, we have acting on initiative, the discovery/rediscovery that comes from the *n* perceived in *c* as being something completely different, as having many additional aspects beyond what we consciously or unconsciously know about it. Who knows what water can be (about) for an autistic individual? The same goes for "us": who knows? It is obvious that this particular "knowing" [*savoir*] must be written as "seeing *that*" [*ça voir*].[4] That? That which can only escape us, which is to say, that which is outside the covering or cape that envelops us, we who experience the use of language, of symbols.

What is our quest? To pinpoint the locatable – a "structure"[5] different from the one that subtends language – which "allows" for acting on initiative.

To go back to the minor event I related earlier, it would be appropriate to pinpoint at *e* – at one of the points of the N that considerably exceeds what we ourselves can perceive – this tapping of my hand on the cluttered wooden table, a gesture that can be expressed in the infinitive as long as it is reiterated by me and is not addressed to someone else – which in this case is quite flagrant: I was addressing the persons who were present, certainly not the youngster who had no business there, except that HE was attracted by an *n* that was more abundant than usual.

---

3. In French, "*Ça va*" ("Fine," "All right," "OK") is the customary reply to the question "*Ça va?*" ("How's it going?" or "How are things?"). [TN]

4. The word play on *savoir* [to know] and *ça voir* [to see that] recurs throughout the text. [TN]

5. In the original text, Deligny added a comment here: "This word, for want of another."

I am drawing attention to this specific "point," which lies at the point of the N and which evokes a pointless gesture without which the acting on initiative would not have taken place or been common. If I say a "pointless gesture," it's because it had nothing to do with the "permitted" acting – "pointless gesture" means nothing if it evokes permission; one would be better off saying "triggered" if that word didn't evoke a mechanism. Does that leave us with "provoked?" I MYSELF provoked nothing whatsoever: neither challenge nor summons nor incitation. No word is suitable. We must be on the right track: the break in the great ring of language use has been respected.

We find ourselves toggling back and forth on the dividing line between this *species* that is our own and the others.

Ethnologists know quite well the phenomenon of instinct that grows, that only waits for ..., and that ends up triggering itself on its own.

Here, what "triggers" (permits, provokes, etc.) acting nonetheless exists at the limit, at "infinity," a nearly imaginary scrap of the real, but only nearly. Of course, we see quite well that we are only dealing with what "triggers," in the ultimate analysis; that was all it took. It is clear that this latent momentum, this contained energy, stimulates the rocking back and forth that turns into intoxication, in the absence of what allows the locatable to become a trace of acting. One has to have seen the gaze of an autistic individual begging for the morsel of a gesture that will liberate the "project" in order to understand properly what I'm getting at.

To say that this gesture beckons is to evoke conscious identity at the outset, the way some evoke the soul. If "another identity" is in question, we need a word other than sign that belongs to the "structure" in S.
We say "marker," or "reference point" [*repère*], which evokes the "structure" in N.

We should also add that there is absolutely nothing we can do about this decisive gesture, and that, in the end, any "gesture" whatsoever – a blink, a shrug – does the job, signals something to be done [*l'à-faire*].[6] But where we can do something, it's because the *locatable* constitutes the humus of our quite ordinary way of life. If we hadn't baked bread twice a week, if some of us didn't insist on putting in gardens, if I didn't write so much, producing all that crumpled-up paper in the wastebasket, with the shards of the ashtray at the bottom, if I didn't smoke, and if we didn't like to model clay in our spare time, for leisure, for pleasure, acting on initiative flashing in on this mish-mash of acted-upon projects, in which the youngster takes part, moreover, but always tangentially, skimming, without concern for the outcome, from which I return to the aforementioned acting in the infinitive, whereas at the

6. The French phrase plays on the homophony between the neologism *l'à-faire*, shorthand for "the thing to be done" and the expression *faire l'affaire*, "to do the job." [TN]

141

point of the N (this "we" capitalized from the seeing point of the one who sees the break in the great ring of the structure of language), carried to infinity, or almost, space and time merge, become the "same thing," something to which the "structure" in S is particularly allergic, and for good reason: it finds itself obliterated.

But where are violence and violation – rape – in this trivial incident that didn't make it into the newspapers or television?

One might see something like an infraction in the fact – presumed then to have been enacted – in the small heap of earth mixed with ash placed in the middle of my table while there were "a bunch of people" around. A provocation?

This is the original flaw in incidences of acting on initiative: they do not respect the pact of concertation, not even in order to infringe on it; they intervene in complete innocence of the moment.

Of course, one can see here – if one wants to truly believe in them – all the possible effects of a SELF [SE] in difficulty or on the verge of expressing itself, a mirage effect to which some hold fast just as others maintain that they have seen the Virgin Mary.

But what is violated, in this acting, is the law according to which every infraction has an author who can and must be identified.

I imagine a judge in search of the guilty party: the so-called "he" who brought in the pile of mud had completely involuntary accomplices who nevertheless cannot be called unconscious, the one who made the clay ashtray, the one who broke it, the one who threw the shards into the oven, and the one who tapped on the table, which he wouldn't have done if the others present hadn't questioned him. One sees how the previously-noted acting comes about, acting whose author is actually an entire "individual," as "common" as can be, who cannot be identified with any "person able to be recognized as such," and we see that I write N, the indistinct "pal," Us.

We see how initiative and individual are one, without however being able to sort out the portion belonging to each, each one innocent of what could be considered a minor offense; the word "individual" then finds a new meaning that no longer really has anything to do with the word "subject," whereas these two words are usually confused, if only so the courts can make sense of them and find out upon whom, "without any confusion," owing to the fact of his or her identifiable identity, to inflict punishment or particular constraints.

Between the lines of this story, some will see a sketch of the stupidity inherent in all judgment, whereas what I have in the back of my mind as I write is to evoke what is the very object of our research, namely, the notion that there is, beyond the conscious identity woven through with effects of the unconscious, another identity, just as common, but in a completely different way, an a-conscious identity on the basis of which "individual" would no longer be one word too many for saying differently what the word "subject" means, as the highly presumed author of his or her acts.

In saying this, I have completely lost sight of the theme proposed for the November colloquium. This is no doubt because, living close to autistic children for a good number of years, I no longer have violence and violation, assault and rape, in my purview. If it is true that they are both as much in fashion as ever, they are the business [*l'à-faire*] of bad subjects elaborated with an ideology that therefore ought to find a way to call itself to account, but that would have great difficulty if it had to judge itself, and then it wouldn't have time to do so, preoccupied as it is with having to shape subjects that a certain form of production requires, via channels to whose secrets the ideology holds the key, and here we find the channels clogged, so they have to spill out onto something. It suffices to see what happens when a sink is clogged even if the clog is far off in the plumbing. It flows back up, spasmodically.

Nevertheless, I come back to the dictionary.
Rape: an act of violence by which a man has sexual relations, with a woman, against her will; the act of violating: violating a sanctuary.
The dictionary is lagging, unless it is getting ahead.
Ideology has trouble extricating itself from its function and from the history to which it belongs with every fiber of its being. And it might well develop more sanctuaries than it thinks, hollow boundary markers that provoke violation, each one intending to prove (to itself) the existence of SELF.

If violence is necessary when it is a question of a woman who has her own will, the "against her will" vanishes when a sanctuary is at stake. And thus it is the bravado around the ONE [ON] that determines rape. It still remains to discover to what extent rape of the other, or violence toward the other, is not of the same order, so that "against her will" could be written as "ITS will," where the omnipotence of the common ONE that has to be defied would be expressed.

If two lovers, both willingly, come together, as we say, then everything is fine, but now we have three or four thugs who come together to do violence. Here it becomes apparent that "coming together as one," even if only for an instant, has quite disparate consequences. When the pin has been removed from the symbolic function, watch out for shrapnel.

Transgression requires an interdiction, and a violation cannot occur if there is no sanctuary. If we bracket the interest that is generally granted to the subject-person associated with a registered identity, what remains is to examine the alloy of the forbidden acts that delineate the project of existing with respect to ONE/SELF.

143

But then what sort of touchstone would reveal the alloy of ideology that makes ITSELF/US believe that it knows what humanness is, and for the good reason that it was ideology that fabricated humanness on the order of the producing that has the obligation of reproducing itself: it is indeed possible that this is strictly the business, the "something-to-be-done" [à faire] of the humanness of the subject.

There remains the humanness of the indistinct individual, who has always already been outside the law, which does not mean that this individual is transgressive in the slightest, since the "he" who has an obligation to distinguish himself is not from the same world.

It is true that, over time, I have lived on occasion – and it was so peaceful that I am sometimes nostalgic for it – among "individuals" for whom violating and doing violence had been forms of acting, sometimes reiterated. I have just re-read the text that I was asked to prepare for the November colloquium and I would be happy to lengthen it, if only because of the title, which must not be read with the eyes but with the ears: *lagirélagi* (theactingandtheacted).

Duly assessed by the experts as perverse, those poor guys of yesteryear.

I recently read a statement by a psychoanalyst in a weekly magazine: "Men are animals dedicated to symbols and crime sticks to our skin, like law."[7]

There must be some truth in this statement, since we don't see males raping females in any species but our own. But we have to acknowledge that we know nothing about the animal that we are or what it is dedicated to. And this is indeed how the a-conscious identity is located, the identity that runs right through us, or so I maintain, if only to honor those close to whom I am living now, individuals who, living in the infinitive mode, act on initiative, which excludes even the shadow of any intent to violate or do violence. There is not an ounce of intention, intention indeed being dedicated to symbols. Which at least rids us of the whoppers relating to the famous instincts against which we supposedly have to fight, and long live the verb. The beast has a sturdy back, the good Lord as well. Which makes two backs for the same beast. We still have to ask who promised us divinity, who engaged us in such a solemn and irrevocable manner. No one, of course, but ourselves.

Fortunately, there are some, the de-voted, the un-avowed, even if they are rare, even if they are autistic, to remind us of an "order" other than that of law: it would be the order of the very nature of the "animal" itself before the vow, it being understood that that "before" persists as a prelude despite the predominance, which seeks to be absolute and exclusive, of the SELF without which there might be some tracing, perhaps, but no writing at all.

---

7. Jean Laplanche, in Le Nouvel Observateur. [Deligny did not supply a full reference. TN]

Art, Borders ... and the Outside

Art ... Borders [*les bords*].

In the dictionary, we see that the word *bord,* which used to speak of edges, borders, has ended up indicating the vessel itself. *Monter à bord,* climb aboard, people say. There remains the sea, which would be the outside.

And we still have to ask whether works of art might not take after flying fish, with an outside that is not of the same nature as the one conferred on us by symbolic domestication and that launches us on what may be called history. If the flying fish seems absurd, nothing prevents us from thinking that despite the endless caulking, the outside oozes and comes to form an ocean that reflects the face of whoever is watching, and becomes a mirror without being one. They say that the ocean gleams but no one sees himself or herself in it.

What I have constantly before my eyes, besides the window that gives me light, is, on the wall, a *tracing* by Janmari, autistic, resistant to what ethnic memory proposes, so much so that I never know if it is a drawing or a tracing. There is a considerable difference. If we are dealing with a tracing, then nothing whatsoever is depicted or represented here, and this is what I believe. This artwork is nothing more than a trace of a gesture, but a trace that I so often see reiterated by hands other than Janmari's, hands of mute children who, provided with pencils, seem to be caught in a somewhat circular rut that we have named a *ring.*

Does this mean that the *ring* demarcates, that there would be an inside and an outside and thus borders? The *ring i*s circular, or nearly so, thus there is only one line, which would be the borderline. If the line were straight, somewhat rectilinear, there would be no suggestion that it encircles, that something is circumscribed, surrounded and grasped.[1]

1. The French word *cerne,* translated here as "ring," comes from the verb *cerner,* "to surround, encircle, circumscribe"; in the figurative sense, *cerner* can mean "to grasp, to understand, to pin down." [TN]

There is tracing, and, quite often, a ring appears. Perhaps it's better to say that it appears to us as something we can name as such, the term "ring" being preferable to "circle" or "round form," despite the fact that the dictionary cannot help speaking to us about "a line that emphasizes a contour." This line, which would be provided with intention, if only the intention to underline, may leave us somewhat perplexed. It is true that a contour can be underlined by charcoal or India ink.

I have said on occasion that lines and language were of the same nature, relying on what I had seen in the acting of so-called mentally disabled children.

Whereas they would get tangled up in their drawings in the same way language tangled them up, shackled them in the truest sense of the word, if I took away their sharpened pencils, instruments that are also instruments for writing, they found themselves unharnessed and wriggled their shoulders. Some of them didn't balk at the chance to dip their fingers in the graphite dust, and from the rubbed white paper a shadow would then emerge, sometimes taking the form of something recognizable, which surprised everyone, the author most of all. Which shows that these gray shadows would have deserved to be called spontaneous, if the word "spontaneous" didn't mean, as the dictionary suggests, "what one does oneself." Because there was not even an ounce of self in these spots rubbed by a nevertheless conscientious finger, but then we are talking about "consciousness of what?" – which is not the same as "consciousness of whom?" In which the subject and the object disappear. The thing and its reflection remain, the shadowy spot on the paper, and there could be something like a similarity between the spot and the thing, the trace of a finger, a fingerprint, where the finger itself had wiped out the creases of skin that make it possible to establish identity.

It had to be shaped or molded, this resemblance between a thing and a stain, if only just a little, and noticing the resemblance required the existence of the S, a sign, a mark, which put us on the same side, the mentally disabled child and I. It was a matter of the blink of an eye in which the strange gaze that humans direct toward things can be located. And, quite often, the mentally disabled child who had more or less willingly abandoned the tracing instrument which is also the instrument for writing picked it up again, not in order to mark the contours of the spot, the thing then taking more precise shape as a demarcated, nameable object, but in order to write his name, even if a forgotten letter transformed Yves[2] into Yes, where some would see acquiescence, which doesn't seem obvious to me at all. But, as we say, everyone sees events from their own window.

---

2. As noted in "*That* Seeing and Looking at One*self*," Yves G. is the main character in the film *Le moindre* geste.

What seems clear to me is that this autistic individual with whom I live in the closest possible proximity, which means I willingly accept his being distant, HE being merely the subterfuge required by the fact that I'm speaking about him, it may well be that he doesn't even have a window. His "tracings" represent nothing; it would be better to say that they do not represent. And yet?

If I judge by the wander lines that are scrupulous traces of the apparent pathways and projects of the "autistic" children who live, here and there, close to "us," there seems to be some similarity between these very traces and the "tracing" produced by each child's hand. The same style. Apart from what the "tracings" of each child may have in common with their wander lines, there are often nuances that make one think that a particular "tracing" and a particular wander line have the same author.

It is clear that the term "author," in this instance, does not correspond to what the dictionary proposes: a "person who is the first cause of something, at the origin of a thing." After reading such a definition, how could you expect everybody not to take himself or herself for God Almighty? How could it be that a "thing" originates from a person?

As for me, writing this text of which I am thus the author, it is quite clear where the lines originate: from two things that are one and the same, traces of pathways, "tracings" that are traces of the hand, but it is true that in tracing wander lines, our hand is not without responsibility.

Does this mean that every traced line originates from the hand? Yes and no, because in the end it is really a whole body that has set itself to frolicking according to detours about which one might think that the project underlying what appears manifestly is to seek agreement between these "tracings," traces of the hand, emanating from the same individual.

About this agreement, potentially remarkable and surprising for those who are moved enough to perceive it and to be surprised, I tell myself not that it surpasses the limits (of understanding) but that it comes from the outside, which is so alluring if only because the horizon recedes as fast as we advance, and strictly speaking what we are dealing with is the infinite, whereas, hemmed in as we are by words, we have to write "infinitives," "to trace" not being the least, where it is a matter of innovating entirely by inadvertence, if only via a detour where it appears that something completely other than going there is at stake, but it is also a question of making the trace of the pathway appear, comparable then to the trace inscribed by the hand of the one who walked the path.

Where is the author, within all these goings-on? He disappears, erased in the same way the idea that art is representing is erased. I was going to say that it is a matter of showing, which is often true, but then what about music? It would be more about tuning, harmonizing; we are not sure whether the French verb *accorder* (to tune, to harmonize) comes from *coeur* (heart) or *corde* (string). But then *accorder* must also mean to create agreement, not consent or conformity but rather discordance from which relations of frequencies will vibrate.

The heart is inside, tucked in, bordered.
It has its limits, which have a history.
The string is outside.

Card Taken and Map Traced

As it happens, I have been a member of a party, the Communist Party – the French Communist Party, since I am French. I was a member, at various times, between 1933 and 1965, and there is no guarantee that I won't take the same card back again.

The word *carte* (card) works well, coming from the word *charta*, "paper." It can either be a "small rectangular piece of cardboard with one side bearing a figure" (playing card), "a reduced scale representation of the total or partial surface of the terrestrial globe" (map), or a "paper establishing certain rights for the person bearing it" (identity card, membership card, etc.).

As we can see, this word is quite vast, and while it has been many years since I had my (Party) card, our customary practice consists in tracing *cartes* (maps) where the wander lines of the autistic children who live here appear; we venture to do this in order to make something other than a sign. One sees that each living area covers a truly minuscule parcel of the surface of the globe.

In fact, what we are looking for is what there may be in *common* between these children and ourselves.

Here we have the word *common*, a word that with only slight changes will allow us to call ourselves communists, since we are looking for what the word *common* can evoke.

That card, taken up once and then again, can be surprising. It isn't the usual attitude of a member, that's the term for it, unless one is astonished that there is a head.

It won't be any time soon that the geography of the body will no longer predominate.

So I have experienced what it is like to be a member, but I was a member who was, for long periods, (at) the head of an attempt that I led, as they say.

To such an extent that I have been told that I was more a leader than a member, but that's all there was to it, I wasn't excluded for all that. What happened was that, on various occasions, I exiled myself from the Party. I always had some map or other to draw with my own hand, and I was led into a drift that drew me away from the Party, without an ounce of resentment. I didn't take the card back. And then, unoccupied, I came back only to leave again. So I never had any scores to settle. I have spoken ill of the Party at times. But when I realized to what sort of horde I was joining my voice, I fell silent, stupefied as I was to discover what the real stakes were in the exuberant pursuit of the Party.

I was a bit premature in leading such attempts. Around whatever project was underway there always arose a certain effervescence that must have been deemed of quite dubious quality by those in charge. But everyone got used to it; I did, and so did they. The worst off, in this business, were the Party members who were in a transitional phase. The transitional phase held up, as long as it was needed, which is to say, the time it took for the project in question to fade away. I was thus a very intermittent leader.

Those who would understand this as a sketch for a guerilla effort directed against the Party would be completely mistaken.

I did actually lead a particular kind of non-lethal guerilla effort, and I felt, we all felt, "based" in the Party of which we were not a part; this was true even for those who were still members.

A member can be said to be detached; always this geography of a generic human body, but whereas a member detached from the human body can't be preserved for very long, the detached Party members persisted and some of them experienced the same emotions as members who were duly articulated with the Party and dependent, as far as voluntary movements were concerned, on the head.

Parties have a history, just as persons do. They are characters, whereas attempts are improvised and no mass movement is at stake. If an attempt generates even a few echoes, and this can happen, its partisans are so diverse, so disparate, that there are reasons not to gather them together in a general assembly. They wouldn't listen to each other, so greatly do their personal ideologies diverge or conflict.

Which shows that an *attempt* is a singular phenomenon; I have sometimes been surprised that attempts don't happen more often. It is more than likely that the urge to attempt something directed at several others is constantly produced but remains unexpressed. No doubt, in order to speak, one must have an identity, a word that ricochets with the question: with what?

And here in fact is where an *attempt* is hampered. Whereas a Party knows where it comes from and specifies where it is going, if only toward another power, an *attempt* has no precedent or doesn't acknowledge one. One might believe that this reflects an excess of self-esteem or the effect of an unfortunate penchant for originality. Nothing could be further from the truth, or else it is merely a question of appearances.

For an *attempt* is closer to a work of art than to anything else. A person who means to create has to stay away from "doing like."

Otherwise, one's "work," that which is proposed, exposed, is useless, if one doesn't see in it some traces of a break with any identifications, whereas it is remarkable that Party members curiously resemble one another and that there is – there was, "in my day" – an exemplary manner of being communist that went back to the ancestors. This is because a Party is grappling with history, whereas an *attempt* is situated within the space of now, now being a historical moment.

Whereas the Party means to continue history and influence it, it always seemed to me to be deprived of a "sense" of history, blind or deaf, take your pick. At the same time, as can be seen in a number of infirmities that deprive you of the use of one of your senses, as a leader of *attempts*, I had another sense that developed and became more refined, a sense that might be called a sense of the moment, for an *attempt* is something very precarious, rather like a mushroom in the vegetal world.

How can you expect the Party to recognize this?

So here you have several *attempts* that look alike, or almost. One is good, edible, and the others are poisonous. On what can one rely in order to decide if a particular attempt is good or deadly?

But must an attempt expect to be recognized, which can amount to being controlled?

To return to the word *carte* with which I began, the dictionary tells us that it is "a paper establishing certain rights for the person bearing it."

This card that I might have, the Party card: would it grant me rights? Over whom? over the Party?

Conversely, and since we know very well that the word "right" can also be written as "duty," would the Party dictate my duty to me?

I seem to remember clearly that that *duty* led many communists, in good faith, to say many stupid things that they later regretted. They didn't pay attention to the word: faith, whether good or bad, is still faith, and whoever searches is always something of a reprobate.

That said, I do not renounce the apparently intermittent sort of solidarity that connects me to the Party, were it a thousand times more vilified than it has been. I'll be told that this is just sentiment? If I am trying to verify the alloy that goes into this solidarity, I see again, naturally, individuals, men and women; I find myself back in the time of the Friends of the Commune. I find scars in my scalp, small ones to be sure, but that linger, if only in my memory, clubbings received in corners of the University, clubs wielded by militants of the far right; and it has been a long time now since the lumps from the rifle butts of the Mobile Guards have faded. There were long marches throughout the city, it was the effervescence of pre-1936, with metalworkers from the Fives-Lille factories who marched ahead of me; comrades, we marched in step.

This is enough to make it clear that I'm a completely obsolete communist, which is understandable, given my age. I am surprised by the echoes that reach me, these days, from an excited base that would call the power of the leadership into question. For this power, which they are said to be arrogating to themselves, must first of all be given to them, or at the least, attributed to them, and by whom other than by those who would like to distribute it.

If I refer to what happens in an attempt such as ours, and which nevertheless is nothing like a political party, every time I have found myself provided with any power at all, decision-making power, it was indeed without my knowledge, but the fact was there and I had to submit to it, even if I thought that it was proof that something wasn't right, but what wasn't right wasn't in my head but in everyone's heads, and I had indeed had enough of it, but what was there to do?

It is a well-known fact that in every gang there has to be a "brain."

And the objective, apart from the project, an attempt is a phenomenon that is quite similar to that of a gang, and which might be expressed as follows: the human persists, despite all opposition. And this all is not nothing.

I was about to say that if there is some abuse of power coming from leaders described as being somewhat "absolute," it is because there is indeed something of the absolute in the heads of those being led, otherwise it is impossible to see where the leaders could stock up on it.

Yet the absolute is not good. It is "that which exists independently of any condition or relation with something else." The need for the perfect being comes from way back in history. Leaders inherit it before they even profit from it and make the unfortunate uses of it with which we are all familiar.

What is at issue is a sort of historical geography as old as the world of man. At its head, there has to be one hell of a figure.

If we come back to our cards, which are neither political party cards nor I.D. cards nor playing cards with kings, queens, and clubs and hearts, and aces, what an attempt entails will become clearer.

Not an ounce of democracy, which is, in our times, an extreme limit that can be seen as provocative. But it is common knowledge that an attempt always has a tendency to get in the way of what is fashionable or in style.

Might we be partisans of an obsolete regime?

Not at all; the regime is ideal, and the ideal of the regime is not to be.

It must be spelled out once again that our subjects are not subjects. But how could you expect to lead individuals who are not subjects owing to the fact that, as autistic and mute individuals, although addressed directly, they have not responded to the call?

Yesterday evening, I listened to two avant-garde psychiatrists on *France Culture*, one Italian and one French, who were in agreement on a formula according to which one should work in such a way as to treat each mental patient as a "subject." Hence the close connection – sought by them – between their professional approach and that of political parties.

Hearing them, I felt quite alone.

Living close to autistic children, who might be thought to be living at the extreme limits of mental illness, and perhaps this is the case, it seems to me that there are also two freedoms. First, that of the subject, and this is the only one people talk about, for the good reason that this freedom can be articulated, therefore legislated. There remains the other freedom, which seems to me to fall under the heading of "species-specific memory."

Here we can discover something about the specificity of an attempt that doesn't situate itself as a precursor to the institutions to come.

To put it another way, this completely minuscule part of the terrestrial globe where autistic children walk and run and whose pathways, wander lines, are traced does not claim to seed the entire surface of the globe, is not at all inclined toward a globality in which an endemic ideological absolute would be found.

Cards and maps don't actually tell us much, except that we have no idea what the *human* is, or for that matter the *common*.

Hence the fact that being a communist is indeed one of the most difficult things to be in a universe where humans strive desperately and stubbornly, as they must, to formulate their rights, whereas common humanity, a humanity of the species, not being of the nature according to which language has provided us, forever, with *rights*, will never have any: they are unformulable.

The Fulfilled Child

It would seem that, in developed countries today, a considerable wave of comprehension directed at children is expanding. When I use a word, I go to the dictionary and look it up. Comprehension: "the capacity to embrace, via thought, the totality of ideas that a sign represents." To tell the truth, I hadn't hoped for as much, despite the fact that any recourse to the dictionary often leads to rich discoveries.

It so happens that we live close to autistic children who live the same life we do, a life of the customary. They are hardly children, even though they are five to ten years old. They are, as one says, "autistics." They live here, in close proximity, "here" being one or another of the living areas of a small network. There are around five or six "heres," and within each "here" there are several of us and several of them, autistics, deprived of the *perorating* that is incumbent on us.

I don't use the term "perorate" with the pejorative resonance the dictionary gives it. The infinitive, built around that which evokes the orifice where language is formed, strikes me as suitable for distinguishing between any one of us and any one of the children, *here* [*ces enfants, là*].[1] If I accentuate the *here*, each time it comes up, it is to present it as an entity that is not included in the pantheon of famous entities. Thus an initial lowercase letter will suffice: *topos*.

So, what does it mean to "comprehend" these children? Does it mean showing them a form of comprehension that would be like a well-intentioned embrace? As one might well imagine, this is our first impulse, or rather was the first impulse, and then that vague impulse receded, like the tide. The children had already been drowned

---

1. The standard French construction *ces enfants-là* can be used neutrally, to distinguish one group from another, but it can also be used judgmentally to single out and set apart; in the latter case, the English equivalent would include stress on the demonstrative adjective, as in "Oh, *those* children...." The use of the construction "*ces enfants, là*," emphasizes the physical presence of the children without any pejorative connotations.

by that wave [*vague*]², or nearly. What still remained to be uncovered between us and them was the *here*: the *topos*.

When I say between, I don't want to evoke a barrier, but on the contrary what we have – at least – in common: *topos*, the living area, outside.

An impulse toward comprehension that collides with the indifference that is common to autistic "children," and that produces drama in households, has a tendency to increase in order to overcome the obstacle. We could have been led to an overabundance of comprehension, which is often what happens to these children, who are said moreover to understand everything, to which we should also add: and the remainder.
Because there is a remainder.

A bit weary of this excess of comprehension when it was clear that the children couldn't take it any longer, couldn't cope with being understood, and when the unlivable was coming to light, we began to think that perhaps *topos* could be the place of the remainder, that is, the place of what appears resistant to comprehension, which – let's not forget this – under the cover of an embrace speaks to us of ideas that are represented by signs. To say that comprehension can only be practiced by presupposing signification shows that something sup-posed is required. So this "sup" that comes to place itself upon the other or to take its place, is indeed the "thing-to-be-done" [*l'à faire*], the contribution of the comprehension that intensifies when it comes up against resistance: thus we have deliberately sacrificed the "sup," we have deposited it outside the living area, so that *topos* remains clean and allows for the research we have been conducting, as cleanly and properly as possible, for the past ten years, which is really not a very long time. As for the number of "autistic children" who lived the same life as we did there, it had to be close to sixty. On transparent paper, we set ourselves to transcribing their pathways, wander lines, and then we held onto these lines, these traces, and looked at them and still do, through transparency; some of them date back ten years and others were made last week. For the most part, we have long since forgotten the *by whom* of these traces. This forgetting allows us to see "something else": the remainder, resistant to any comprehension.

Far from being disappointed by this, we were rather relieved. This sort of embrace left a place for a certain respect, which we found in better taste. Respect for what? For something self-evident that becomes clearer and clearer over time. Numerous "crossbeams" appear in the transparency of the papers where the wander lines are transcribed, the "crossbeams" being *heres* where the wander lines intersect, overlap, in space and across time. It is obvious that, through various aspects of their

---

2. The French word *vague*, used as an adjective, can be translated as "vague"; used as a feminine noun, it corresponds to the English "wave," in both the literal and figurative senses. [TN]

manners of being, transcribed as trajectories, these children, *here*, are one and the same, a manner of speaking that could lead to confusion; let's say that what appears is what they may have in *common*.

On the one hand, we have the *perorating* [*pérorer*] that is incumbent on us, and that we have in common, and on the other hand we have the *locating* [*repérer*], if we indeed want to accept the primordial infinitive common to the children deprived of the perorating by which human beings distinguish themselves from what is called the animal kingdom. Locating is not a mystery. It is well known that an "autistic child" does not look (at us); one should say "eying" to evoke the way they have of seeing without looking. There is *that* [CE] way of seeing and there is seeing the SELF [SE] or an OTHER [SE]. It takes just one character (s), one that is a little twisted, to evoke what I call the fissure between our viewpoint – which is capable of seeing itself – and the "seeing point" of an "autistic child." Contrary to the unconscious, which I have heard does not take place (has no place), this fissure that I am evoking takes place: *topos*, and, as far as we are concerned, what is at stake is a living area where both a life of the customary and a life of research go on side by side.

To return to the comprehension that, as I see it, exists only on the basis of an abuse of signification, I refer to an excerpt from the presentation of a recent book: "From birth, a child of man is a being of language ...; however small he may be, a child to whom a mother or father speaks of what they know or suppose to be the reasons for its suffering ...,"[3] etc. Here we find the supposition that can be thought to be necessarily appropriate to make about a child who is preparing for *peroration*. There is still something within this formulation that astonishes me: "a child of man," which resonates as a term for a species, whereas it is in fact the image of an evolved human-that-we-are that the child must be capable of incorporating (into himself or herself). This can be seen clearly in looking at our maps, by this I mean the fissure between *that* seeing and seeing the SELF or an OTHER, here the fissure is filled, and the ethnic memory is supposed to have to – and supposed to be able to – substitute for species-specific memory.

What I wanted to get at by speaking of the fulfilled child [*l'enfant comblé*],[4] and in order to play with the accent, as others play with commas – and one knows quite well that these typographical symbols are the least of symbols – is that the child appears to be the fulfillment [*comble*] of the "person" in the same way that the poet says that woman is the future of man. I have spoken about typography, about the accent that is the least of signs, whereas we need to return to topography: a topography of living areas where these crossbeams appear and where what is *common* to these children manifests ITSELF [SE]. I have emphasized the completely unexpected SELF which occurs

3. Françoise Dolto, *Lorsque l'enfant paraît*, vol. 1 (Paris: Seuil, 1978), p. 10.
4. *Comblé* is the past participle of the verb *combler*, "to fulfill," used here adjectivally; *comble*, the corresponding noun, can be rendered as "fulfillment," "limit," "height," or "depths." [TN]

here merely as an effect of language: where the fissure that runs between a manifest mode of being and a manifested mode of being will be found – for comprehension demands, if only surreptitiously, that in every mode of being there be something manifested – in other words, that there be a sign. And yet the very existence of a sign, however small, requires the acceptance of a convention that we must indeed sup-pose as recognized, acquired; hence the twisting of the character that allows us to think that locating THIS is locating a SELF. Here the *common* disappears in favor of the one and the other without which perorating takes place, as it were, in a vacuum.

When I speak of this specific *common*, it is easy to see that what is at stake is not the common of ordinary mortals. Nothing allows us to think that that *common* is conscious of being mortal, or better: of mortal-beings. Hence some will tell me that there is no being. In the same way "a child of man is a being of language" can be restated this way: a child of man can be – and can be born – only of language.

It is as if one had to take sides. For, in the end, in speaking about species and about the *locating* that comes from the species memory that is supposed to have been sup-planted by ethnic memory, I am speaking about nature. And yet nature, and what may be immutable about it, is held in contempt by people of progress. That said, what the progressives forget is that *perorating* has a function that is just as immutable, one that can be expressed most simply as cleaving the common so as to separate the one from the other, and to allow each to be conjugated, which can mean attempt-ing to become one with someone else or to recite oneself, a verb incarnate, past, present, future. It is obvious that time,[5] in the living areas, does not conjugate. The infinitive reigns, being the tense outside of time, the species memory always reacting to the here [*topos*] and now; what may have happened, "in time," to each individual, has only secondary importance at most in relation to what, as if by reflex, shows on the surface, on the level of the manifest.

I shall take an extremely simplistic example: a duckling is innately endowed with a latent swimming ability. If there is no water in the surroundings, swimming does not take place – *topos* – and remains null and non-occurring. And, as I see it, the same holds true for the *common actings* that, despite being reiterated, arise from ini-tiative, since it is not a question of "doing as"; these are *acting(s)* that, without *topos*, do not take place. About a youngster who is a bit backward, it is easier to think "But what is he missing, what has he missed?" – which might be, for example, on the order of love – than to wonder "But what is missing THERE [*Mais qu'est-ce qu'il Y manque*], here, now?" THERE [Y] being the term apt to evoke the water I was talking about in the *topos* of the duckling.

---

5. The French word for time, *temps*, is also the word for tense (as in the tense of a verb). [TN]

158

It is very convenient to think that these innate common *actings* that come into play rather like reflexes, since they elude the detour through consciousness, have become *makings* or *doings*, through substitution of the ethnic (memory) for the species (memory). However, this is not at all the case. We see these *actings* emerge every day, stunningly, without subject or project, and without object. For the duckling, water is not an object: it is something *real* that is indispensable in order for swimming to be possible. If this duckling parable is getting stale, take frolicking, a *common* form of *acting*, situate it on an upper floor of an apartment building, and wait for the complaints. Well, all right, frolicking is something that's going to be *done*, a few hours a week, on some ad hoc terrain. In this case it's a matter of *doing* sports, which doesn't have much relevance, except in being particularly gifted for domestication.

If we ricochet from frolicking to exulting, which is not a rare thing for anyone who lives in close proximity with autistic children, we find ourselves grappling with a manifest happiness alongside which our own forms of happiness can seem quite paltry. Could there then be two kinds of happiness?

I believe so, as I believe that there are two kinds of freedom, and that between the two the gap is unbridgeable. There is the freedom of the one and of the other, always in the process of being legislated, recognized, validated by power; it is the right of/right to, whose boundaries are set in such a way as to be circumventable, as in an equestrian event; then there would be – and not "there is" – the freedom of the *common* that owes nothing to perorating. Those who expected some sort of fantastic [*faramineux*] extravagance would be quite disappointed.

It is not by chance that I use the word *faramineux,* from "*bête-faramine*," an imaginary animal from western and central France, from the Provençal, *féram*, "ferocious beast," and from the Latin *ferus*, "wild." Here we find ourselves knee-deep in folklore. And I have read on occasion, in texts purporting to be analytical in inspiration, that the *real* is the worse-than-hell and the worse-than-anguish, it is chaos and violence. Only someone who has never lived with beings who are up to their eyebrows in the real could peddle such legends.

To say that Janmari's body – Janmari having been autistic for over twenty years now and part of my life for the past eleven years or more – to say that his body is fragmented is to assume that HE has a body, in other words, that he has incorporated the image of a person that he hasn't digested. In order to be, one must thus have, if only a body, a body that is, as it were, "commoned." And yet the *common* I speak of, resistant to the intrusion of language, neither communes nor communicates.

That said, it is only too true that ethnic memory has always been busy pumping away the duckling's water and putting it in bottles. The undeniable advantages of the (symbolic) domestication of man by man come at this price, and they have always been exercised at the expense of the species memory, the latter deprived of what would be its *topos*, and, by the same token, there have to be children who are not children, resistant to the inevitability of that domestication of man by man so long as the surrounding environment lends itself to this resistance and proposes detours other than perorating, in which a certain "all" can be conjugated.

What is at stake, of course, on our part, is a good dose of taking sides, for which I have found the infinitive "to miscreate," which can mean to evade or dodge beliefs, and above all those that are most widespread, or to create something other than what is taking place.

That "or" is an "and," for the two approaches – one of which is not believing (in) this excess of belief proposed by perorating, and the other is to innovate who knows what that would allow for locating to be exercised – go hand in hand.

Those Excessives

Intellectual?

Given that we don't quite know what this means, better to rely on the dictionary. In the case of intellectuals, it says: "Intelligence has a predominant or excessive role."

Excess in everything is a flaw. I don't feel too implicated, myself. I believe I have known some intellectuals, and I have found them very much alike. So we would be dealing with a kind of caste. Every one of them had convictions.

Conviction: "firm opinion." That's fine. But in following the historical course of the word, we find this: "proof establishing someone's guilt." There is some truth in this. When I had dealings with intellectuals, it didn't take long for me to start feeling guilty. Very quickly, they identified my ideas. They exercised a habit no doubt acquired during their education. What I was able to write or say was dissected, x-rayed, and turned as it were into fingerprints of those from whom I had borrowed a good part of what I was proposing.

In this connection, I was surprised by many things; my remarks were confronted with works that I was quite certain I had never read and that I had never even heard of.

For those intellectuals, it was as though their own culture were being projected back to them like a mirage.

When those intellectuals happened to be communists, it didn't make things any easier. As petit-bourgeois, they weren't really quite comfortable being communists, and so the "someone" that I was, among other things, had to drink with them. In the realm of politeness, it was the least I could do. To such an extent that I found myself being told that the stories I was writing sounded something like Jacques Prévert. I was so proud. Actually, they said this to warn me.

Since then, I have dealt with others, who, although communists, didn't risk joining up. But their convictions were no less annoying. And it was the same mirage effect: convictions as strong as theirs inevitably overflowed and were projected onto anything they read. And, within their utterances, I found my own writings marinating in a sauce in which they had identified lingering traces well known to themselves.

One day, one of them, more or less a communist, came to see me. He had spotted Hegel, for sure, in my bullshit, whereas, shame on me, I had never read a word of Hegel. But it hardly matters. They didn't hold it against me, quite the contrary, that wasn't the issue. The other one who stopped by came, he said, to see what I saw from my window. It was obvious that this was the reason for his detour.

At the time, I was surprised, but in thinking about it again it seemed to me that I understood how an intellectual, besides possibly suffering from an excess of culture, is deprived of, severed from, deficient in something of great importance, which I am going to call *topos* in order to make it an entity that does not rule in the same pantheon as Eros and Thanatos.

Of the professors from the Faculty of Letters where I was a student, not all were intellectuals. A good many of them didn't seem to suffer from an excess of intelligence, far from it. But some of them had written books that were fairly well known. In fact, to my eyes, it was not easy to distinguish one from another. What they said, the very content of their discourse, seemed completely secondary in relation to the fact that they all spoke from the same place which was called a (professorial) chair. They spoke from the same chair. *Topos.* And yet this site is not clean, I don't mean in the housekeeping sense, but in the sense that they were all like birds on the same branch. Now, the branch is much more important than you might think when one is a bird oneself. And the one-upmanship of opposing convictions is of very little importance as far as this *topos* is concerned; in other words, the place *from which* something is said outweighs "that about which" one is speaking.

That fact is so obvious that the chair in question ended up becoming the site to which all and sundry owed it to themselves to gain access, in order to perorate there, if only to wipe out the privilege by sharing it. So much so that the privilege thus shared began to proliferate in such a way that I then had to wonder, and I still do, whether the site itself, in this case, hadn't ruined the most striking and powerful things that had been said there.

You will tell me that on occasion people speak from more or less anywhere. This is true.

But *topos* is a particularly susceptible entity.

If you simply put a microphone in front of a speaker's mouth and spread the recorded "statement" wherever you like, posting via whatever medium you like, you can say that whoever has spoken, the one speaking, is "posted." And if we see him, as we do on television, it changes nothing, quite the contrary: the speaker is "posted" and amalgamated, however confusedly, with all the others who are "posted" there. And here the phenomenon of the (professorial) chair is reiterated; here a good number of intellectuals stand out. We shouldn't be surprised by the loss of interest in these exchanges of roles, the role lying first of all in the fact of speaking from that place, *topos*.

So this is how one can understand the detour of the intellectual who came to see what I see out of my window, a window behind which I write and describe what takes place "here." It is well known that exiles who could be thought of as no longer having any place are all the better heard; *topos* in this case is respected.

But, that said, a book is also an aspect of this *topos*, an ambiguous and misunderstood entity. We know perfectly well that if the one who writes is respected, he or she is just as much suspected. There is a kind of cleft between the masses, the plebes, and those who set themselves apart, even and perhaps especially when it's a question of speaking for the masses. Place falls within the order of *topos*.

If I were asked in what respect I'm not one of them, not an intellectual, I would simply refer to what Paul Valéry says on the subject. Apart from the fact that I have (a) place, this place being that of an attempt, whereas the "trade of intellectuals is to mix everything together under their signs, names, or symbols, without the counterweight of real acts," my own "trade" is to live close to children whose acts I believe to be nothing but "real(ity)."

And if I mix names, symbols, and signs together, it's in the style of a third-rate handbook.

The smallest discovery we may happen to make about what eludes signs and symbols, what cannot be named, provokes an avalanche of significations, and I have to do my shoveling with a pencil or a pen, leading to a calloused hand, not on the palm, but precisely where the pencil with which I'm writing rubs and hardens a small recess of epidermis which becomes all lumpy on a knuckle of my third finger.

And this is just fine. It doesn't take much for a man to be proud of himself.

The Human and the Supernatural

There is the supernatural and there is the human.

Anyone who has lived for a long while in an insane asylum where a good number and variety of individuals and children are confined will have in memory the full spectrum of ritual stances from the various religions, present and past, as if brought to their culmination.

Some see a parody here, since the individuals in question are insane. And for an autistic child, the act of placing one's hand on a hot stove, without the reflex to withdraw it, can make one think that feeling can be interrupted.

Another individual, growing up, hands joined, gazing at the sky: one would think he had come straight from a painting evoking some mystic from the days of old.

There are strange coincidences here, consistent enough for the insoluble problem of form and content to be posed.

So here we have gestural forms that appear to have no content. Is this possible? It seems more reasonable to think that, for the same form, there can be several contents.

We know of the rocking that often occurs in mute children, while in certain religions, perhaps most, prayer must be accompanied by rocking; mere language is in some way surpassed. Whereas for the children affected with what is often viewed as a symptom, it is a question of a vacancy of language. The same attitude corresponds to the same content, the same vacancy, the same lacuna, suffered by some and sought after by others.

The other day, completely by chance, I discovered photos from an initiation ceremony for the Carmelite order.[1] The woman who was about to enter forever was lying on the ground, her body becoming one with the cloister tiles, and I saw again the autistic child who has been near me for more than ten years in the same posture, except that there was no surrounding cloister, and that, if the nun was taking on this posture, it was precisely at the moment in the ceremony when she had to take it out of respect for the customs, whereas in the case of the autistic child, one might think that the posture was taking hold of him.

The difference seems considerable, and also the distance.

On the one hand, there is what comes from the heavens. On the other, there is what comes from human beings deprived of the slightest intention, unless some intention is assumed. Here we find, at both extremes, the abandoning of the subject, of the subjective – deliberate on the part of the Carmelite, and completely involuntary on the part of the autistic child.

We may say that the Carmelite abandons all her roles in order to limit herself to a single one, which begins with this posture of the body sprawled on the floor, face down.

It is said that soldiers often are found like this during a battle, their arms stretched out as if on a cross, their faces in the mud.

Have they chosen their fates?

I say this because I wonder if the choosing that some see as what distinguishes humans from the species whose postures are, as they say, "programmed," is nothing but an illusion. Which would amount to saying that the subject, the self – everyone's self – that we all value so much is the perceived reflection of an illusion.

We cling to it, to this self of each one of us, but religious beliefs are not the only ones to offer an opportunity to shed it, insofar as possible.

This aspiration to – of – the supernatural is found in the superhuman efforts that are called for during revolutions that do not speak of any god, but rather of mankind. The fact that these revolutions run out of steam and sometimes fall short or turn bad provokes such a resurgence of the religious spirit that it is permissible to think that the image of humanity that inclines and carries people toward the superhuman during times of revolution is perhaps quite close to the supernatural image of mankind that religion proposes. The materialist revolutionaries simply think that

---

1. A Catholic religious order established in the late twelfth century. [TN]

they are going to promote this image of mankind, but by means other than the ones through which religion operates.

And what if the illusion were there, within this projected image that humanity means to realize; the paths toward it differ, but the image, the project, are always/already given.

Those who live with religious beliefs know the origin of that gift; but what about the others, those who reject the supernatural origin of mankind? They don't seem to wonder very much about the source of the gift, namely, what they think and feel about "man." This is actually what shocked me when I read what Itard had written about his "wild child" from the Aveyron region, around 1800. He attempted to ascertain whether this child, having lived isolated from other human beings for almost his entire life, had an innate sense of justice. This is a wholly extraordinary idea that proves to what extent there is confusion between the innate and the acquired. As far as "man" is concerned, it may be better to say that the innate is radically rejected and thought to be null and void, a non-occurrence.

And yet, having lived close to autistic children, I think the rocking that many of them share – and that is found in ritual postures conducive to prayer – is innate; consciousness of being – of being oneself within the gaze of the other – is at least partly abolished and does not exert its control. It may appear paradoxical that in moments when consciousness of being is stirred by the wind of the mind, even if we need to capitalize the word "Mind," this rocking can be found. But is it not also a question – at least to a certain extent – of abolishing the self of each one of us, the self whose control is fertile in ways of being that religion condemns?

In fact, the spectrum of postures that a human body can adopt is not that broad, and we must indeed play the instrument given us; we have no other.

A long time ago it was said that, in order to believe, one had to begin by kneeling; the rest would follow as a bonus.

And yet kneeling is one of the most constant postures among the children about whom the least we can say is that we have to suppose – out of our own concern for seeing them as similar, a concern that certainly comes from good intentions – that the S who kneels is indeed an S. Under the impulse of this good intention, it seems to be understood that our own feelings are what predominate. If we find ourselves kneeling, it's because we have intentionally adopted that posture. And we make a gift to the other of our own intention, so great is our generosity with respect to him or her. Once again we discover the image of human beings that is supposedly the same for one and all, and that seems to have something immutable about it, immutable being a term that, when applied to the innate, is enough to indicate that it escapes us.

Thus we are grappling here with two immutables, one coming from what is specific to the species, and the other coming from the self-image that humans have given themselves – or that, as many believe, has been given to them.

At the intersection of these two immutables, these two gravities, there are identical, common postures that seem to be the culmination of what the innate – left to itself – provokes, and the culmination of what the most dematerialized image of "man" proposes as a recourse.

To such an extent that the unconverted, materialists and atheists, no longer know what do with their bodies and their hands.

One can certainly close one's fist in a threatening way, something that neither a believer nor an autistic individual nor a fascist would do. But are we really dealing only with a threat, or the feeling of being threatened?

If I rely on what I see, the rallying gesture of autistic children would be rather to open the hand – and not at all to extend it for a handshake – within the field of the gaze which is not the field of the gaze of the other, and then, in this offered, open palm, endlessly gazed at, what is there? No mirror, in the hollow of this hand, and no image like the ones given to children at their first communion. Nothing. Skin and lines. It is here that chiromancers read the future. We know what this has cost the Gypsies, recently and even in earlier times, when they were sometimes presumed to be witches. All this to say that strange relays come into play with respect to the same objects. For the Nazis, it was enough to say that the Gypsies were dirty, racially speaking, whereas they themselves were clean, well bathed. We see that the accusation was less serious than the earlier one, even if the consequences were equally so.

And what about autistics, in all this?

For the Nazis, the only choice was to exterminate them or, at the very least, prevent them from reproducing.

For others, animated by a strong feeling of likeness, no such thing exists; the image of mankind given or received necessarily has to be reproduced as such.

I still wonder if the same abuse isn't involved in racism; the border that separates races, for some, is taken much further and becomes more subtle: it would only be a matter of an ethics, which would be that of the unconscious.

Far be it from me to make such an amalgam between two positions that provoke two very dissimilar postures. For one side, it is a matter of hatred, for the other, love.

What I take as a warning is what alerted Claude Lévi-Strauss, among others: namely, that if people decide that they are similar only among themselves, they draw a boundary: they have a common image of what they are, an ingrained image.

And it could very well be that the human lies beyond that boundary, which comes from an image, even if it is only an image of the body.

The Charade

The unconscious?

There is psychoanalysis, it's true.

For me, psychoanalysis is a curiously foreign language. I thought I could learn it, by reading texts written in the only language I know, French. Impossible. The same misadventure had befallen me when I was younger, with English, Latin, Greek, and mathematics. However, this time the texts were written in French, a language I'm rather fond of. I couldn't understand it. I told myself that I was dealing with a kind of double language. I occasionally spent time with people who spoke psychoanalysis. I spoke as well, in my native tongue. It seemed that my remarks were being returned to me translated, interpreted, as one says, and I no longer understood them. This produced a bizarre effect, as if the others who were there were frolicking in the middle of a swimming pool whose water I couldn't see.

And then I got used to it, all the more easily when I met an autistic individual who, clearly, could no more understand our language than I could psychoanalysis.

Sometimes I would ask myself whether I hadn't purposely become resistant to this language. When I saw that Janmari was a stranger to mine, I stopped questioning my own intentions, since it seemed so clear to me that, as far as intentions were concerned, there weren't any. Thus I was over it, in the clear. I mean that I acquitted myself without any other form of trial. At peace, I could try to see whether by chance this language, which like all languages constitutes a whole that has its own coherence, might not be eclipsing something else that persists around the edges, as is the case with any eclipse: an opaque body makes a screen haloed all around with a light that seems to emanate from the body itself, just as we see a halo of light around the head of a saint.

There still remains the thought that the head of the saint itself hides something from us, something that, through an effect of optics, seems to emanate from it, but that is really nothing. It's merely the remainder; what had been concealed persists on the threshold of perception, whereas the saint, of course, has no intention of hiding anything whatsoever, his or her task being to reveal, if only the truth.

I even reached the point of telling myself that any truth conceals, eclipses the real, and that the aura that I saw, via the presence of an autistic child – provided as I was then with a sort of third eye, like the one spoken of by Tibetan monks, among whom it was standard practice to make a hole in one's forehead – glimmers of the real that was hidden by the fact of the consciousness that is incumbent upon us.

Being neither a monk nor Tibetan, I hadn't made a hole in my forehead. Janmari was there, constantly, with his own "seeing point," perceptibly distant and different from our viewpoint, which is more or less unanimous among all those who, as soon as they are born and even before, have been initiated into symbolic existence.

The real: it seems to me that I have come across this word in texts written in the French language, no doubt about that, but owing to the fact that that language is double and at the very least has double meanings, goes in two directions,[1] it swept the words away from under my nose, and then, now you see them now you don't, who knows what became of them in that waltz whose music I didn't perceive.

It is completely discouraging to hold a word in sight, and see it spin around, pair with others, join a constellation, like a string of beads; in fact, it escapes you like a ball on a playground; others play with it cheerfully, but what are they playing at, what's their game? It's a mystery. There are no goals, no baskets or nets. They are having fun, that's for sure; the game is making them laugh. After all, words don't belong to anyone, and we would be wrong to feel ourselves deprived of them just because others use them in a way that suits them.

So what about the real? It comes from *res*: thing.

I have mentioned that I have read, and sometimes even re-read, a good number of pages written *in* psychoanalysis. I have called it a foreign language. But where might the foreignness come from? Perhaps it's that the thing, the real, doesn't exist in that language, to the point that autism is envisioned like a charade, the subject going silent and seeking refuge in identification with some object in which obliteration of the subject would be seen.

---

1. The French expression *double sens* signifies "double meaning," but *sens* can also signify "direction." [TN]

The autistic individual – and our Janmari, in this case – would thus be playing a role, his manifest attitude being a charade, his attraction toward *the thing* explained by the fact that S would be moved by a sort of identificatory tropism.

No things, then; there is only something like an object since there is, *a priori*, something like a subject and, when the latter is lacking it's because it goes to ground and obliterates itself. To put it another way, when an object becomes a thing, it is nothing.

I don't know if *psychoanalysis* speaks like this; but a language doesn't speak: it is spoken by some subject who uses it and, as we say, expresses himSELF or herSELF. Is this to say that all subjects who speak the same language are in agreement? Certainly not; it is thanks to language that we are able to discuss, argue with, congratulate, and accuse ourSELVES and EACH OTHER. Here we can see the importance of the WE in each case where we are dealing with the SELF. For those who do not have the same WE – the same language – there are no more reciprocal feelings, there is no more consent or resentment.

Thus it is the WE of psychoanalysis that escapes me, the S of the subject being in some way the center of gravity of its coherence.

If I read that Janmari is a subject who would identify himself with anything whatsoever, and in so doing would be obliterating himself, I see an inkling of intention, an ounce of intentionality, or, if you will, the indication of the existence of the S at the center of the human system, just as, for a very long time, the earth was maintained at the center of the solar system; it actually had been the center forever, as everything that we had been able to feel in that respect attested.

And it is true that, watching Janmari live, there's no question, he does turn around us, and we need only rely on what we can feel in order to suppose that he wanders like a soul in pain deprived of the ability to identify with someONE. But this way of feeling can come from the fact that each one of us is someONE, and that this ONE of the existing subject has an undeniable propensity for self-projection, as we say, as if every ONE of us were a soul having a hard time identifying, and then the charade comes from us, and not from the autistic individual, the fear of nothingness inspiring us, this nothingness being supposed by us, moreover; and it is in shamelessly identifying ourselves with the "he" in question – who is not "he" – that our only option is to interpret that he is identifying himself, for want of us, with a piece of manipulated string, a scrap of a thing that for Janmari is not "one" but that for us, can only be ONE (object) supposedly circumscribed, that is, named or almost, the real being indeed fragmented owing to the effect of the language that is incumbent on us, an effect that doesn't concern Janmari in the least, except that it deprives him of that by which we are *things*, and indeed real [*réels*]. To insist on the plurality of the word *réel* suggests that each one of us is a singular being, which is no doubt true for us – felt by us – but not for Janmari. It would be better to say we are reality [*le réel*], if only ever so slightly, except that we have long since lost the habit of being real. And rather than invoking habit, we ought to speak of attitudes.

Because from Janmari's seeing point – the third eye – the real has innate *forms*; why not say the word: I have nothing to lose.

I'm speaking in a different language.

It is hard to imagine a law, even if it were the law of language – and I have come across this term in writing – that would not result in a good number of formalities.

For those of us who see autistic individuals live, their manner of being appears strangely formal to us; repeating occurs constantly.

If there must be forms, is it the case that Janmari would lose himself, in his "ways," whereas we would find ourselves, in our "ways" of saying?

That is something of which I'm not fully convinced.

How can something that has never existed be obliterated? and in order for a SELF to lose itself, it first has to be.

If we find ourselves, within our own ways of saying, it's because we are already there, a position has been taken and a "seeing point" occulted, eclipsed. Who will state, and in what language, the distance between two bodies, the one that exists only in order to be seen, and knows it, and the other that exists only in order to see, without consciousness of being?

Freedom without a Name

I have hesitated and I am still hesitating over the very words that make up the title of this text.

I first wrote "freedom without a no." As usual, I started with a gesture from Janmari, who has been close by for ten years, as autistic as can be; the gesture most often noticed is his hand reaching out toward something. On close examination, it was obvious that the thing in proximity to the extended hand was attractive or repulsive. No mimicry came into play to tell us more about this ambivalence, unless we were prepared to see, in this gesture, the very origin of the sense of the verb "apprehend," where both grasping and fearing are involved.

To tell the truth, it would be better to come to terms with it: Janmari's gestures mean nothing, and do not constitute any sort of sign, any gesture, ever.

From there to thinking that, from his seeing point, our own gestures are not signs, nor do they signal, it was but a small step that we took quite cheerfully without any hope of return.

Suddenly, the climate brightened. We had been relieved from our perplexity or our distress, and the customary life of the tiny units in the network was established around this mode innovated by Janmari according to which our gestures wove what was to be done, with, in addition, a special sort of respect toward the mute children who came to live close to us, a mode that we have named *the adorned* [*l'orné*]. What is at issue is clear: our attitudes and ways of being are adorned with "detours" that are in no way necessary and that express nothing, represent nothing. So it is that the establishment of a rather gentle tradition, the adorned being ceaselessly reinforced by small events that serve as its humus: the actings multiply, diversify, gain magnitude. It suffices to see what happens once we put a halt to *the adorned* and bring signs back into play, as we have been shown that we were supposed to do from the start, and even prior to our own birth: the *actings* wither and disappear.

But what can be said about a freedom without a no and without a yes? It loses its name.

If any beings resistant to power exist, they are indeed the autistics. To such an extent that power and freedom appear to be placed under the same banner, or rather are of the same origin, which frankly is not news.

As for *the adorned* that lies beyond "yes" and "no," it is neutral. This is the discovery. Except that the sonority of the word "neutral" has nothing engaging about it, and if *the adorned* remains neutral, we lose its brilliance and renown, to say nothing of the elation that comes from the impulse to lash out at the other. And then everyone knows the sad fate of the sexless beings that bustle about in hives and anthills.

So let's take another word, and let's say that *the adorned* is refractory, a better word for it considering that living areas, for the most part, have in their adornment some stones whose presence invites "detours," if only within our trajectories and the course of our projects, stones that are in some sense refractory to the slightest intention.

Is it possible that we ourselves have no intentions, here? Probably not. But the fact remains that the stones refract our intentions, stones *located* by the children, from which we get *actings* that can surprise, our own projects finding themselves refracted in disparate, broken sequences, very often deprived of the "something" that is the object – the project – of our own "doings."

So, freedom?

If we act in order to do (something), Janmari, autistic, benefiting from what can be located within these "doings," dares to *act*; and not in order to do or make. He has very little concern, actually, about the identity that is anchored by a name.

And here we find freedom adrift, no longer having anything to do with the slightest of projects. But is not what drifts off this way the word itself, the word "freedom," its name, which is written everywhere, and do you know what they said at the school I went to when I was little? "The name of a mad man is written everywhere." Who knows where this saying came from, the one we repeated so cheerfully.

At whom, or at what, was this a way of lashing out?

Perhaps it was a way to deal with the fact that everyone would like his or her name to be written everywhere, and let those who achieve this beware: they would be mad, and it would serve them right, *because the name of each and every one cannot be written there,* everywhere. There would not be enough room, and even if there were enough room, if every name were written, none would emerge from this gibberish. Slabs of marble remain, affixed to the stone of monuments: names are written. Not the names of the mad, but of those who died in a war, and quite often under the banner of freedom, those whose names tell us why they died, those of whom there remain nothing but names. What is remarkable is that, in the dictionary, one of the antonyms of the word "freedom" is the word "fatality." We ought to change the signs on these monuments and put what the dictionary proposes: "determinism, destiny, fatality" in place of "freedom, equality, fraternity."

All this is quite well known.

If I return to ants or bees, which are tirelessly busy and which are neutral, being sexless, they are also called workers. Which explains their drive.

All this to come back to something a psychoanalyst said, that, as far as our species is concerned, suckling is (a) cultural (act). This shows to what degree nature is denied, considered rubbish and out of place for a species so special that even the word species no longer concerns it. I wonder what to think, in this geography, about the 98.6 degrees that we are bound to protect at all costs if we want life to persist. Am I digressing? Not at all. What is at issue is still the difference between *doing* and *acting*, between the acquired and the innate.

Because, in the end, we know very well that freedom is not found in "nature."

So what do we learn from Janmari, an autistic individual if ever there were one?

That outside the name [*nom*], where the no [*non*] is chanted[1] – or perhaps we should say outside the no, where the name is chanted? – a stone can serve as a reference point, owing to the deficiency of [*au défaut de*] anything that could serve as a sign.

I could have said "for want of" [*à defaut de*], but I chose "deficiency" since I think that there is something wrong with the fact that in order to name, if only freedom, one must still have at one's disposal the use of a name as such. Hence perhaps the misadventures of this noble project in the name of which we find ourselves struggling with a fatality that might well turn out to be inescapable; universal understanding seems to be as one with the horizon.

In the same way that what is understood comes from what can be uttered – and it is indeed necessary for the individuals involved to prepare themselves to utter, that

---

1. The French words *nom* (name) and *non* (no) are homophones.

177

they be ready, otherwise the understood flows past like water over a duck's feathers and does not take place – the identifiable demands that identity should lend itself to being, not that it be voluntary; it must also not be refractory.

Is it possible that Freedom, like the Unconscious, lies only within History? and then we still don't know what it is: freedom-consciousness-of, freedom-project, the limit between the one and the other and if I move my boundary, I'm infringing; letting you do as you will, letting you move yours, I am infringed upon. Freedom, a fixed idea, unchanging as we once believed species were unchanging. And so you see here, where mute children come to live, what a strange democracy it is where the opportunity to say yes or no is replaced by a stone, the yes and no coming from the same ray of light which, when refracted, allows for an entire catalog of multicolored nuances to shine through, to such an extent that, if a democracy is established and we expect it to be popular, we would be better off speaking of the refractory.

It is obvious that what is named and what is refractory do not go well together; the light beam of rights and duties, refracted as it is from the yes and the no, shatters into countless particles whose fog comes to enshroud our own heads in which everything that can be said, all that can or could be said, which is no small feat, ruminates; in vain.

To think what the freedom of an "autistic" other may be requires naming it other, and then what becomes of the other's freedom not to be other, if he or she is even slightly refractory to this involvement of the reciprocal and to all identification?

It is easy to see the potential abuse in this a priori assumption that everyone, from the outset, would volunteer to become "man or woman," a necessity then toward which there would be only aggravated inaptitudes, as there should be, through countless subtle words of advice, correction; isn't correcting them – these children, here – what their parents' distress urges us to do?

And, in the spirit of the times, you hear some good ones; hot air balloons rise up full of readymade ideas, the most sumptuous of which ostentatiously display the word "freedom."

That said, displayed, proclaimed, supposedly on the side of history, what persists as a prelude, in our eyes, is the quivering gesture, the indistinct yes/no, which goes hand in hand with desire/fearing where apprehending emerges, having become a verb.

Where it appears that I don't write desiring/fearing, or desire/fear, for how could I, since "freedoming" [*liberter*] does not exist.

Refracting exists, and what would be refracted would be the least of words: and/or, among others.

What seems to be obliterated, then, is never that through which humans distinguish themselves and find themselves objects of the "distinction" that goes on culminating in order to arrive at the point where fully realized humans are actually nothing more than humans who realize themselves fully, in complete freedom.

It was in vain that Darwin said all paths lead to man if they are seen from man's perspective, the perspective of man deprived of "nature."

"The most perfected of animal societies are merely distant and pale sketches of human society, even though they announce and prefigure it."[2]

And here we are, Janmari and I, at the transition point, hand quivering and overloaded with wanting to *say* [*vouloir dire*].[3] I believe that his hand passes through that point, and that we are indeed dealing with laws of nature, nature being refractory to the point that freedom becomes lost within it, loses its name, but then, perhaps, what marvelous findings....

I very consciously retained the "re" that is on call and installs itself once nature is evoked, nature which from the outset is situated in the past; we may wonder why.

It is easy to see that this quivering of the hand is in no way a parapraxis, a Freudian slip. But rather an *incomplete* action.

But can we say that these incomplete actions will one day be completed?

No, unless the S emerges, the S that (more or less conscious of its own end) will determine that its gesture signifies something, and we see quite well then that this something is not at all some, and is not a thing, but a sign.

In order to make a sign, there have to be two, whereas this quivering of the hand, this incomplete acting, perpetuates itself "in a vacuum," it would perhaps be better to say "in silence," the heard having just shattered against the refractory. So we cannot say "the heard"; we should say "the hearable."[4]

---

2. Jacques Ruffié, *De la biologie à la culture* (Paris: Flammarion, coll. "Nouvelle bibliothèque scientifique,"1978 [1976], p. 360.
3. The French phrase *vouloir dire* ordinarily corresponds to the English "to mean," "to signify." Here, the stress on the word *dire* draws attention to the literal meaning: "to want to say," and thus to the question of expression. [TN]
4. The French neologism *entendable* comes from the verb *entendre*, which can mean both "to hear" and "to understand." [TN]

This quivering of the hand, demand/refusal, is it an "intentional" movement, like those of which ethnologists speak, when they know to what extent words are inappropriate? Because, in the end, what would be the intention in a gesture that says nothing definite?

To warn them, they'll tell me, to warn those nearby. But what can those nearby do about it if the author of the gesture does not know what he or she wants?

Do we all have a quivering hand, like the outline of a flapping wing propagating through the entire flock?

It could indeed happen that the manifest confusion subsides. The very thing that seems to have been denoted, having served its purpose, no longer has a reason to be. It literally no longer takes place.

Here it can be seen that acting (which is not about taking or fending off), the incomplete acting – I mean without end – suffices (unto itself).

Do we believe that we ourselves are in the clear, we who, from birth, have evaded autism? It suffices to see the hand-clapping that applauds, at the theater, if only what causes the applause could last forever ... or is it the fact that it is over that is applauded, the one not excluding the other, because in the end, what a shame if that which produced joy in the moment endeavored to last forever.

Are we now far from Freedom?

Perhaps not so far if we suppose that freedom is evoked from choice.

Let's return to Janmari, autistic as can be. His rocking sets in under many circumstances, one of which seems to be particularly refined: being planted at a fork in the pathway, which leads to a great deal of indecision, and the rocking veers toward vertigo, eyes closed, the droning at the back of the throat going toward a *crescendo*.

I know very well that THEY will tell me that each of us takes pleasure where we can find it and that after all, it's his right to gorge himself on hesitation.

"He is quite free."

But can rights prevail under the aegis of "to each his own," which becomes "what he wants" for which the "right to" is called upon, from whence power would be compromised; but as compromise is the ordinary fodder of power, here we find it more dashing than ever, faced with an influx of rights demanded of whomever they may concern, whoever may have the authority to convey them.[5]

Merely saying "Janmari is quite free" resonates from the fact that by naming him we know at once what free is or should be. And yet, where this freedom is concerned, structured as it is by law, Janmari could care less.

The very name of freedom comes to be refracted upon the rocking that can veer all the way to vertigo; the word concerns us [*le mot nous concerne*].

And it is indeed outside of this particular "ring" [*cerne*] that the laws of nature – of which we understand ourselves to be bereft – are played out.

---

5. *À qui de droit* is the equivalent of "To whom it may concern" as the address in a letter to an unknown recipient. But the French phrase more explicitly addresses the unknown person(s) who have the right, that is, the power and authority, to grant a request. [TN]

Pretend Not to Notice

Pretend not to notice. *Faire semblant de rien.* This can be said in French; I'm always afraid of giving the interpreter a hard time [*du fil à retordre*];[1] each language has its locutions and idioms. Joseph Conrad thought that turns of phrase like these formed character; born in Poland, he spent his childhood in France and adopted the English language, feeling more English than the English; having adopted the language and its turns of phrase, he very much wanted to be adopted by those whose mother tongue he used as his own native language, language becoming a place.

Is this to say that he pretended to be English? Apart from pretending not to notice, there is also pretending to do or to be [*faire semblant de faire ou d'être*].

My place of adoption, which could stand as my native country, is not a foreign country; it is a much more singular ethnic group, one of its characteristics being that it has no language, since it lacks the use of language; I am referring to autistic children, some of whom are growing up, and to us among them.

Living in such a place, close to autistic individuals, it is clear that to make a sign is to pretend, whether we are talking about a gesture of encouragement close to what ethologists call a movement of intent, or rather the gesture indicating "no" with the head where it is not possible to see a movement of intent. Our head pivots right to left and left to right and so forth; at best, such a movement would entail pretending to look from right to left in order to look to the right, and this would be a sign of indecision, Buridan's sign,[2] whereas this is not the case, the "no" is decisive and in no way marks the slightest hesitation.

---

1. This expression translates literally as "some thread to twist again"; it thus introduces another play on the motif of spiders and their webs. [TN]
2. A reference to a paradox incorrectly attributed to the medieval French philosopher Jean Buridan: a donkey, stationed halfway between two identical piles of hay, would purportedly starve to death for want of any reason to choose between them. [TN]

That said, if Janmari – the autistic youngster who, without wanting to, directs this approach – sees me make that sign, the acting that has been bottled up until then will begin to flow, liberated; to put it another way, my sign of denegation, which ought to be prohibitive, becomes a gesture of permission.

All this to say that Janmari doesn't perceive the semblance, the sign made by the head being a semblance of saying. That this mimicry on my part is so fully crafted and convoluted that it resembles nothing having to do with doing could be expressed by saying that there is nothing to it but making a sign.

The sign made resembles nothing? It resembles the sign one has to make when one wants to signal "no." The semblance thus lies in the resemblance; signs have to resemble one another, after all, if only among themselves, or else they risk being completely meaningless gestures or acts of mimicry.

The sign "no" that liberates acting whereas it ought to prohibit acting leads us onto the trail of thinking that *acting* has nothing at all to do with *making*, making going hand and hand with making a sign that is a semblance of saying.

If we follow this trail a bit further, we arrive at the fact that our mode of being is to pretend to be, and that Janmari, loyal to his own mode of being, does not perceive the semblance. In speaking of Janmari I'm speaking of autistic individuals – which puts us in the position, we who live in constant proximity to them, of not knowing what we resemble, what we look like, and this is exactly what happens to us.

If, as the dictionary states, semblance is appearance, we have in some way disappeared. To appear [*apparaître*] is to seem [*paraître*] and to seem is to pretend [*faire semblant*], to pretend to be something or rather someone. This someone that we are, would it be a matter of semblance?

We shouldn't be surprised by this, accustomed as we are to the necessity of making and doing, if only of making a sign or doing what has to be done.

Concerning this *doing what has to be done* – and even making the slightest sign requires the "has to," which, if it is not respected, will result in the sign not being understood – Janmari couldn't care less, which is merely an idiomatic way of putting it because if he had even the tiny bit of S' (self) that would allow him not to care, he wouldn't be able not to care. At best, he would like not to do anything, this is why he would always be pretending since wanting would be involved, wanting going hand in hand with consciousness of being and of doing what one has to do in order to be recognized as being, and thus of pretending, as one has to pretend. The gaze of the impersonal "ONE" is pitiless and does not forgive spelling mistakes, the least of signs being spelled out in order to be identifiable.

One could believe that living this way, deprived of knowing what we look like or resemble – and it is clear that I have to write res*sembler* (resemble); *semble* (seem) would not be enough, for semblance requires resembling – one could believe that, living this way, deprived of appearance, we lead very hard lives.

Actually, it does seem that this transparency is often felt as being completely unbearable by those who approach us, impelled by the winds of good intentions. They would gladly strip themselves naked if they had to, on the condition that that could be seen, could "see itself." The condition has not been fulfilled; in order to make oneself naked, one still has to do it, and pretend in the sense that, in order to see oneself, there has to be some similar being who perceives the intention of being undressed; about this, the children couldn't care less. Whereas what those who approach us – wearing their goodwill on their sleeves – do is write some sort of memoir, which has the virtue of keeping them company; this is just what ethnologists would do.

As far as we are concerned, deprived as we are of any semblance, we have ended up getting used to it. After all, it is possible to live without a shadow; one gets accustomed to anything.

And what then appears, like new stars in the sky of the conquerors, is the possibility that human beings are only semblances, which is more often expressed as a claim that humans are beings created by the symbolic.

If I look at Janmari's hands, it seems that they are not made to count to ten even though they are surprisingly dextrous, dextrous being an unfortunate adjective, as his left and right hands are equally skilled.

The fact remains that with these hands he never pretends anything, not even to do or make something, despite the fact that his wealth of acting renders his presence very precious.

In no way inspired by the semblance of being, he lives in the infinitive, which is a mode of being common to the autistics who look at us from somewhere other than semblance. From somewhere else, but where?

And it's no use looking at ourselves or looking at each other or seeing ourselves again on a video screen, we never see what makes us similar, that is, what makes us resemble the person we are in our own eyes, which see only the semblance: what the dictionary calls "appearance."

And the dictionary goes further: parenthetically, it proposes "(opposed to the real)."

185

Opposed? This is not the case for us; we are not opposed to the real; we have nothing against it; we have no idea what it is.

Joseph Conrad, Polish by birth, French by childhood, and English by adoption, is wrong to say that words are the worst enemies of reality. He had to feel in Polish, think in French, and speak in English; thus he was at odds with a trilingual reality; reason enough to condemn words of which he nevertheless made remarkable use.

Words are not the worst enemies of reality; they create it and we are the creatures of that creation.

As for exiting from language, we really can't escape it; it's no use pretending not to make signs since we are on foreign soil, we never manage to be anything but shams [*faux-semblants*], rather as one says "false witnesses." But what can be said about a false witness? He does not lie about the fact that he was there; he lies about what he has seen and, quite often, what it seemed like to him....
In other words, he pretends to have seen something other than what he saw.

However, as far as I'm concerned, no matter that I have witnessed Janmari's comings and goings with my own eyes, I am still a false witness, my intentions having had nothing to do with it. Can we condemn someone for being a false witness in the absence of an intention to be one? Probably not; even this crime, then, is pardonable.

Still, this false witnessing that is nourished by shams, "false semblances," even if it is inevitable, is irritating. Is this to say that there is a true-semblance? Verisimilitude [*vraisemblance*] exists, at least in the dictionary. There is no such thing as false similitude [*faux-semblance*], at least it can't be found in the dictionary. But how would semblance be true or false? The role of semblance is to create likenesses; this can be rephrased as "similar beings," which we are, except for Janmari, of course.

The Obligatory and the Fortuitous

To speak of war is to speak of the obligatory, or rather of the obligation to make war, or if not to make it then at least to be in it. What may seem quite surprising is the readiness and ease in which each and every one of us accepts this obligation, whatever the identified subject thinks of war, which, unlike meteorological phenomena, would not come about if men were not led to make it.

Making war looks like an obligatory phenomenon, then, whereas those who are its manipulators or manufacturers think they don't want such a disaster. This leads one to believe that such a constraint, felt as a misfortune, will be refused by those who are themselves called upon to produce and reproduce it.

To believe this would be to have very little knowledge of men who, their own wanting being countered, fall back on the obligatory and, according to what I saw of them during the last war, far from being tormented by the sudden deprivation of what could be called their freedom, they are actually relieved, giving back to those responsible the power of wanting that they nevertheless seemed to cherish. Which leaves one to think that each and every one of us must in some way have the obligatory ingrained within us.

So much so that this business of making war, which resonates with monstrous atrocities, is always felt as highly probable and even inevitable, even if it means saying that human nature is at stake, the nature of the said humans intervening when one cannot help but observe to what degree humans, who pride themselves on wanting what they want – as opposed to animals, which endure – find themselves grappling struggling with a *having to* that they did not want at all.

From this starting point one of the most common words of the most ordinary vocabulary, I mean freedom, a notion generally based the free exercise of wanting on the part of each of us, appears the way dead stars – and we know they are dead – appear to us, endowed with their brilliance and radiance, and yet with a nuance that is not negligible: these stars are not dead, for they have never lived.

War then appears to be within the same orbit as La Boétie's tyrant,[3] who can exist only by the wanting of each and every one of us, whereas no one of the each-and-every-one-of-us had wanted it, thus it is a mirage that, as mirage, has the peculiar property of crashing down on the heads of those who have never done anything but fear it.

If we examine more closely what gives human beings – if indeed humans exist elsewhere and differently than within this same orbit of mirage – their feeling of freedom, we end up with consciousness of being, a phenomenon that supposedly can give us the ability not to submit to the obligatory; and in looking under a magnifying glass, as we would look at a drop of water, at a particle of this consciousness of being, we perceive that it is teeming with signs, to such a degree that it is hard to sort out whether consciousness is exuded by signs or if it is the other way around.

It might be that there is in the sign itself, in the slightest of signs, a considerable portion of the obligatory, whether the obligatory is a necessity of consciousness or whether the sign itself exists only as obligatory, with an effect that consciousness feels.

This is what struck me when I was an educator responsible for instructing retarded children. I was young, I had my ideas and I worked my heart out; this work consisted in trying to draw the children out of their apathy, which seemed colored by an aversion to writing, reading, and counting. To mention only counting, I would show them the five fingers of one hand, spread out, and the children would draw as many sticks as they saw fingers; once they drew these sticks, they counted them and wrote down the number 5 – at least that is what those who participated in the exercise did; those who didn't remain contemplative and almost ecstatic at seeing the use of the appendage I had at the end of my arm; some of them who wrote numbers skipped the part about lining up the sticks and proceeded by taking a poll, glancing over at what their neighbors had written and once they had observed that 5 was in the majority, they drew it as the result of their inquiry; I hesitated to criticize this way of operating, which seemed to me to require at least as much intelligence as going by way of the sticks, where each stick represented a finger; but what also happened was that the conscientious ones wrote 5 first and then traced the number of sticks corresponding to the number that was immediately expressed.

Some will think that we have gotten far away from war, whereas this is not at all the case; we are right in the middle of it: once the use of 5 had apparently been acquired by three-fourths of the group, we had to go on to 6, which led me to use

3. Étienne de la Boétie (1530-1563) was a French judge and political philosopher whose influential "Discourse on Involuntary Servitude" dealt with the mystery of why people consent to be ruled by tyrants. [TN]

the five fingers of one hand while the fingers of my other hand remained closed except for one which pointed toward the sky as if it were responsible for evoking the fact that in addition to me and my gesticulations there was someone else who saw everything from up there. One shouldn't think that it's so easy to go from 5 to 6; I saw 5s forming, as if molded from the previous week's work, and, next to the 5, as happy as could be to emerge once again, the 1, which might have thought itself forgotten or the victim of some dark ingratitude; as for justifying the way the numbers were drawn, the twisted, bulging 5 with a cap, the 1 straight as could be, the 6 a bit like a cherry whose stem would go off to the side, it was better not to think about it; that's how it went and that's all there was to it, until several months later, it was actually a policeman who, standing on the crest of an arched bridge, looked at me, both his arms raised with one hand spread wide open while the other one remained closed except for one finger which pointed toward the sky and beyond, where I had some chance of arriving sooner rather than later, given the 6 that was inscribed in my military dossier: all those born French according to the records in the second half of the year preceding the one during which the previous war was declared had that same number in their military dossiers. And the policeman who was signaling me from afar had no desire to teach me that 5 and 1 make 6, but that the 6 had been drawn, as one would say in regard to a lottery, with the difference that I hadn't bought a ticket, at least to my knowledge.

I was indeed mobilized, and the fact that the motives for the event to which I was imperatively convoked escaped me had no importance whatsoever; as for my mobility, it was completely determined by the rails on which the night train traveled, and it was frankly one of the most profound mysteries of human nature that all the males of the same age were magnetically drawn, at the same moment, toward their home-town barracks, just as eels at any given moment head toward the Sargasso Sea, except that for these individuals of the same species, it was not about reproducing; it was actually the complete opposite: what they had to reproduce was war, which in order to be made, had need of us, whereas we had no more wanted to make war than we had wanted to be born, or than we had decided to have five fingers on each hand, or than, in order to write a 6, we needed to have a circle with a tail that is pointing up but slightly crooked and that escapes from the side of the little circle the way a stone escapes from a slingshot.

From the moment when the obligatory is a necessity without which the slightest sign would not exist, one shouldn't be surprised that the margin of initiative attributed to each-and-everyone-of-us is reduced to such a degree that all that remains, if we really care about it, is to believe in it, for want of being able to prove that freedom exists; it still remains for us to find out why they teach us its necessity.

It is true that the teaching I had received from a very young age, at home, up until I started university studies, not to mention the movements that I belonged to, had taught me disdain and hatred for the outdated phenomenon that bore the name war, so much so that I found myself completely unprepared when I found myself incorporated, as we say, into a unit that was part of the spearhead of the French army and more specifically in Holland during the days that followed May 10, 1940, a date that is being spoken of again.

What surprised me was not so much being there without an ounce of wanting on my behalf; I had a long-established habit, ingrained, as it were, of submitting to the obligatory, although I had practiced freedom during breaks, clandestinely entering empty classrooms in order to smoke a couple of cigarettes, which was strictly forbidden; what astonished me was the feeling of light casualness that I could tell my fellow recruits shared; the obligatory that we had to live with had reached its utmost limits, to the point that, when we got into the truck that transported us, we had no idea where it was going, and the driver had no idea either, his duty being to follow the truck in front of him; and so it was for the whole line of them, and moreover for all the lines of motorized machines, no one knew where they were going; those who had the power to give them a destination had no idea where those lines might be and even if they had seen them from afar, they would not have been able to locate the head or the tail of these segments, which nevertheless were moving like the cut-off sections of an earthworm, seemingly endowed with autonomous existence, the popular belief being that each segment regrows a head, and thus a tail.

Some will say that this was an exceptional disaster in history, which I would very much like to believe; but this is not my aim, history being for me a place where I have never found myself; or rather, I have always lived so completely within it that I am quite unable to say anything at all about it for the same reason that we don't expect a fish to talk about the water that it has never had the opportunity to see unless it has been taken out of it, and then it dies, an event that abolishes the privilege it would have been in a position to enjoy.

In reality, if I can speak of the obligatory, it is because I live close to children for whom the obligatory is an unknown element, whereas it is in this element that we evolve, and some feel that we do so freely; so that autistic children look at us somewhat in the same way that we look at fish in a bowl.

Since I have spoken of elements, I shall say that we evolve within the obligatory whereas they react to the fortuitous.

That said, one of us can become unconscious, if only after taking a blow to the head, which doesn't mean he or she would be the unconscious personified.

The same can be said for the autistic individual, who is not autism personified, if we are willing to grant that, if the unconscious has taken on legitimacy, it could be that we should consider the autistic aspect of human beings in a way that differs completely from our usual approach, which is to say that someone is autistic.

What can be said about obligation? "Bond of duty by virtue of which a person may be constrained to give, do, or not do something." "A moral bond that subjects the individual to a religious, moral, or social law."

What about the fortuitous? First of all, it is positioned as an antonym of the "necessary" and the "obligatory," and the word resonates somewhat like *fors*, an archaic term for "except" that calls to mind chance and the unexpected, the exception.

But since it's a matter of calling to mind the autistic element of human beings, blind to the obligatory of the sign, we shouldn't be surprised to find that words don't have the necessary scope.

I was talking about the war and I'm coming back to it, particularly on the point that those mobilized, put into a situation of non-wanting or rather wantlessness, were none the worse for it; I speak of wantlessness as one speaks of weightlessness or zero gravity. Those who wanted to make war from the outset were quite rare; as for those who didn't want to make war, all they had to do was be there and the rest would obligatorily follow, even to the extent of getting killed, just like those whose wanting operated freely. Deprived as we were of having to want/not want anything whatsoever, we were the "immutable man of history (who) borrows an admirable capacity to adapt" from the fact that he can end up being "indifferent to any sort of hypothetical supposition," to borrow some phrases from Joseph Conrad; from this we can see that the men in question were equipped with an astonishing "power of endurance."

And yet, as far as we were concerned, it wasn't so much a question of endurance; the war of 1940 wasn't the war of 1914 and the journeys with neither head nor tail in no way resembled the trenches of Verdun; quite simply, our assumptions were off. It was fairly clear that we had good odds of getting ourselves killed by the planes dropping bombs and firing machine guns on the convoys; we were caught in a huge trap. Within this situation, everybody's mood was rather laid back and light-hearted; if I consider my own frame of mind, which must have been quite common among many of the others, all projects having completely escaped me, living became an infinitive; the infinitive was an autistic mode of being, and the fortuitous then took on the importance that it may have for the children who live here, apart from any wanting, not even, as far as they are concerned, wanting to make a sign. We passed through deserted villages, and if our part of the convoy chanced to stop in one of them we would explore the houses, rummaging here and there without purpose, even if, as if they were above and beyond this "exploring" enacted in the infinitive and without intentionality, some grabbed bottles of wine or other trinkets that they turned into treasures, and inside the jolting truck that was taking us toward a completely unpredictable destiny, they continually took inventory of their treasures. I had to say "as chance would have it ..." as if the wanting we were deprived of could not disappear and chance is easy to blame, just like nature when the nature that man has provided for himself and that makes him hunger for the obligatory is lacking, and this was indeed the case since by dint of not wanting war, we were in the process of making it. Does this mean that we were autistic? To say that a man is unconscious does not exhaust the fact that the unconscious is something completely other than the permanent or passing state of a man. One can say that there are autistic children; one can also say that there are stupid children, which does not exhaust the fact that stupidity can be found in each and every one of us. If one envisions autism as a failure of wanting, the individual freed from obligation and living according to a mode of being innocent of Being, it is not at all certain that autism is reserved for those who appear to be autistic.

Besides the surprising power of endurance about which Joseph Conrad speaks, Conrad who knew the men who lived aboard ships of yore, what we can find surprising is the power of the carefree state that man is fully capable of taking on; given over to chance, he finds himself freed. The obligatory does not concern war alone; instruction is obligatory, and this decision on the part of power seems to be unanimous, which is quite easily understood.

But whatever the legitimacy of the obligatory and its necessity might be, what is inescapably lost in it is the necessity of attraction, and then men and women, and more so children, risk dying of boredom, which is easy to chalk up to a congenital apathy. And yet we see to what extent the fortuitous is restrained when the obligatory reigns without shame; the way things are going, it is obvious that the influence of the fortuitous only keeps on growing and becoming more refined; it would appear that no one can do anything about it.

But I was talking about war and its subterfuge, as old as footpaths, according to which one must prepare for war in order to avoid it. For one can be amazed that so many men who didn't want to make war allowed themselves be mobilized; it is because they had been told that mobilization was the best means for preventing war from taking place; such was the proposed motive, and, as far as motives are concerned, the dictionary suggests that to be more amply informed we should look up the term "versatile."

The big surprise for those who see autistic children living, not tied by the primordial obligation that makes us who we are, is that they are not at all versatile; which leaves one to think that the fortuitous might have its own gravity and its own order, one that is under no obligation at all to the symbolic order.

Connivance

A colt about a week old behaves like a miniature stallion with his mother the mare; she shifts a bit and that's it, and nothing in her attitude suggests that she is in any way offended or bothered.

There is nothing surprising in the fact that a week-old colt already manifests the entirety of the ways of being that will be his as he ages and when he is up to it. Is he whole? No more and no less than every being born of a specific species, and in which the species is found, whole.

But then we come up against the notion that human beings do not belong to a species, so that human beings, deprived of a species, are no longer whole, are castrated from being, cut off from "to be," if we indeed want to understand the infinitive, and all this in order to allow for Being, which thinks itself in the subjective and wonders whom it is to resemble.

If the broodmare is neither offended nor worried, it's because she has no sense of Being, just as the colt, once grown, will not hold onto a shocking memory of his moments of exuberance, and for the same reason, namely, that his memory will not be a memory of himself.

Which amounts to saying that humans, all of them, who are of the order of Being, are castrated from being, condemned to wanting to do or to make since they are deprived of acting, in the sense in which acting is reacting in a mode specific to the species, our reality being of the symbolic order, if I understand what is said about it, repeated and posited as a primordial truth. It is highly probable that I would have found nothing to say that would challenge this truth had I not found myself being the one who had to say something about our role on this earth when we have occasion to live in close proximity to autistic children, some of whom have grown up.

That said, it is as if they aren't whole, the sexual for them being as ungraspable as any sign that we can make, even if, in our eyes, it would be the slightest possible gesture.

In order to do or to make, one has to want, if only in order to make love, as we say. The fact remains that we talk about making war, too, and many have found themselves in the process of making it without having wanted anything at all.

Which invites us to look a bit more closely into this propensity to make love, which is supposedly unanimous and instinctive, whereas perhaps some find themselves making love somewhat or completely as if they were at war quite simply because the draft had made the decision.

And yet it may be that, finding themselves at war, some pretend to make war, just enough to avoid being identified as not making it; the situation is not quite the same with regard to love, for the proximity of the other does not allow one to dodge the issue, especially to the extent that the other knows the role that one has the duty of playing as partner.

As for situating the contribution of language to this always hazardous enterprise, it is all the more difficult in that there is language as such, what every one of us can say in formulated words, even if in silence, and there is Being that exists only in stating itself, even if no one understands anything of what it is saying (to itself). That no one can hear what is being said takes nothing away from the predominance of the subjective Being whereby we are subjected to the necessity of wanting, wherein some see precisely the superiority of this species that is ours, it being well understood of course that it is not a species.

And we see quite well how speaking of the powerful [*puissants*] in this world is not at all a matter of evoking the contrary of what those beings who are powerless [*impuissant*][1] would be, *impuissant* being a term with no relevance whatsoever to the autistic boy I saw grow up purely innocent; some will see cause for pity here, whereas I think that cause for pity exists only from the moment when the being in question feels his own impotence, whereas this is not at all the case; and innocence is not felt as such unless it stops being innocence, one of the antonyms of the word innocence being awareness.

Now, the individual I'm speaking about is in no way aware and lacks nothing, acting being a way of reacting to what he perceives, and it does seem that in everything he perceives, nothing at all is evoked that could be called the other.

---

1. The contrast between *puissants* and *impuissants* reintroduces the sexual dimension, as *impuissant* is the word for sexual impotence [TN]

From this we may think that he is deprived, which is very generally what is thought. We would still have to make presumptions about what we are deprived of by the phenomenon of the subjective Being that goes hand in hand with the existence of the other; about this subjective Being there is general agreement that it is a creature of language and it's a short step from language to sexuality, if the sexuality in question is understood as that of Being, an entity that can also be called the human being as such.

The lowercase being remains, existing in the infinitive mode; deprived of language, this being is deprived of sexuality as much as of aggressiveness, but not deprived of vigor, skill, and activity.

It is easy to understand that the exercise of aggressiveness, like that of sexuality, requires a certain connivance.

This word connivance came to me even though I wasn't expecting it. A word can turn out to be illuminating, rather like a glowworm. Examined a bit more closely, the word "connivance" turns out to come from late Latin and evokes the action of blinking or winking.[2]

Thus the dictionary tells us that it comes from a secret understanding, a complicity that consists in hiding someone's error or fault, through a tacit agreement, wherein aspects of the sexuality characteristic of human beings are found.

That said, this blink of an eye that belongs to the domain of signs is constantly being produced without anyone noticing, neither the one nor the other.

This is where connivance disappears whereas the infinitive "to blink" persists, if only for moistening the eyes, which without this reflex would rapidly lose the faculty of seeing.

Hence the choice I have made to put this text under the heading of the word "connivance," which came to me by chance. There is the blinking of an eye in order to moisten a delicate apparatus and there is winking, which requires some sort of wanting that does not intervene when what is at issue is the specific role that eyelids play.

Which puts us on the trail of the fact that if Being has quite consciously done away with its foundation in order to evolve toward its destiny as subjective Being, this operation is, fortunately for us, incomplete; and the same completely insignificant movement of eyelids can become what forever links the fate of two beings madly

2. The English word comes via the French *connivance* from the Latin *connivere*, "to blink," "to shut one's eyes to something." [TN]

in love; everyone knows the pre-eminent role of amorous ogling in love play, and no one dares to think about the sad fate of a woman in love who, having withheld her winking for too long, her fellow conniver being temporarily absent, goes blind and will never again be able to see the object of her passion.

Which amounts to saying that the least of signs is a much more perilous exercise than we are led to believe, and that if we remain dependent too long on the sign itself and on the effects we expect from it, we risk losing the use of our senses.

This blink of an eye that moistens the eyeball can be used in order to establish the connivance that is indispensable for the exercising of a sexuality of which the autistic individual who lives in the vicinity is innocent.

Does this mean that between him and me, "me" being any one of us, there is no connivance? It is obvious that this is not the case and that this connivance is alert, lively, anxious, enthusiastic; it has all the more acuity in that, if there is agreement between us, it is tacit to a point that goes beyond innuendo, the slightest wanting to speak being out of the question. And this complicity feeds off all our oversights, stubbornly insisting as we do on taking the other for an other, and it can happen in particular that shutting the eye by reflex in order to moisten the eyeball is the tiny gesture that allows acting to emerge as if by reflex, the word reflex obviously being the most suitable term when it is a matter of distinguishing acting from doing.

Here we are grappling with a mode of being where connivance is established in a mode other than the one in which subjective Being is established. Which suggests that the species, cast aside even before the dawn of humanity if only to allow for this dawn, persists in hovering around us and accompanies our trajectory, in our quest for a mode of connivance from which we are separated. Must I write that we are separated from ourselves? That would mean including the wanting of Being, whereas this wanting is perhaps a result of the separation, a subterfuge rendered necessary owing to the emergence of Being in a subjective mode.

The fact remains that, to broken language – or better, to any insignificant sign – there corresponds the manifest nonexistence of sexuality.

What does this mean? Perhaps simply that we live according to a certain mode of connivance that we feel is the only possible mode to the extent that we owe it everything, including being born.

The fact remains that our eyes blink, completely without our conscious knowledge, as if being couldn't care less about the pretensions of Being and were determined not to die from dryness.

The Missing Voice

To be sure, there is the voice [*voix*] and, to rely on sound alone, there is the path [*voie*].[1]

The path is made for going, whereas the voice seems made for speaking.

Thus one might think that it was thanks to the voice that speaking occurred.

Similarly one might think that the path is there and all one has to do is go where it leads.

Following the traced path is thus within the grasp of the humblest of beings.

And yet, in watching an autistic being living, one perceives that, despite being equipped with the adequate organ, he or she remains without a voice if we accept what the dictionary says: that the voice is the organ of speech.

So there would be the organ and there would be speech; an autistic being can easily make himself or herself heard. On occasion, the autistic being close to whom I have lived for quite a long time barks by yelping, and in yelping is more like a fox than a dog.

Why had he chosen the path of acting like a fox rather than like a papamama?

The farmers in the neighborhood of the surrounding area used to get their guns and remain on the lookout for the predator.

What a strange detour, if he wanted to be heard or understood by us. Moreover, he seemed completely happy; he seemed to be having the time of his life.

---

1. The French words *voix* and *voie* are homophones. [TN]

And it is quite clear how, if we had come across him at the edge of a deep forest, we would simply have written the legend of the fox-child.

Many other such tales have been written.

There remains the surprise at the strange use of that organ of ours. But such is perhaps the fate of organs; they do not always conform to the use traced out – to come back to the path – by the predecessors.

The voice is a trace? If so, then one has to follow it. But we know very well that the obligatory invites avoidance, and from this comes freedom.

But every trace invites avoidance; the autistic being in the presence of a path creates detours that are whimsical, to say the least; in them one can see the exercise of a certain sense of initiative.

We could content ourselves with such an interpretation and rejoice in the fact that the autistic being is not a processional being.

That said, if instead of contenting ourselves with what things seem like to us we study the traces of the detours that evade the path, we notice that they coincide more often than they ought to with old paths and trajectories of which we were unaware.

Here the autistic being becomes a pilgrim – a word that used to mean "stranger" before coming to mean "traveler."

Strangers, autistic beings? That's the least we can say about them. The least and perhaps the best.

But is it possible that strangers can be such, to the point of showing no attraction whatsoever to our voices, and that, making no use at all of their own, they leave us, with respect to them, deprived of the use of ours?

This is nevertheless what happens, except that we do not intend to be deprived of a right that has become quite fashionable.

The voice that we cannot give: are we going to use it in order to interpret the stranger?

But the stranger is not a language.

Would it be a question of guessing what the autistic being may want?

And what if this being were deprived of any wanting whatsoever? Then we see the intervention of the *a priori* of likeness [*semblabilité*], which erases a great deal of the respect due to the stranger and even the simple recognition that a human stranger can exist. To consider the other as a likeness – of oneself – is an honor whose weight has crushed so many hardy ethnic groups that the idea arises of holding back the burden.

When the voice is lacking, the individual is thereby deprived of the ability to express himself or herself – whereas expressing oneself has become the most precious privilege that everyone, it seems, claims – or should claim.

But this is to see the voice only as noise that escapes from the mouth of an individual.

If the voice is lacking, it does not penetrate within the individual. And yet in order for the voice to come out of the mouth it has to have already come in.

It seems indeed that if, in autistic beings, the voice is lacking, it is because the voice has missed them as beings – or that these beings have missed their voices, as we would say of a tennis player who wasn't in the right position to receive and return the ball.

He missed the voice or the voice missed him.

But then how can we say that the autistic being is silent? This would be like saying that the tennis player who wasn't there when the ball arrived had not wanted to return it; how can one return something one has not received?

What we notice, when the voice is lacking, is that the organ persists and the modulated sounds prove that the vocal chords are indeed there and that they vibrate.

But we notice something else as well; in the place of the instrument that has been abandoned for want of use, another one springs forth, one that, oddly, is not destined to take over for the one found to be out of service.

And yet, as far as we are concerned, we are completely incapable of playing this instrument, and we may wonder whether it is not the existence of the instrument that made the – autistic – individual incapable of taking up the voice; so that the autistic being would no longer be someone who is lacking something; he or she would be the bearer of an excess of something, something that could be called an exacerbated sense of coincidences.

And the use of this instrument makes the autistic being a being for whom nothing is lacking. For autistic beings, reality is perfect, fulfilled, they demand nothing more; and it is precisely because they ask for nothing that they don't perceive the answer.

People will tell me that it's a great pity if I rely on the fate reserved to those who are strangers – but strangers to whom? To us? Rather, they are strangers to the language that then becomes the native land of mankind.

If I observe the life of an autistic being close to me without taking myself as a standard, when he looks at a drop of water creeping down a stone wall, it seems quite clear to me that he expects nothing other than nothing, or no one; above all he is not expecting someone else whom he could always fear would get mixed up with things that don't concern him or her, including the autistic being's own happiness. Austistic beings care nothing for anything the voice might allow.

In a new place, he explores with meticulous attention. He still asks for nothing. Can we say that he expects to find something, that he is searching? If we were to start acting the way he does, it would be because we were searching; but it is clear to us what searching implies; exploring is not the right word either; but I have already come to terms with this; no word at all, ever, no way of saying would ever be suitable for indicating what it is like to be a voiceless being, and for a very simple reason: because, as far as we are concerned, the voice dictates us and it is not surprising that it is found within our own practices, which can thus be quite easily expressed.

So it would have to be understood that to explore is an infinitive that has no end, though this takes nothing away from the scrupulous minutiae of the investigation – far from it.

That said, it is by way of the explored that it turns out, many years later, that the smallest thing discovered can be evoked by coincidence with another thing discovered within what we call the present.

The extraordinary subtlety of this "meaning" of coincidences disturbs us and quite often provokes a situation in which what is enacted by the autistic being is completely inopportune – from our viewpoint.

But we see quite clearly where opportunity lies; it is a matter of the port.

The autistic being is at the port, has always been there; he has no intention to reach any port whatsoever.

It is death; or it is wisdom.

When the-Human-that-We-Are Is Not There

This *journal* is written on the basis of what happens to ME.

M, what is it, or rather, where is it?

It is, at the end of one of Janmari's reiterated "autistic" journeys, a house found around ten years ago near a fountain. In one room, four walls and a window, a chestnut plank that is more like a workbench than a table.

A few steps away, a workshop has been populated with wander lines, traces of paths followed. Currently, images filmed in the living areas where other "autistic" children come to live are being projected there.

Janmari is always here, close by.

I sometimes see him.
I sometimes see the filmed images.
Sometimes one or another of those who live in the living areas will say something when they pass by.
Sometimes books are brought or sent to me.
Sometimes I listen to the radio, and thus to the echoes of what is said.
Sometimes echoes of books I have written reach me.
Sometimes parents of "autistic" children come to stay in our network and then they leave. Do they come to see ME? This particular me has become filmed video images of what they have seen of their child while he lives the very customary life of one or another of the living areas.

I say this in order to explain the warp and weft of my work, written from day to day. And in order to indicate its scope, I'm copying what I was just writing to the editorial secretary of a journal, who had been speaking to me about Albania.

I told him that between the common that I was trying to evoke and communism, there is not, as one might believe if one were to rely on the sound of words, an isthmus that one could easily cross without getting one's feet wet.

There is a fissure, a rift, that is truly impassable, the common being an attribute of a species and communism being the business[1] [*l'à-faire*] of human beings, who are more inclined to dominate, that is, to believe themselves.

Respecting the fissure and allowing the common to exist is no doubt the most difficult work that humans have given – or could give – themselves.

What I'm trying to say from here on is inscribed within this project, which has no end, by which I mean that it will never end.

Someone had to bring me *The Ego in Freud's Theory and in the Technique of Psychoanalysis* in order for me to discover the *real* evoked according to the "meaning which man has always given" it: "it is something one always finds in the same place ... but if it has moved, ... one also tells oneself that sometimes it moves under its own steam ... and our own displacements have, in principle, with certain exceptions, no efficacious influence on this change of place.... Prior to the exact sciences, man thought, as we do, that the real is what keeps turning up where one expected it. At the same time of night one will always find one particular star on a particular meridian, it will turn up again there, it is indeed always there, it is always the same. It's not for nothing that I take the celestial landmark before the terrestrial, for in fact the map of the sky was drawn up before the map of the globe."[2]

The citation is long. This is because of the maps evoked, whereas we trace them ourselves. And then there is the earth and the sky, and (to) the truth, and the ONE, and there is the reference-word of which we have made, in our own network jargon, a keyword that has satisfied us for years.

The real is "something one always finds in the same place."

We sometimes named the markers [*repères*] – which, for children deprived of the use of language, "served as points of orientation."

This didn't get us any further, quite the contrary.

---

1. See above, "Acting and the Acted," p. 141, n. 6.
2. Jacques Lacan, *Seminar, Book 2: The Ego in Freud's Theory and in the Technique of Psychoanalysis, 1954-1955*, ed. Jacques-Alain Miller, trans. Sylvana Tomaselli (New York: Norton, 1991), p. 297 (hereafter, *Ego*).

One has to understand the importance of this "in the same place."
We let ourselves get caught up in naming, if only "places," the "primordial" one being the place of water, the watering hole.

It is easy to understand that in naming the stars, we fix them. And so it was that human beings, before the advent of the exact sciences, were able to orient THEM-SELVES.

It took us a long time, months, years, to notice that in fixing reference points, named places, we were losing the infinitive TO LOCATE [REPÉRER], a term without a subject and without an object, without anything that would be nameable. For, in order to name, one must have already been named, which has happened to us, whereas with these children, if they hear their names they remain resistant to them and do not utter them, at least that is the case for most of them.

And yet the fact that their name is located by some of them has nothing to do with the fact that it may have been "understood," perceived as a name.

To such a degree that in naming reference points, we remained in our own denomi-nated world, equipped with the *perorating* that is incumbent on us.

The fact that the living area became a constellation of named places was one of the no doubt ineluctable avatars that came from the use of *perorating* that is our privilege, the real becoming evacuated to who knows where, outside, as is appropriate each time language gets involved.

That human beings use the stars for their own ends in order to locate themselves in time and space is hardly shocking. It's an old story. As for discovering what is real about it, that calls for a different approach.

The same goes for us: using our map of the area in order for the children here to be a bit more like us, to conform, requires us to imagine what the reference points are for them. And as soon as one recalls the mythology that arose at the same time that the use of the stars allowed the-humans-that-we-are [*le bonhomme*]³ to locate himself in time and space, something here calls for prudence.

It will become clear why I speak about the-humans-that-we-are, and not about man-kind.

---

3. *Bonhomme* is a versatile French noun that is often diminutive or somewhat dismissive; it can be used to designate a snowman, a gingerbread man, a stick figure (as in children's drawings, or in the game of hangman), a child, or an adult male with no special distinction: "a regular guy," "an ordinary bloke," "a decent fellow." In this chapter, it is used to designate the very large subset of human beings who have access to language and the symbolic, as opposed to the generic *homme* ("man"), used to encompass all members of the species, including autistics; In this essay, *bonhomme* is rendered as "the-human-that-we-are." [TN]

We can deal with the legends woven from the named points that were stars, which remained intact; they were not touched by the stories.

But here we have children, here and now, close at hand.

From their journeys we keep the traces, which make a map.

We know perfectly well how mythology is elaborated: the-humans-that-we-are project themselves. From the self that is projected on a large scale, the image that the-human-that-we-are makes of himself or herself is reinforced. The mythological component incorporated within the-humans-that-we-are is thus considerable.

I shall be told that this component is necessary for the-humans-that-we-are. We still have to discover to the detriment of what this image predominates, and why, I mean to what ends?

While a few autistic children circle around us and wander off, is it really necessary to search so far away?

The fact that their deviations are very often so *common* that we can draw up a map of the *crossbeams*, a constellation that surprises by its persistence through time and through each one of the children, provides us with as strong and consistent an image as the image that is provided to us through communion, so to speak, of the-humans-that-we-are, of their bodies.

If I say this image is communed, instead of saying it is common, it's because it re-quires participation on the part of each and every one; unless we say is that the one of each is born – comes to be – only through this participation in a generally accepted convention.

One has to realize that this image of the body – of the-human-that-we-are – is ac-quired – by which I mean it is in no way innate. It is one thing to see hands; as for *having* hands, it is, as we say, a whole other story.[4]

Because, in order *to have*, if only hands, one must also have awareness of *being*.

The two verbal auxiliaries turn up here, primordial infinitives without which the-hu-man-that-we-are would not exist.[5]

---

4. The equivalent French expression used here, *une autre paire de manches* (literally "another pair of sleeves"), extends the imagery related to body parts. [TN]
5. The verbs *avoir* ("to have") and *être* ("to be") function as auxiliaries in French much as in English: *il a vu*, "he has seen"; *il est vu*, "he is seen." [TN]

When I say: "to see hands," one must be skeptical.

It would be better to say "to look at." Because there is a clear difference between seeing and being seen.

As soon as there is some SELF, we are dealing with looking.

When looking predominates, it is at the expense of what?

At the expense of *seeing*, as I believe an autistic child sees, without even having any awareness of being.

All this in order to say where our maps are going to lead us: to the discovery of the real.

They are fully inside it, up to the eyebrows.

Lacan returns to this idea of place. The real is outside, always there, in its place, and man before the advent of the exact sciences seems to have worried about what he had *to do so that* all these named points by which the real manifested itself should stay in place, and so that "his ... actions – actions in the real sense, that of speech – were indispensable to [had something *to do* with] sustaining things in their place."[6]

It was I who italicized the term "to do" in the passage, while what is at stake are "actions in the real sense, that of speech."

I firmly believe that all *doing* and *making* is language, if it is only doing one's business,[7] or making love, or whatever you like, including making war, as the case may be.

The fact that, when we're dealing with the stars, the real is outside is not open to doubt. But the real perceived by a human being who is not conscious of being, this too is the real. Can one say that this real is inside?

It seems to me that Lacan would answer that there is nothing to this: "Everything which is human has to be ordained within a universe constituted by the symbolic function. [...] If the symbolic function functions, we are inside it. And I would even say – we are so far into it that we can't get out of it."[8]

---

6. Lacan, *Ego*, p. 297.
7. Like "doing one's business," the French expression *faire ses besoins* is a euphemism for urinating or defecating. [TN]
8. Lacan, *Ego*, p. 29, p. 31.

Therefore it is outside where the part of the human that would be resistant to what functions "in the symbolic" takes place.

This may well be, and it is probably not a discovery.

We still have to set out to discover this "outside," even though Lacan warns us that we, who are endowed with the perorating that is incumbent on us, are inside, and we can't get out.

One can understand how tempting this approach of going to take a little look "outside" can be.

It so happens that we have guides who are waiting for us.

But where the approach becomes particularly difficult is that, instead of being there, outside, in their places, at the right point, as the stars in the sky would be for who knows what adventure, it turns out that they follow us, more like will-o'-the-wisps than stars – and just try to get your bearings in this dance of little beings who may well precede us only in that they follow in our footsteps from the day before yesterday or three years ago.

So, apparently, a big gamble is involved. Especially since they ask nothing of us, except perhaps to do what is needed to make these children become like us, and that's all there is to it.

And yet we find ourselves setting off on detours that seem to be never-ending.

But "like us" implies a necessary belief in the validity of this "us," of the-humans-that-we-are as we think and conceive of ourselves, after millennia of symbolic domestication, and Lord knows what advantages humanity has drawn from this.

But at the expense of what? – this is what we still have to find out. There is no advantage without damage.

Moreover, it is quite possible that the detours that appear to separate and distance us from our sought-after goal are the sole possible passageways for children who are hardly "children." We have no proof of the opportunity provided by these "detours," but we do have quite a number of clues that invite us to pursue our approach "outside," outside of what functions in the symbolic mode, if only in desperation.

For having used the term word "reference point," which has become one of the keywords of our jargon, we have been fulfilled by it, that's for sure.

Are we speaking about us? About each one of us?

It is true that words fulfill us.

And, what is fulfilled, or filled in, is in the extreme case the rift, the fissure, the fault between the inside, where the symbolic functions, and the outside, where the real takes place.

And despite this rift, this deep-seated fault, language does not stop making us *believe* that it is fulfilled.

The question remains as to why language keeps trying to fill in the rift sliced open by its mediation, which could be expressed as its order.

Perhaps language also serves a cause that is not eager to be identified. Perhaps this cause is in part allied with all power. Thus it would be understood that language fulfills us in such a way that it erases that which delivers us to any power, as subjects. What is at issue is law and a certain order in which we are entrenched. On the other side of the trench, there is another order, other laws, those of the real.

As for knowing what detours have had to be taken to get there, go ask those who have searched. It is inarguable that most of them have paid a more or less high price for trying to go see, outside, and it is not over.

That the-humans-that-we-are then took credit for what suited them among these discoveries, for what he could make use of, is just as inarguable. What was at stake was the nature that they dominated.

As far as their own nature is concerned, one can imagine that it's not going to be so simple. Which is a way of saying that ethnic memory, fortified by millennia of beliefs, is not ready to admit that what persists, or rather might persist, of species memory deserves respect, for there are, as they say, conditions, necessary *circumstances*.

Here we begin to glimpse an entity so discreet that it is not included in the pantheon of capitalized entities such as Eros and Thanatos, I'm speaking of *topos*, which evokes space, the here-now.

And here we are again, in the living areas of our network.

In reading Lacan, one is caught up in a game that could be called a labyrinth. One is caught up in vertigo. One knows that one will not escape from it. One follows all the same. I take the risk: Janmari's presence allows me not to lose the thread.

If I speak of Janmari, one might believe that we are dealing with someone very particular, and this is true. Actually, something about his ways of being, which I describe, is common to all the autistic children who live "here." Thus they don't belong to him. When I write Janmari, it's a bit as if I were writing "they."

If the symbolic function creates a universe, here we are, with Janmari at the threshold of another universe, a real one, where another function is practiced.

To be clear, I shall call *perorating* [*pérorer*] the master verb of that which functions in the symbolic realm, and *locating* [*repérer*] the master verb that is practiced within the other universe.

When Lacan writes: "From the moment man thinks that the great clock of nature turns all by itself, and continues to mark the hour even when he isn't there, the order of science is born. [...] And like the slave, he tries to make the master dependent on him by serving him well,"[9] we understand that if nature's great clock works all by itself, that's acceptable, but if the human functions all by itself, this is intolerable; it's unbearable. If human beings already do not tolerate this dependence, this "slavery" with respect to nature's great clock, how would they tolerate being dominated by the human, if we call human that which *really* exists, governed by laws other than the law of language which human beings can recognize since they owe to it a certain freedom? Humans recognize themselves, find themselves there. These are the least of things.

I follow the labyrinth with no way out, and I find something: "A door isn't entirely real. To take it for such would result in strange misunderstandings. If you observe a door, and you deduce from that that it produces draughts, you'd take it under your arm to the desert to cool you down."[10]

It turns out that, for those who have lived close to autistic children, a door is not nothing. And it is even by looking at the various ways of being of these children in regard to doors that we came up with the term "the customary" [*le coutumier*], which still persists in our jargon.

---

9. *Ibid.*, p. 298.
10. *Ibid.*, p. 301.

That a door is open and allows for passage, that's acceptable. But the requirement that the door be closed again right away – common to a good number of children here – is peremptory. Here we have a fact that lends itself to a proliferation of meanings. But if we accept the hypothesis that the door can be something that is completely real, the common *acting* of re-closing the door simply indicates a certain respect for the real as it is, not that everything has its place, as one would say of an object; the thing and the place of the thing are the same thing.

In the universe where *locating* functions without the intervention of perorating, there is not some thing, in the way we would say there is someone. The some thing is already the object, cut off from the rest, from all the rest, by the very fact of being nameable.

So there would be something like an order of things, moreover, that would be just as shifting and mobile as the order of language, and just as immutable.

This *acting* – of re-closing the door – that proceeds from the *locating*, thus signifies nothing at all, to my mind, it is a manifest attitude, not manifested. Still, within this *acting*, there is such a peremptory requirement that on occasion, for want of the possibility of carrying out the *acting* freely, as it were, it is quite possible that a hand gets bitten or a head hits a wall, which leaves us speechless, and which would drive us toward living behind closed doors (*huis clos*) in an impasse that would be hell or at least its antechamber.[11]

I go back inside the labyrinth, which means that I'm not playing the game, since there is supposed to be no exit. I go back there completely: "If you observe a door, and you deduce from that that it produces draughts...." This happened to me personally, when I had just barely reached the age of reason. I had been taken to the sea, and the waves that wouldn't stop coming, one after another, amazed me. Seeing boats rocking back and forth, I deduced that the movement of the boats was what created the waves, and, already gifted for my age, I experimented with my fresh new discovery by placing my hand flat in a puddle of water and moving it around, leading to the formation of waves; delighted, I saw them come to die one after another on the edges of the puddle.

What does Lacan say? That the one who would take the door as something real would carry it under his arm in order to produce air currents in the desert.

I once saw an autistic child fan himself and cool off his cheek with the movement of pages of a book, the thumb releasing the pages, one by one, each page becoming a fan. Doing this, he was on cloud nine.

11. *Huis clos*, translated as No Exit, is the title of a play by Jean-Paul Sartre in which one of the characters utters the now familiar line: "Hell is other people." [TN]

Which goes to show that the order of things is not so imperious that it does not give way, possibly, to what can be handled. Here we are delivered from hell.

Let's keep advancing into the labyrinth: the door – which must not be taken as something "entirely real" – is "the symbol *par excellence*, that symbol in which man's passing, through the cross it sketches, intersecting access and closure, can always be recognized."[12]

During the time that my grandfather watched over my education – I was at the age when I created waves with the hand of a master – each time he heard someone speak of the cross, he said: "and the banner…,"[13] an expression that resembled "the Army and the Church."[14]

I only later learned that a banner was a shirttail. All this to say that my grandfather was somewhat of a non-believer, a trait I inherited. A bit later, I made my first communion. At the time, there was a household detergent and a bleach that were sold under the name La Croix (The Cross). I lived in the north, my native region, and on Saturdays the housewives washed the floors of the houses with abundant help from soapy water and a mop. The hallway door was left wide open to the paved sidewalk where the water poured out. Then, caught up in their momentum, the housewives would clean the cobblestones of the sidewalk, the water swept off into the gutter; and I have seen women who held back the water from the gutter and used it to wash the cobblestones in the street all the way into the middle of the road; the width of the washed cobblestone corresponded roughly to the width of the house, so that the road seemed to be oddly tiled.

Does the story of this weekly frenzy take us away from the door? Perhaps not as much as it seems. What is at issue is the doorstep, and the threshold.

So this is what we can say, within a living area, about the frame of a shelter, and about the traces that we keep, traces of paths of the children here, wander lines.

That there is a *crossbeam* even before the door is there and before the customary paths have been established is something that may be surprising; the threshold identified is then the doorstep.

---

12. Lacan, *Ego*, p. 302.

13. *La croix et la bannière* (the cross and the banner) is an old French expression evoking the difficulties of the Crusades. Originally referring to processions where both religious and military symbols were displayed, it is now used to describe any difficult situation. [TN]

14. The French expression used here, *le sabre et le goupillon*, is another way of referring to the linking of military and religious power. The word *goupillon* (aspergillum) is the instrument used by a priest to sprinkle holy water. [TN]

For me, it is merely about catching language in the act of exerting itself.

The *pas de porte* (doorstep) is then the passage, or the fact that, there is not – yet – a door.[15] Either the *pas* (step) is the action of allowing the support of the body to pass from one foot to another, or the *pas* is an auxiliary of negation. What still remains is the trace of the human foot.

If I lose myself as much as I like in the dictionary, it is to find traces of the pre-supposed: the foot, the door. Since the door is not there yet, we would be dealing with an expectation; any *crossbeam* is sturdy enough. And we see how language ends up completing our surprise before the persistence of these crossbeams, which, I remember, are merely the traces retained from the *theres* where the wander lines converge, crisscross, and sometimes stop, all of them, *there*.

We see quite well that everything we suppose is established to the detriment of some-thing else that would escape being said. And here we are limited, confined, to our universe, with all its "comprehension."

It's acceptable if this *crossbeam*, attracting the gaze because it is said to be at the thresh-old, does not hide the others toward which the so-called would not know what to say, in points that could only be named *there*, and that's all there is to it. We see where the traces retained from these wander lines are necessary, and all the more useful in that we have forgotten the "whose" of these traces and in that we don't see what they are coming to do *there*.

In the same way that every hand, before being someone's hand, is that of a species, every wander line, the path having in fact been walked or run by a child, very often ends up at some crossbeam, as if the crossbeam were the project, whereas this is not at all the case if we understand by project "what one proposes to do or make"; everything is here: the ONE/SELF of the-human-that-we-are, and the *doing* or *making*, and the pro-posed where the proposition resonates, each act presumed to be the to-be-done of language.

Here I'm merely demonstrating the most common way of thinking, not in order to destroy it, but to show that from the outset it fills in the rift between the two universes.

Admittedly, these *common* crossbeams indicate "some thing," except that, once again, this some-thing runs a great risk of being understood as being an object, through which the ghost of the the-human-that-we-are-subject would reappear.

---

15. The French noun *pas*, "step," has a homonym in the negative particle *pas*; thus *pas de porte* can mean "doorstep" or "no door." [TN]

For a long time we thought, regarding those crossbeams, that indeed there had to be something there that served as a reference point.

On occasion we found traces, virtually imperceptible, of paths of yore that in fact used to go through here.

On occasion, a dowser, divining rod or pendulum in hand, would show us where we should drill if we wanted to see water spring up. And for a long time now, this *where* has led to a crossbeam.

There may be some truth in these coincidences, whereas other crossbeams remained without any cause that our senses could detect, our senses being not very sharp, to tell the truth.

One still has to consider that a living area is a territory, and that the *locating* that keeps on functioning in the infinitive provokes common *actings*, and that if Janmari stares at what we would call the palm of his hand, this way of staring being common to a number of autistic children – and staring is not looking – one should not be surprised that, within a living area, this rocking back and forth begins to occur for him in the same place where it happens to a good number of others who are "others" only for us.

Sometimes we managed to situate the *there* of the rocking where our own customary pathways proved to be densest owing to the fact that they often intersected *there*. Perhaps we have here some indication that, between *that* way of *seeing* [*ce voir*] and *seeing oneself* [*se voir*] which in French differ only by virtue of a more twisted letter, we are dealing with a difference not only in scope but in function: the very organ of seeing does not operate the same way, which is not at all surprising. When what is at issue is looking, the-human-that-we-are, the object of peroration, is incorporated within the objective.

When what is at stake is locating, seeing / seeing again / foreseeing are a single verb; the tense is unknown, absent, as if there were a retinal persistence of a magnitude other than our own that allows us to reconstitute the movement starting from some twenty fixed images moving past in a second, whence the cinematographer, while as far as Janmari is concerned, this retinal persistence plays out over years. Thus the necessary hypothesis of a memory other than our own that functions, with the-human-that-we-are incorporated not only into perception but throughout all the commotion that plows, turns over, and modifies what has been recorded within everyone's memory, which is merely a certain form of memory.

One shouldn't be surprised to see that *actings* can come about, completely inopportune, starting from this locating.

Autistic children come and stay here, and come back; sometimes they come from far away, which means a long journey in a car. After an initial stay, and thus an initial journey from her home to here, the child returns home for several months and then comes back for a second stay. And on several occasions, during the second journey back from home, the child shows distress, making a scene. At first everything was going fine, and then suddenly....

I leave you to imagine what parents might say to themselves about this, whether they express it or not. Where else would one want to locate the cause of the distress other than within the child's intention, that she doesn't want to leave home, her parents, or that she is frightened in advance of the elsewhere to which she is being returned.

In fact, in practically every case, (and it wasn't always the same child), it turned out that the car had not taken exactly the same path as the first time. As soon as the initially traveled path was left for a detour in order to avoid heavy traffic or to take an alternate route, distress broke out. To locate is to see-see again-foresee.

This said in order to counter the presupposed.

Which does not mean that one must take the same path every time.

So, what must one do?
I leave this question in suspense, while insisting on the idea that suspending abusive comprehension marks the beginning of a better approach.

So should one explain to the children where they are going and why?
Why not. You never know. But it is quite clear that any explanation intervenes to the detriment of what it would mean to respect the locating that is beyond us and that provokes the acting that leaves us speechless because it in no way takes into account our own moments and the life that we try to lead (for) ourselves.

What would be a mode of existence based on this *locating*?

I have used the parable of the raft: our presence created a raft adrift, borne by an element so rare in our universe where the symbolic functions that only a few puddles of it remain here and there, and mainly during the tornadoes of history where crazed humanity exterminates itself and then something human reveals itself in the light of day, right in the middle of murderous history, as if inadvertently.

But we are not there, at the heights of history, we are here, in the Cévennes, in these times; the heights of history are, for the moment, taking place elsewhere.

The image of the raft had the advantage of explaining how the big ideological waves [*vagues*] – which can be described as big trends [*vogues*] – when they fell back on top of us, passed us by, the links holding us together being supple enough to allow, between us, the gaps, through which convictions, wherever they came from, passed through the floorboards.

It is easy to see what I'm afraid of: beliefs and their excesses, not that I believe one should not believe (in something), but it was obvious that, here, our element, or rather, the "element" that we were looking for in letting ourselves drift, was not in this something.

Here we see that the parable was merely an illusion, because how can a raft drift when it is borne by an element that is precisely what it is looking for?

Actually, we were stuck, like Noah's Ark on Mount Ararat.

To be even more simplistic, if to locate and to act are primordial infinitives, they are comparable to what it is for a duckling to swim.

If there is no water, the swimming in question does not manifest itself, owing to the lack of the essential "there," and the duckling appears for what it is: poorly endowed for running and pecking the ground with its beak.

All this to say that the primordial infinitives take place, as we say, only if the site – *topos* – allows that to happen.

I have also spoken of drifts that, planted within the customary – the raft – allowed for some maneuvering. When one believes in something too much, even if only in an image, it carries you away.

In fact, it was within language itself that those drifts needed to be planted. But how on earth can you plant drifts within language?

There is for example, the S of what can see itSELF [*SE*] become untangled and become the C of *that* seeing [*CE*], C being the initial letter of this common word which denotes that seeing is common and thus eludes us because we are limited to what can be seen, the-human-that-we-are included. Which leaves this common seeing speechless where a form of identifying is practiced that is a prelude to endless actings as long as the *topos* allows for it.

Topos? Here we are in front of an infinity, the site of the human.

And if it is right to say, as I have read, that the unconscious does not take place, does not have a place, the specifically human does not either, but what occurs, if there is even just one propitious little puddle, proves that it could take place, in a universe other than the one where *doing as* reigns, whereas *acting* comes from initiative.

Coming back to Lacan and to the door, a "symbol par excellence" and not something that is "entirely real," I would say that the risk in forgetting the real is believing in symbols, believing in them to such a degree that a student, hearing his teacher tell him to leave the room (*prendre la porte,* literally "take the door") really takes the door, and if there is enough wind he takes off like someone holding onto a hang glider. One of two things happens: either one lets go of the door in time, or one decides to become an angel.

The door: symbol, access, and closure; and the threshold that forms a *crossbeam* as if crossbeams were so many impassable thresholds, for want of the "element" that could be called the locatable, and for which our universe is so incomprehensively foreign that it is a pity.

So that one doesn't make the mistake of supposing that I am describing the autistic child as the prototype of a better humanity, I allow myself to drift within my own memories, and I see myself: while the psychology course was taking place in the amphitheater of a university where I was indeed enrolled, I find myself in a bar, not far off, on the edge of Place Philippe-le-Bon; history must always get mixed up in things, if only by specifying place names. To get to the bar, I had to cross Rue de Valmy. And there I am, playing a game of 421.

Everyone knows how it works: three dice, which at that time were made of bone. Three little trinkets made of bone, marked by black points, one point on one of the sides, two on another, and so on, all the way to six; so we have three dice made of bones all marked in the same way; thirty-six sides that await two or more players. It's best to have a cloth on the table, or an enclosed surface of some sort, like that of a tambourine, because on a marble tabletop the little bone trinkets will slide, whereas they need to roll, side over side until they stop; the side that lands on top offers the points indicated by its markings. Serious players never use a leather cup to roll the dice, even though one ought to be used in order to ward off potential cheating. The cup remains there, a scorned witness to legitimate suspicion. But, as we shall see, following the rules and using this cup would deprive the players of their reason for playing – a reason of which they are unaware.

Thirty-six tiny sides or faces, thirty-six tiny masks to handle, this is important. There is something at stake in the game: the loser(s) must pay for the drinks. But to find out who is to pay, it would suffice to play a simple game of heads or tails, or to draw straws, or to use some other stratagem of the same order.

But in order to handle these dice, which roll, something else is at stake, something human, whereas in a casino this element is absent when a croupier spins the roulette wheel and a tiny ball bounces around, frightened.

Glimpsing a bit, thanks to our Janmari, what acting had to do with it, I seemed able to grasp why the game of 421 was more appealing to me than the professor in the flesh, his bones not being visible.

What was it about these thirty-six tiny masks tumbling from the toss of a hand? Locating can exert itself, and in the gesture of the hand that throws the dice, lets them go, sends them to leap about, there is something of *acting* that intervenes, as I see it, like a reflex, or almost.

It is true that on the cover of the book by Lacan that I had borrowed for several days, one saw soldiers from ancient Rome or from who knows what ancient era playing dice while they were in the process of making history, and on the cover of another book that has just reached me, *Un parmi d'autres* (One among others), by Denis Vasse, published in the series "*Le champ freudien*," what one sees on the cover is the judgment of Solomon, an excerpt from the fifteenth-century book of hours of Queen Eleanor of Portugal, the cover shows a tiny baby and an executioner holding the baby by one hand while with his other hand he is raising a saber crossed with an axe. Solomon is seated calmly on his throne, holding his scepter in one hand while the other is open, palm up. He doesn't look at the inside, not being autistic. What he has said was that, to cut short the dispute between the two women whom we see, one standing close to the throne, the other kneeling, all that was required was to cut to the quick. Here the efficacy of words is made manifest.

But I was talking about the dice, which are located, that is, all their sides are perceived, by the persistence of which I spoke: seeing, seeing again, and foreseeing all intervene to guide the handling, so that the three sides facing up, the "bearing faces," each show a specific, remarkable point. And when this happened the players rejoiced, winners and losers alike, which means that what was really at stake was not at all winning the round.

That locating/acting should dodge the detour of consciousness made us dodge cheating by the same token, for intentional *doing* or *making* have nothing to do with *acting*. And I have often seen players who, having very consciously noted that on the side opposite 421 there was 653, strove when they saw 653 to throw the dice so each die would flip over, and they couldn't do it. If they did succeed, the throw was annulled, so clearly had everyone seen the cheating coming and being carried out, the dice merely sliding without turning, which isn't allowed.

Only acting is capable of such virtuosity in handling, precisely because all perorating is absent.

And it is the dictionary that taught me that chance [*hasard*], of which we had made an entity, was spelled *hazart* in the twelfth century; the word came from the Arab word, *az-zahr*: a die, having come into French from the Spanish *azar*.

A veritable windfall from which I infer that the slightest gesture, apart from its ability to serve as a sign, which is a conventional gesture, can also *hazard* – and thus mis-create – with or without dice.

And yet we lugged this big wooden die around, so big that we really couldn't have handled three of them.

It is true that we ended up stashing it in the hollowed-out trunk of a tree struck by lightning, and in front of the split trunk we placed a flat rock, which was actually a sink made of bluish gray stone, and one could still see the marks of the chisel that had cut into the stone, a flat chiseled-out stone that vibrated every time the wooden die was tossed onto it and rolled, held back by the rim. The hole that pierced the stone wasn't a problem.

It is quite probable that the resonances of this stone, in each one of us, would awaken long-dormant memories of school days: an oak, a carefully-positioned stone – who among us hasn't been a Gaul, to some small extent, at one moment or another of his or her history-drenched existence. That there was bravado, on our part, and a manifest preference for these old rites at the expense of modernity, is entirely possible. Our small stone table rang clear, but it seemed to me that, throughout the living areas, these old assumed rites ended up weighing on our consciousness, and that the detour via the stone lacked joy.

Janmari never tired of it, the big wooden die placed very carefully back inside the old split trunk, and on occasion this struck stone led to surprising initiatives on his part, if only going off to look for a coffee pot discarded years earlier, over behind a low wall, in order to use it again and make coffee, rejoicing in this as one does with rediscoveries.

That the only initiative is to reiterate should not be surprising: to identify is a form of seeing-seeing again-foreseeing-acting that comes from afar; all re-seeing may intervene.

The fact remains that, as far as we are concerned, the-human-that-we-are is still here, in the least of our gestures, even when the gesture of *hazarding*, taking a chance, is at issue. Hazard a detour by way of a stone, a die thrown, and a SELF [SE] intervenes that remembers, if only the Gauls.

Which goes to show that we don't escape this reiterating, which as far as Janmari is concerned comes from locating, whereas, as far as we are concerned, it comes from the perorated.

Moreover, this detour I held so dear, the detour by way of the stone, was never anything but a matter of reiterating the crossbeam-detours that appear on our maps and persist after ten years of traced wander lines.

Even when we are dealing with very customary paths, and the children follow or precede us – but what does precede mean when we're talking about the path from the day before or the day before yesterday, and sometimes the path has been used for months – the wander lines make a detour, detours, ineluctable arabesques all along the regular path.

What comes to the surface from the attitude manifested during these detours, which aren't merely a matter of frolicking around, as one might suppose, is a certain gravity, if indeed the mask manifests [*manifeste*] any sentiment whatsoever, which is not obvious, for if the mask, the mimicry, are part of what is manifested [*manifesté*], an accent appears, the slightest of signs, and one that I'm always afraid is a supposition on our part.

Nevertheless, these detours are not a matter of exuberance – "an overabundance of life that is translated [*se traduit*] into behavior and expressions." Obviously, I find the dictionary fulfilling: "an overabundance of life that translates ITSELF [SE *traduit*]...."[16] As Lacan says, we'll never get out of the impasse.

Can we say that the child – the autistic child – who takes this route, follows these wander lines, which make a *detour*, makes a *detour*, whereas it is rather the ineluctable aspect of the detour that takes him, seizes him, and this "*him*," what is it, which can be said as who is it? It is not a matter of each one, these crossbeam-*detours* are often shared, and if it is the detour that seizes the boy, here we have a *detour* that becomes an entity endowed with intention regarding the children, an evil spell, so to speak, that hovers over them quite simply to prevent them from doing as we do, and to keep them from following the paths we normally follow.

---

16. In this reiteration, the highlighted reflexive pronoun suggests an active reading of the verb; the English equivalent would be "translates itself." [TN]

The detours intervene as a matter of course.

So it is that the fissure between the customary and the habitual appears. But we are the only ones who perceive it.

If I look up customary in the dictionary, I find: "who has the custom of doing something...."

Custom: "way of acting established by usage." The fissure has been filled in.

To find the fissure, if only a little, I had to propose that "customary" be thought of as an infinitive,[17] like taking communion, except that, as far as the meaning is concerned, it's just the opposite; "customary" evokes an acting on a common initiative, foreign to the-humans-that-we-are, to whom consciously or from the depths of our souls, it occurs to take communion, which can be expressed as *making* an act of faith.

Where does the fissure lie between taking communion, which belongs to the order of *doing* or *making* and our customary, which belongs to the order of *acting*.

Whereas I have read that the unconscious is that which insists, this fissure persists. If I say that the fissure weaves in and out, I endow it with an intentionality of questionable quality. The dictionary tells me that the *fau* from *faufiler* ("weaving in and out") would ricochet off *fors*, which means *hors*, "outside"; the fissure comes from the *hors*, the outside, the real, and persists unbeknownst to us.

Filling in the fissure is the work of the symbolic function itself; all believing takes back up what it can within its formulated project, regarding this gravitation specific to the common that, being of the order of the real, has now and forever been OUTSIDE.

Each species has its own way of locating.

This word *commun* (common) itself seems to have been found there in order to fill in the fissure. There is *comme* (as), there is *un* (one).

In writing this, I'm rehashing. I don't believe it could be otherwise. There are words like old tree stumps. When it comes time to get rid of them, to see what lies underneath, a groundbreaking ceremony isn't enough. It takes at least one more pass.

17. The French adjective *coutumier* (translated here as "the customary" when used as a noun) has the same ending as a class of French verbs; thus it is a homonym for the invented infinitive *coutumier*. [TN]

219

Moreover, it's not a question of uprooting or destroying some word that has come to lodge itself at the borderline of attraction; rather, in evoking this attraction, the word stifles it. An infatuation is involved, an "obstruction" – and being infatuated used to mean "suffocating by swallowing too fast." The communist impulses probably suffocated from seeking to swallow everything. Understanding everything is too much, and even then, there is what remains, which is not nothing: the real.

That this locating allows for seeing – even glimpsing doesn't take as long as the blinking of an eye – all the sides of the dice, including those that are hidden from us while they are being looked at, this seeing being a re-seeing, opens the field of pre-seeing where acting is produced, quite often inopportunely. Acting truly has no end, no "port," if a port evokes the project of a harbor, a destination.

Whereas the construction project was to paint wooden planks, Jean L. from Le Serret spent a great deal of time wondering why the autistic Gilles T. set out, as they say, to hold the brush in such a way that the plank to be painted was covered only with a line that ran all the way down the middle of the plank and that was all, a straight line, the width of the brush.

In fact, every time Gilles T. draws, it's a line, no matter what the surface. Thus we are dealing with reiterated acting, which can look *like* resistance to doing; I insist on the *like*, for of course I don't think that way. The fissure passes between *acting* and *doing* and there is resistance to doing, refusal, only on the part of children relatively conscious of being; the-human-that-we-are is there, and so is the project and everything that follows, including not giving a damn about it. And the path that must be taken in order for the child to decide to *do*, or to *make*, has nothing to do with what would allow *acting*, which awaits a completely different detour.

From the paintbrush held in the hand of an autistic individual, a straight line emerges no matter what the surface may be, and no matter, of course what our own project may be, which may be to *make* him – the autistic individual – draw, or to *make* him cover the plank of wood with paint as is required. This *as is required* says quite a lot about our own project.

Here we have two children, both mute. They are in the process of peeling an orange. Without scrutinizing every little gesture too closely, we know quite well that one of them is going to peel the orange meticulously and scrupulously, and then wait, the orange in his hand, the *acting* completed. The other one hurries, and even though the orange is still covered with patches of white coating, gobbles it down. The first child is autistic, the second is not. For the other, the child who eats, the-human-that-we-are is there. For the first one, the project remains suspended, as we see it, the "port" being the mouth and everything that follows. The sequence, from a peeled orange to a chewed and swallowed orange, does not occur; there is a missing link. Peeling the orange meticulously is an instance of *acting* without end.

So what shall we say? That something is lacking in this act. What is lacking in the child whose act seems to remain suspended, is, strictly speaking, the-human-that-we-are, which is presumed to be the end goal. Peeling an orange to eat it is a *doing* where the end prevails over the care, the scruples, that appear during the *acting* of peeling.

Here is something to induce wonder about morality, which then appears as an effort to restore to this gluttonous human-that-we-are a modicum of disinterest, of indifference toward *self*,[18] whereas during the slightest instance of acting, the *self* not being there, what is involved is a sort of tangent that merely brushes past the projected surface, the small demanding world constituted by each and every one of us.

I should emphasize that such *actings* are quite common, constant, incessant, and are produced without apparent difficulty. At every moment, they are produced around us.

These actings that are tangential to the-human-that-we-are remain (as if) unresolved. Seeing the other eating his orange does not intervene in the locating that allowed for a scrupulous peeling, which requires a degree of dexterity that cannot be compared to the gesture of bringing an orange to one's mouth.

Here we see what is involved in *acting* without a project, and what is involved in the common outside-of-the-self, not that the-human-that-we-are has gone outside of himself, or has overcome his appetites, his desires, what have you; there is nothing of the-human-that-we-are here. I will be told that the same can be said of monkeys, who can peel oranges perfectly well and eat them.

This indeed is the proof that each species is quite singular, and in passing let me mention that once I saw a macaque, who was living alone with us, put on an amazing show before swallowing what was, for him, a treat. I can even say that the fonder he was of something, the more exuberant his preliminary high jinx. Starting from his gestures, we had enough to recreate a whole tribe of monkeys on the look-out, ready to seize the treat, hence the dodging, swerving, and detours of this lone macaque who ended up retreating to an inaccessible location, on top of a window, and the treat was eaten, teeth showing in a menacing mimicry. Toward whom, or rather toward what, if not the rest of the troop, which was not THERE, and yet? Which shows that it is not by chance that *y*, the "there" of being there, here, makes a fork.

---

18. In the French text, the old spelling *soy* is used here, marking a subtle difference from the contemporary concept of *soi*, "self." [TN]

We can often gloss over the missing link between peeling and eating an orange with some sort of gesture that initiates the succession of events leading up to the swallowing of a barely-chewed orange.

The reparation in question is so crude that the damage is flagrant. We are taking a shortcut, that's all, avoiding the necessary detours, which would be of a different nature than a recommendation that can be expressed by something like: "What are you waiting for? Eat your orange."

The stupidity, the malfeasance, of such a remark is striking. It is quite obvious that this way of speaking couldn't care less about the rest of the world, I mean about the real, the other, latent universe in which *acting* would pursue its scrupulous course without end to an unbelievable degree.

It is even here that *believing* and *fearing*, which go hand in hand with *perorating* and *locating*, do not meet.[19] As far as *believing* is concerned, it is inconceivable that there is no end, whereas *fearing*, which functions as an infinitive within the real, from the springboard of *locating*, requires, in order to function, that this real be in some way adorned with the detours that have been lost, erased by the fact of the *perorating* that has taken place, the-human-that-we-are incorporated, and this is then the only way out. One indeed has to pass by there, the *there* being what is recognized.

We see that everything is here, in this missing link that is needed for *acting* to be articulated. It is the very link that is found when domestication is at issue, whether we are dealing with a horse or any other animal on the verge of being used. And we know well that in this case, a peroration limited to a few phonemes does the job: "Giddy up! Gee! Haw" are conventional terms that are very effective.

Is there any harm in this? Everything depends on the point of view of the one looking on, who may prefer to see a band of wild horses running loose, or, on the contrary, may appreciate masterpieces of dressage that entail a certain respect for the animals.

But clearly this is not what I mean, my aim being to posit that, as far as the human is concerned, species memory, under the grip of symbolic domestication, is unexplored, and apparently unexplorable. It was ages ago that language cut to the quick of the common itself, at the beginning of time, or almost.

And here *we* are, in close proximity to autistic children, first-hand witnesses to this inveterate inaptitude for restoring what we have ended up calling the adorned, that

---

19. *Le croire et le craindre* (Believing and Fearing) is the title of a book by Deligny (Paris: Stock, 1978).

is, the detours traced in the real, traces of the human on the basis of which the locating would find itself in its own element.

When Janmari set himself apart a little while ago and began to rock back and forth, with glasses, sugar cubes, and spoons in position on the table while the coffee was waiting in a bowl on the corner of the stove, what were we to do? Forget the abusive interlocution and focus on the gesture, any gesture for that matter, and the coffee-drinking will be unleashed.

Regarding the gesture made, we may think it constitutes a sign. *Ite missa est*: there is nothing more to be done, and the-human-that-we-are is restored, but in such a rudimentary form that the damage, the contempt, is flagrant. Even without speaking of contempt, there is at the very least misunderstanding. The hiatus, within the very course of *acting*, would warrant something other than the gesture that we know will fulfill its function, will fill in the gap, and reclose the space that has been opened up toward the *outside* – of all good sense – where the real exists.

If I say that the gesture does not constitute a sign, whereas it seems to invite and allow, and even if we have made a sign, I fully understand that people won't take my word for it.

This gesture, what is it, most of the time? It may amount to tapping the table, and that's enough. I am convinced that Janmari's way of looking begs for something else. But what? The scope of this "something else" is such that it provokes vertigo, and tapping comes in to close off any avenue of escape for the symbolic function.

If I say, despite whatever the-human-that-we-are may think of it under the impetus of doing what he can, that this *tapping*, even if what is at issue is a sign, is not a sign, because Janmari has never ever made this sign, which is nevertheless the slightest of signs.

For those familiar with Janmari's extraordinary dexterity where the slightest of gestures are concerned, there is something astonishing here.

In every sign, a convention is involved; the other, toward whom the sign is made, is assumed to be capable of making the same sign, otherwise, the sign is never more than a gesture, a gesture of nothing at all, tapping on the wooden tabletop, a gesture that Janmari is not in the process of making as a sign, because he could permit himself to drink coffee once everything else was ready, prepared to tap on the table if that were all that was missing – which never happened.

Proof that the lack indicated by the hiatus in *acting* is of a different scope from the one that ricochets off the sign.

I fully understand what can be thought: that what is lacking, in this case, is the the-human-that-we-are who is not there, not embodied within Janmari.

Unless one assumes, as I do, that there are two forms of lack, as there are two forms of happiness, and thus two forms of freedom.

For being jubilant happens quite often to Janmari. But to be jubilant is not to be happy. And about this freedom that we grant him, the freedom to be exactly like us – based on the evidence, he obviously couldn't care less. Which leaves us speechless, even though we have gotten used to this disdain, we have ended up seeing it as the glaring proof not of his inaptitude for being like us, nor of our inaptitude for being like him, since that "him" is non-existent; so, then, proof of what? proof that granting is not enough.

I see in the dictionary that Giraudoux wrote: "the granting of leisure to the working class." The dictionary is a truly remarkable assistant. Granting speaks of granting rights, and to grant is "to grant favor or thanks."

What I mean is that thanks and rights are not enough when what is involved is the other freedom, the one that originates within the real.

Completely by chance, I hear the word "liminary" [*liminaire*] on the radio; it is quite apt and allows me to say that if I speak of the common as others speak of the unconscious, the common is liminary; while I have occasionally called it refractory [*réfractaire*]. In these two words, the endings resonate, completely by chance.

It might be said of a libertarian communist that he is communary, which would be a way of evading the suffix "ist" attached to the names of political parties.

To say that the common is liminary reminds us that it is initial, primordial, and always/already eliminated, "banished outside the threshold," the dictionary tells us, adding, about the verb "to eliminate": "to discard, to cause to disappear after making a choice."

And yet the symbolic function does not leave us the choice: the symbol plays the role of a door, access and closure, and beyond the threshold, there is the *outside*.

One can even say that language exists only by virtue of the inflexibility of this choice; that it only maintains itself at the risk of disappearing, which will happen only once human beings have disappeared, which is in the process of happening, owing to their notorious inability to respect the *liminal*.

I have written that if the unconscious is that which insists, the common is that which persists. Today I would write that the common is that which preliminates, even though this verb is not in the dictionary; which would mean that locating/acting precedes, and not within time as one might believe, but within the slightest moment, the "place" having always/already been given over to the-humans-that-we-are, who can do nothing but make ourselves believe what we believe, including that, starting from the one, the common can appear in the light of day, which never happens.

If I say that *acting* is common, we see quite well that it is not a question of understanding one another, or of loving one another.

If the *acting* of scrupulously peeling an orange remains suspended – and, then, a gesture, we might say that what is involved is an offering without a "to whom" – this acting, it is true, is common, and that's all there is to it.

Nothing *to do* with *acting*. I have nothing against the act of loving one another, except when it is passed off as a panacea – "a formula by which we claim to resolve everything" – the common that I want to attempt to evoke is immediately eliminated, as it is "supposed" to be, "supposed" by those who exist only by virtue of being subtracted from the real – which has been eliminated by peroration – and left then to their fantasies.

Setting out to seek the laws of the real was a way of respecting it. But taking up again what Lacan says, the passage I cited at the beginning of this notebook reveals that our task is a tall order, the real being "something one always finds in the same place ... but if it has moved, ... one also tells oneself that sometimes it moves under its own steam.... And our own displacements have, in principle, with certain exceptions, no efficacious influence on this change of place...."[20]

So here we are, smack dab in the middle of the exception itself, our own movements not being for naught for those children who can be assumed to live within the real. Which would mean that we are real, which I believe, and that our "movements," even the least of them – the slightest gesture – are, from a certain *seeing point*, real.

But this real aspect of our movements – and the slightest of them can have more importance than an entire panoply of demonstrative gesticulations – eludes us along with the harmony that locating "awaits," has always "awaited," forever broken, fragmented, and *acting* thus always appears to us as interrupted, fragmented, suspended, shattered by the rigidity of our enacted projects deprived of the preliminary detours without which *locating* loses itself, disappears, merely blinks.

---

20. Lacan, *Ego*, p. 297.

And we see snippets of *acting* in reiterating, tangential to what we are and what we propose – not to mention what we assume.

The-human-that-we-are inhabits us, he takes up residency, he watches, *that* way of seeing is immediately eliminated, because *that* seeing and what can see ITSELF cannot be reconciled. On the part of SELF, it's a conquest, it's a matter of acquiring – if only the knowledge and comprehension of the real and its "laws," as we say, and this something – this something real – that "one always finds in the same place" cannot be found; the "place" is taken.

Whereas *acting* might be said to consist in arabesques, all making or doing obeys a project, follows it, being rather economical and even stingy with its functional gestures, which have as their function *to do* or *to make*; which shows how the objects produced that are necessary for our freedom eliminate the endless arabesques without which the other freedom also has as much trouble existing as the duckling, without water, would have trouble swimming.

All one has to do is see a blacksmith *doing*, which has happened to me. Apart from what he was doing, quickly and well, there was a festival of tiny hammer blows on the anvil, for no apparent reason, which rang clear. Just as though something of the wayward *acting* persisted despite the hustle and bustle. This chiming of tiny hammer blows that caressed the anvil, that quivered and bounced back from their own momentum, had a boundless joy about it.

Janmari, as I know him, would be quite capable of spending – a strange apprentice – most of his time in such *acting*, handling the hammer so it would bounce back, excited to the quick by this momentum coming from the metal, Janmari, completely *envibrated* as he sometimes is by the sound of a fountain, his hand placed flat on the bronze or the stone, no doubt so the vibrations that come from hearing or touching will reunite "somewhere" in the place that calls ITSELF him – not that he says this himself. And then put yourself in his place, and you will be in a position to approach what it means to be jubilant. This is what I mean when I suggest that there are at least two forms of happiness, as there are two forms of freedom.

A strange *topos*, the one that lends itself to perceiving *in* what I must indeed declare to be this Janmari, *here*, the *in* not being included within the universe in which symbols operate, human, nevertheless, whatever people may say.

In rereading pages from this journal, I land on the cross ... and the banner. It must have been when I was about seven or eight years old that I learned that banner meant a strip torn from a shirt, and when I look back, it feels as though I was in some way vaccinated by this against the attractions of medieval competitions, where each lord had his own banner, and against the processions in which banners flourished; a good stretch of history and belief had thus been hidden from me, by the word evoking a piece of shirt, which to tell the truth was like a transparent screen. Seeing the Middle Ages and the processions through that screen, a strip of shirt, I could no longer believe in them, and if I come back to the way I made waves, with my hand flat in a puddle of water, it's because when I evoked this memory several days ago, the real of the gesture followed in its wake, several days later, as if aspirated. That hand, flat against the cold surface that lets itself be pierced and then reforms itself above, my hand however suddenly lighter, and, when I raised it back out, it seemed like it was aspirating water, but barely, and I had felt the beginning of one of those endless gestures in which the "my" of that hand was being lost. It was about making waves in order to see, to see how waves made themselves, since they indeed have to make themselves or be made, but in the same wanted and even reasoned gesture, *acting* was occurring, and it led me to feel something like shame, at being there, hunkered down, a few dozen steps from the North Sea, and all alone; shame? More like turmoil, and as for what I think about it now, it's that my hand was outside, a human hand and nothing more, abandoned, or almost, offered to the risk of experiencing the real, and if I was at fault, it was in believing that I was capable of understanding how waves were made. And I was conscious of that fault, or almost, whereas the turmoil of acting was of a completely different order than that of fault. Quite simply, I lost myself, which can also be written as: I lost ITSELF. Something perilous was going on.

Peril: "risk to which something exposes one"; "that which threatens existence."

The dictionary says what it can, and so do I. This turmoil, this peril, this attraction, described as a threat?

What is involved is *fearing*, which is not the same as being afraid; I wasn't afraid of anything and above all not of drowning, in that puddle, nor was I afraid of seeing my hand disappear. And I tell myself that this *fearing* is common, and that it's a matter of exulting. Which goes to show that when the real is at issue, vocabulary is of no use, nor is grammar.

"And the human then
appears as being what remains,
somewhat in tatters,
of the Arachnean traversed by
the sort of blind meteorite
that is consciousness."

Le Serret, June 1975
Background map and tracing
45.57 cm x 30.5 cm

The map of "Le Serret" designates a more expansive portion of the territory than the living area that is usually designated by this name. The broad lines in black pastel (the main one of which crosses the entire map) transcribes the journeys of an adult, Jean Lin. The wander line of an autistic child, Anne, is traced in India ink. The adult and the child are accompanied by a flock of sheep, whose hoofprints are sprinkled throughout the map. The ringing of sheep bells is represented by tiny clusters of dots. The sounds of a flute and a bell are represented in three places (at the top, in the center, and at the bottom) by three strokes. At the top, Anne strayed from Jean Lin's path; the *black flower* marks a stopping point and a rocking motion. In the center, a chaotic zone of lines and schematically-drawn stones designates the place where they stopped to cut wood (note the sketch of a machete). Farther down, in two places, the child's wander line deviates from the main path for short detours or *swerves*.

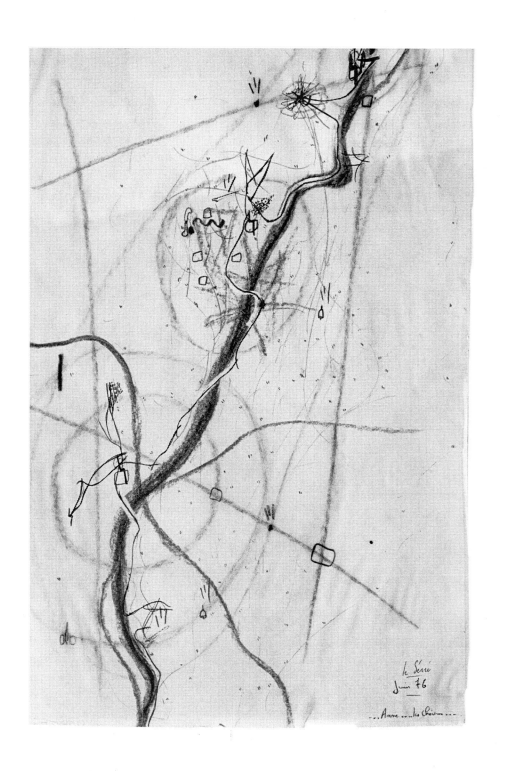

le Serre
Juin 76

... Anne ... les Chiens ...

Monoblet, November 1976
On the opposite page: Background map and tracing
Following pages: 8 tracings, reproduced without the background map
36.6 cm x 49.7 cm

The background map is a freehand sketch of the kitchen in "Y House" and
its furnishings (table and stools at the top, stove and sink at the bottom). The
entrance to the room is on the left.
The wander lines are drawn in India ink on tracings superimposed on the background map. They transcribe the movements of the three autistic children while
bread is being made. The "eyes" mark the children's places around the table. The
"hands" are recognizable, as well as the strings of saliva (with which one of the
children is playing), represented by little wavelets.

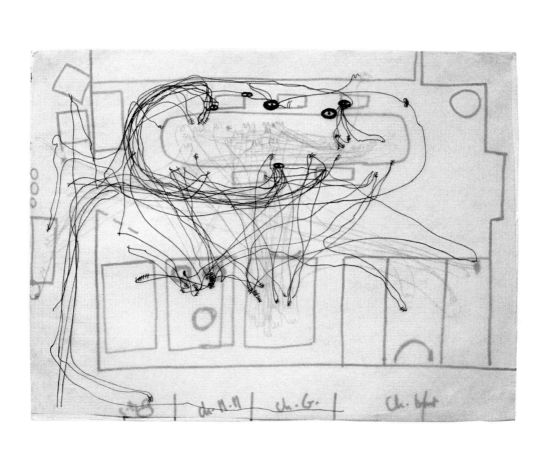

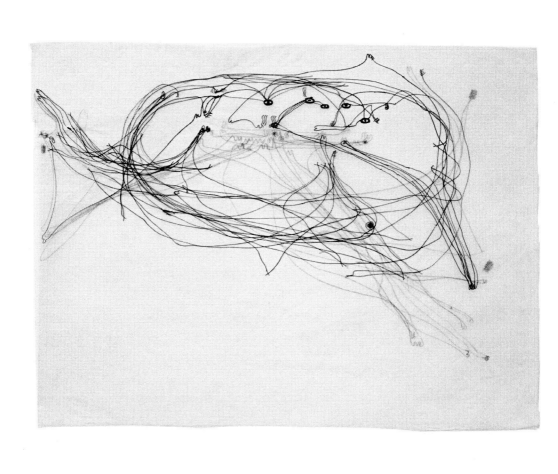

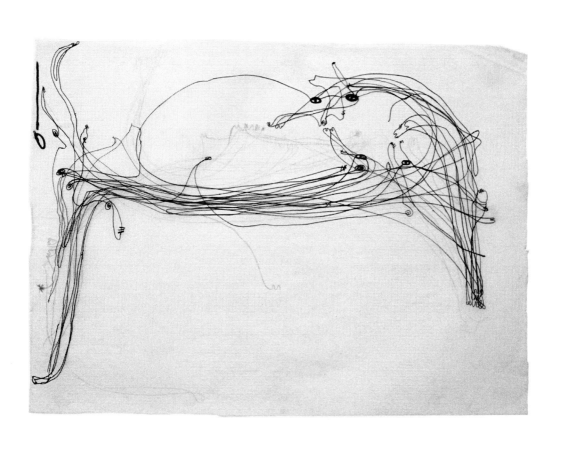

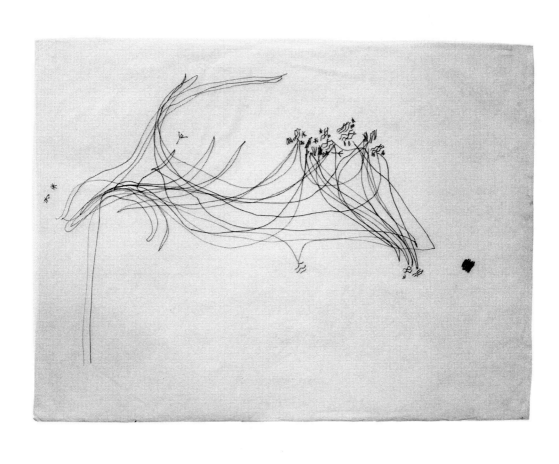

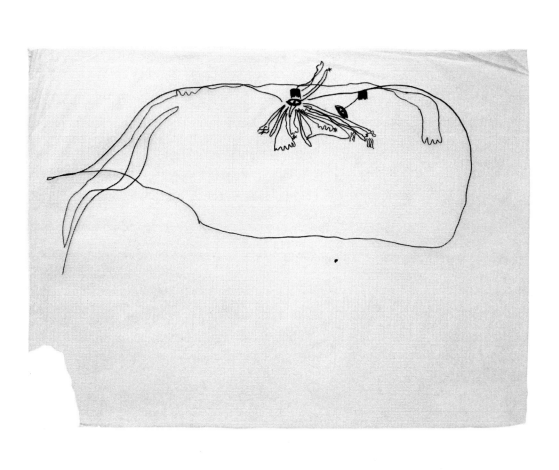

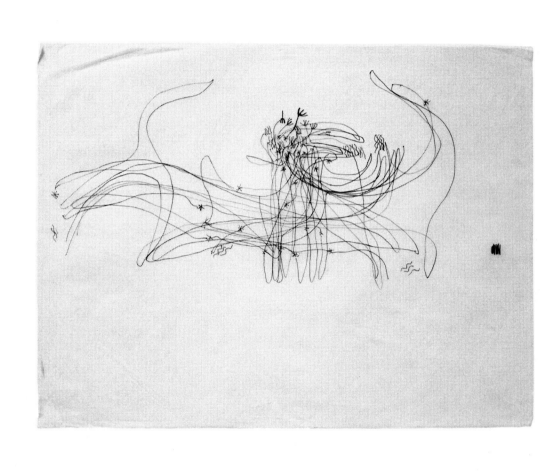

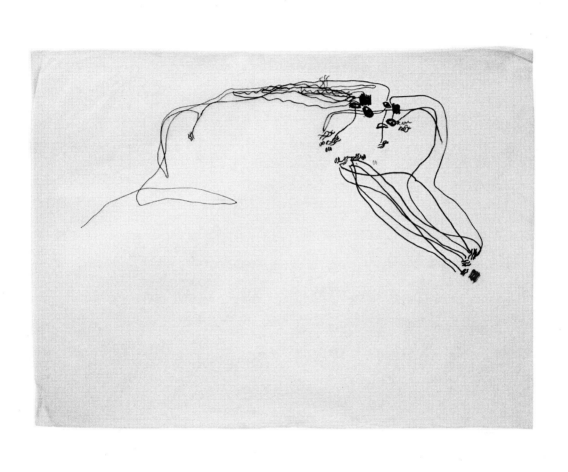

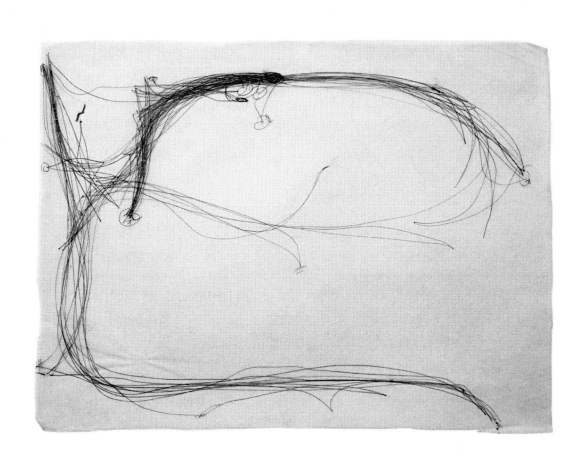

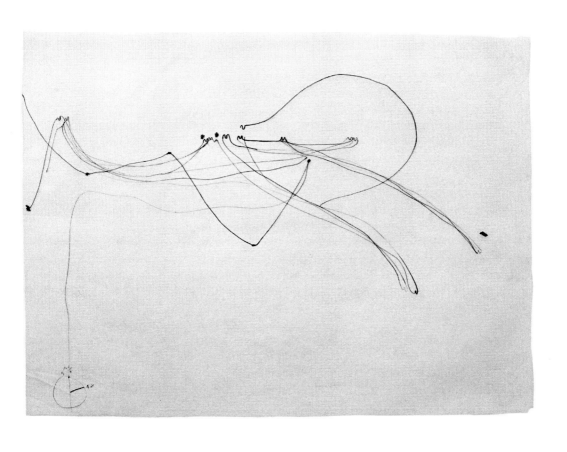

Monoblet, August-September 1977
On the opposite page: 5 superimposed tracings
Following pages: these 5 tracings reproduced separately
59 cm x 69.5 cm

The "Y House" comprises two levels. The kitchen and dining room are on the ground floor; the bedrooms and a long, narrow garden pressed up against the outer wall are on the upper level.
Each tracing transcribes the movement of an autistic child between the kitchen and the dining room (on the left), and in the garden (on the right). The gap corresponds to the part of the wander lines between the two places (in the stairwell and the second-floor bedrooms) that have not been transcribed. The wander lines were traced on different days and at various times of day.

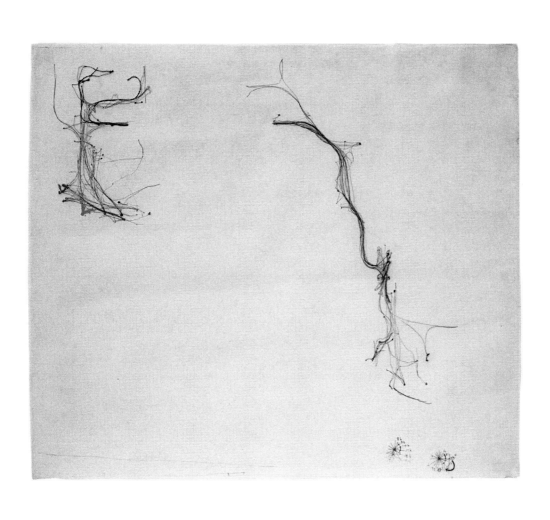

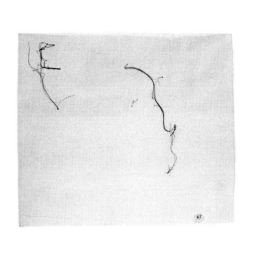 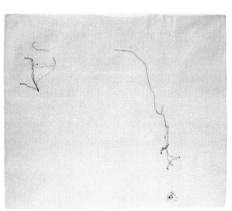

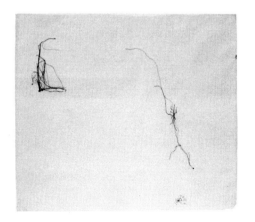 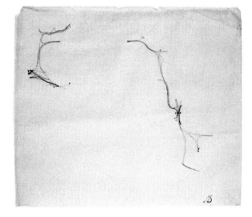

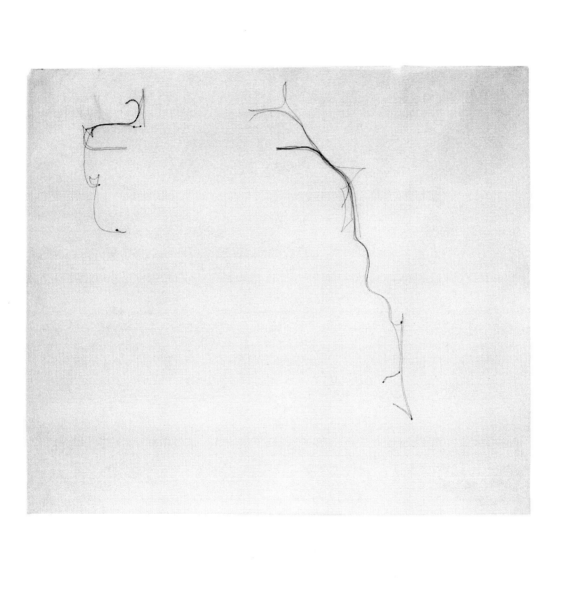

Monoblet, September 17, 1977
Two superimposed tracings
59 cm x 69.5 cm

The tracings each contain transcriptions of the wander lines of two autistic children, "during dishwashing time," between 5:15 and 6:00 p.m. The shape of the space suggests that the children are in the garden. The transcription includes lines in bister (invisible on the black-and-white reproduction) that designate the more limited pathways of an adult (probably corresponding to the dishwashing process).

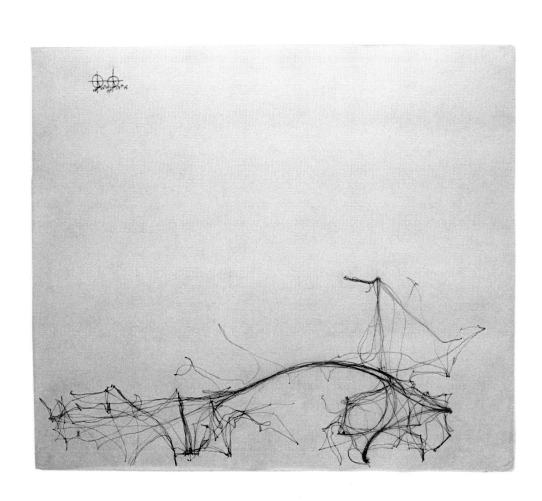

Monoblet, September 17, 1977
Three superimposed tracings
59 cm x 69.5 cm

The tracings each contain transcriptions of the wander lines made by three
autistic children while wool was being dyed, between 4:00 and 5:10 p.m.

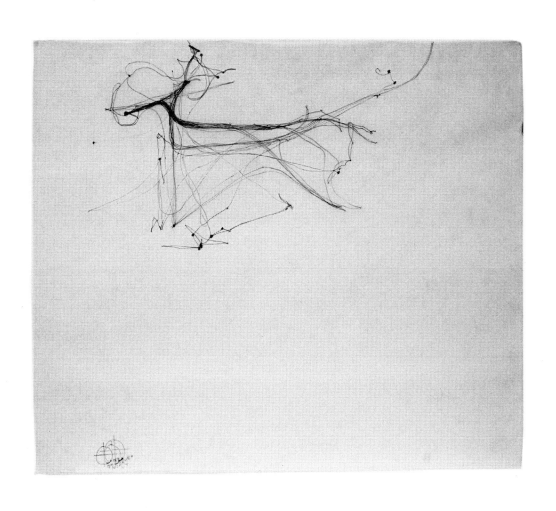

Original Publication Data

Part I

"The Arachnean," *L'Arachnéen et autres textes* (Paris: L'Arachnéen, 2008), pp. 9-96.

Part II

The first nine texts in Part II also appeared together in French as *Les enfants et le silence* (Paris: Galilée/Spirali, 1980) and in Italian translation as *I bambini e il silenzio* (Milan: Spirali, 1980).

"*That* Seeing and Looking at One*self*" ("Ce voir et se regarder"), written for a conference titled Madness in Psychoanalysis, held Dec. 1-4, 1976, in Milan; first published in *Recherches,* no. 24, special issue, "Cahiers de l'Immuable/3. Au défaut du langage" (1977), and reprinted in the conference proceedings, *Madness in Psychoanalysis*, ed. Armando Verdiglione (Paris: Payot, 1977).

"Acting and the Acted" (L'agir et l'agi"), first published as "L'agire et l'agito" in *Violenza e Psicanlisi,* ed. Armand Verdiglione (Milan: Feltrinelli, 1978).

"Art, Borders ... and the Outside" ("L'art, les bords… et le dehors"), first published as "L'arte, i bordi ... e il fuori," *Spirali* 1, no. 2, special issue, "Arte" (Nov. 1978).

"Card Taken and Map Traced" ("Carte prise et carte tracée"), first published in Italian translation as "Tessera presa e carta stracciata," in *Spirali* 2, no. 1, special issue, "I partiti" (Jan. 1979).

"The Fulfilled Child" ("L'enfant comblé"), first published in *Nouvelle revue de psychanalyse*, no. 19 (Spring 1979).

"Those Excessives" ("Ces excessifs"), first published in Italian translation as "Quegli eccessivi" in Spirali 2, no. 5, special issue, "L'intellettuale" (May 1979).

"The Human and the Supernatural" ("L'humain et le surnaturel"), first published in Italian translation as "L'umano e il sopranaturale" in Spirali 2, no. 9, special issue, "La religione" (Oct. 1979).

251

"The Charade" ("La parade"), first published as "La Parata" in Spirali 3 no. 1, special issue, "L'inconscio" (Jan. 1980).

"Freedom Without a Name" ("La liberté sans nom"), first published in *Dissidence de l'inconscient et pouvoirs*, proceedings of a colloquium held in Paris in 1978, ed. ArmandoVerdiglione (Paris: 10/18, 1980).

"Pretend Not to Notice" ("Semblant de rien"), first published as "Parvenza di niente" in Spirali 6, no. 1, special issue, "Contro Jung" (Jan. 1981).

"The Obligatory and the Fortuitous" ("L'obligatoire et le fortuit"), first published as "La guerre" in *Spirales* 1, no. 1 (Feb. 1981).

"Connivance" ("Connivence"), written for a conference titled "Sex and Language," New York, April 30-May 2, 1981; first published in *Spirales* 1, no. 5, special issue, "New York: Sex and Language" (June 1981).

"The Missing Voice" ("La voix manquée"), first published in Italian translation as "La voce mancata" in *Spirali* 0, no. 38, special issue, "Verginità" (Feb. 1982); reprinted in French in *Spirales* 0, no. 16, special issue, "La couleur de la voix" (June, 1982).

"When the-Human-that-We-Are Is Not There" ("Quand le bonhomme n'y est pas"), first published in *L'Arachnéen et autres textes* (Paris: L'Arachnéen, 2008), pp. 191-219.

Jason Wagner, Drew S. Burk
(Editors)
Univocal Publishing
123 North 3rd Street, #202
Minneapolis, MN 55401
www.univocalpublishing.com

ISBN 9781937561109
This work was composed in Garamond.
All materials were printed and bound
in January 2015 at Univocal's atelier
in Minneapolis, USA.

The paper is Hammermill 98.
The letterpress cover was printed
on Lettra Pearl.
Both are archival quality and acid-free